OBJECTIVE

IELTS

CAMBRIDGE UNIVERSITY PRESS
Cambridge, New York, Melbourne, Madrid, Cape Town,
Singapore, São Paulo, Delhi, Mexico City

Cambridge University Press
The Edinburgh Building, Cambridge CB2 8RU, UK

Published in the United States of America by Cambridge University Press, New York

www.cambridge.org
Information on this title: www.cambridge.org/9780521608725

First published 2006
4th printing 2012

A catalogue record for this publication is available from the British Library

ISBN 978-0-521-60872-5 Teacher's Book
ISBN 978-0-521-60882-4 Student's Book with CD-ROM
ISBN 978-0-521-60885-5 Self-study Student's Book with CD-ROM
ISBN 978-0-521-60873-2 Workbook
ISBN 978-0-521-60874-9 Workbook with Answers
ISBN 978-0-521-60881-7 Class Cassette Set
ISBN 978-0-521-60880-0 Audio CDs (3)

ISBN 978-0-521-60872-5 Paperback

Designed and produced by Kamae Design, Oxford

OBJECTIVE

IELTS

Michael Black
Wendy Sharp

Teacher's Book

Intermediate

CAMBRIDGE
UNIVERSITY PRESS

Contents

Map of Objective IELTS Intermediate Student's Book

OPIC		TEST SKILL AC = Academic GT = General Training	TASK TYPE	LANGUAGE FOCUS V = Vocabulary, G = Grammar, P = Pronunciation
it 1 mmunicate! 8–11 mmunication	1.1	Reading (AC / GT) Speaking	True / False / Not given Short-answer questions Part 1	V Paraphrase V Ways of communicating
	1.2	Writing extra (AC / GT) Listening	Spelling errors Note completion	G The passive P Spelling and numbers
t folder 1 12–13		Reading	**Yes / No / Not given**	
it 2 ealthy diet 14–17 od and drink	2.1	Listening Speaking	Note completion Part 1	P Weak and strong forms V Adjectives describing food
	2.2	Writing extra (AC / GT) Speaking	Using appropriate language Part 3	G Comparing things or talking about similarities and differences G Adverbs of degree
iting folder 1 18–19		Academic Writing Task 1	**Describing processes**	
it 3 y attractions 20–23 sure in the city	3.1	Speaking Reading (GT)	Part 1 Multiple matching	G Cause, purpose and result
	3.2	Listening	Note completion	V Descriptive adjectives V Adjectives ending in -ing and -ed P Word stress in related words
t folder 2 24–25		Listening Reading	**Matching**	
it 4 ys of learning 26–29 ication	4.1	Speaking Listening Reading (GT)	Part 3 Multiple choice Multiple choice with multiple answers Reading effectively	V Words used in academic writing
	4.2			G Review of present tenses P Word stress
iting folder 2 30–31		Academic Writing Task 1	**Handling data 1 – line graphs**	
vision Units 1–4 32–33				
it 5 covering the past 34–37 tory	5.1	Reading (AC / GT) Speaking	True / False / Not given Multiple choice Note completion Part 3	V Types of building V Collocations related to research
	5.2	Listening Writing extra (AC)	Labelling Task 1: A description of a place	G Review of past tenses
t folder 3 38–39		Listening Reading	**Sentence and note completion**	
t 6 at is job satisfaction? 43 rk	6.1	Listening	Flow-chart completion Sentence completion Labelling a diagram Table completion Multiple choice	V Work V Collocations with *money*
	6.2	Writing extra (GT) Speaking	Task 1: Letter of application Part 2	G Past simple or present perfect?
ting folder 3 44–45		Academic and General Training Writing Task 2	**Understanding the question and planning your writing**	

TOPIC		TEST SKILL AC = Academic GT = General Training	TASK TYPE	LANGUAGE FOCUS V = Vocabulary, G = Gramma P = Pronunciation
Unit 7 Selling dreams? 46–49 Advertising	7.1	Speaking Reading (AC / GT)	Parts 1 and 3 Multiple choice Headings	V Word formation
	7.2	Listening	Sentence completion Matching	P Sentence stress G Relative clauses V Advertising
Test folder 4 50–51		Reading	**Headings**	
Unit 8 Time to waste? 52–55 Leisure activities	8.1	Reading (GT) Speaking	Table completion Part 1	G Talking about the future
	8.2	Listening	Short-answer questions (lists) Short-answer questions	P Vowel length V Leisure activities
		Speaking	Part 3	
Writing folder 4 56–57		General Training Task 1	**Writing a letter**	
Revision Units 5–8 58–59				
Unit 9 Climate change 60–63 The environment	9.1	Reading (AC)	Summary completion	
	9.2	Speaking Listening Writing extra (AC)	Part 3 Note and table completion Task 1: A diagram	G Countable and uncountable nour V Collocations related to the environn
Test folder 5 64–65		Reading Listening	**Summary completion**	
Unit 10 A place to work or live in 66–69 Buildings	10.1	Speaking Listening Writing extra (GT)	Part 1 Note completion Task 1: A letter of complaint	P Polite intonation V Phrasal verbs and collocations wi *house* and *home*
	10.2	Speaking	Part 2	G *-ing* forms and infinitives 1
Writing folder 5 70–71		Academic Writing Task 1	**Handling data 2 – bar and pie charts and tables**	
Unit 11 Animal life 72–75 Animals	11.1	Reading (AC)	Multiple choice Multiple choice with multiple answers	V Definitions relating to social organisation
	11.2	Listening	Sentence completion	G Articles V Compound nouns P Diphthongs
Test folder 6 76–77		Listening Reading	**Multiple choice with multiple answers Multiple choice**	
Unit 12 Sport: just for fun? 78–81 Sport	12.1	Speaking Listening Speaking	Part 1 Table completion Part 3	V Sport V Word formation
	12.2	Reading (AC / GT)	Matching	G *Should, had better, ought to*
Writing folder 6 82–83		Academic and General Training Task 2	**Connecting ideas 1**	
Revision Units 9–12 84–85				
Unit 13 Choices 86–89 Making decisions	13.1	Reading (AC)	Locating information Multiple choice	V Collocations with adverbs
	13.2	Listening	Multiple choice Note completion	G Conditionals
		Speaking	Part 3	
Test folder 7 90–91		Reading	**Locating information**	
Unit 14 The importance of colour 92–95 Colour	14.1	Listening	Matching Listening for specific information	V Words and phrases related to cha P Linking words
		Writing extra (AC) Speaking	Task 1: Describing changes Part 3	V Colours V Adjectives describing personality
	14.2	Listening	Short-answer questions	G *-ing* forms and infinitives 2 V Confused words V Comment adverbs
Writing folder 7 96–97		Academic and General Training Task 2	**Making a general statement, giving examples and using comment adverbs**	

Content of the IELTS Test

Each candidate takes four IELTS test modules, one in each of the four skills, Listening, Reading, Writing and Speaking. All candidates take the same Listening and Speaking Modules. There is a choice between Academic and General Training in the Reading and Writing Modules.

Listening 40 questions approximately 30 minutes

There are four sections to this part of the test and they are always in the same order. Each section is heard **ONCE** only. During the test, time is given for you to read the questions and write down and check your answers. Ten minutes is allowed at the end of the test for you to transfer your answers from the question paper to an answer sheet.

Section	Format	Task types	Objective Test folder
1 and 2	The first two sections are concerned with social needs. There is a conversation between two speakers, followed by a monologue.	Questions are chosen from the following types: • multiple choice • short-answer questions • sentence completion	TF 6 TF 3
3 and 4	Sections 3 and 4 are concerned with situations related to educational or training contexts. There is a conversation between up to four people and then a further monologue.	• note completion • summary completion • labelling a diagram • table/flow-chart completion • classification • matching	TF 3 TF 5 TF 10 TF 8 TF 2

Reading 40 questions 60 minutes

There are three reading passages in the Reading Module with a total of 2,000 to 2,750 words (Academic) or 2,000 to 2,500 words (General Training). All answers must be entered on an answer sheet during the test. No extra time is allowed to transfer answers.

Academic	General Training	Task types	Objective Test folder
Texts are taken from magazines, journals, books and newspapers, which have been written for a non-specialist audience. They deal with issues which are interesting and accessible to candidates entering undergraduate or postgraduate courses or seeking professional registration. At least one text contains detailed logical argument. One text may contain non-verbal materials such as diagrams, graphs or illustrations.	Tests are taken from notices, advertisements, official documents, booklets, newspapers, instruction manuals, leaflets, timetables, books and magazines. The first section, 'social survival', contains texts relevant to basic linguistic survival in English. The second section, 'training survival', focuses on the training context – either training itself or welfare needs. This section involves a text or texts of more complex language. The third section 'general reading', involves reading longer, more complex texts.	Questions are chosen from the following types: • multiple choice • short-answer questions • sentence completion • note completion • summary completion • labelling a diagram • table/flow-chart completion • headings • Yes/No/Not given • True/False/Not given • locating information • classification • matching	TF 6 TF 3 TF 3 TF 5 TF 10 TF 4 TF 1 TF 1 TF 7 TF 8 TF 2

Writing 2 tasks 60 minutes

Task	Academic	General Training	Objective Writing folder
Task 1 allow about 20 minutes for this	Describing graphic data / a diagram You will be assessed on your ability to: • organise, present and compare data • describe a process • describe an object, event or sequence of events • explain how something works You must write at least 150 words.	Writing a letter You will be assessed on your ability to: • write a personal or formal letter • ask for and provide factual information • express needs, wants, likes and dislikes • express opinions, complaints You must write at least 150 words.	**Academic** WF 1 WF 2 WF 5 WF 10 **General Training** WF 4 WF 10
Task 2 allow about 40 minutes for this	Writing an essay You will be assessed on your ability to: • present the solution to a problem • present and justify an opinion • compare and contrast evidence • evaluate and challenge ideas You must write at least 250 words.	Writing an essay You will be assessed on your ability to: • provide general factual information • outline a problem and present a solution • present, evaluate and challenge ideas You must write at least 250 words.	**Academic and General Training** WF 3 WF 6 WF 7 WF 8 WF 9 WF 10

Speaking approximately 11–14 minutes

The Speaking Module consists of an oral interview between you and an examiner.

Part	Format	Timing	Objective Test folder
Part 1 Introduction and interview	The examiner introduces him/herself and asks questions about familiar topics, for example, your home, family, job and interests.	4–5 minutes	TF9
Part 2 Individual long turn	The examiner gives you a card, which contains a topic and some prompts, and asks you to speak for 1–2 minutes on the topic. The examiner asks one or two questions to round off the long turn.	3–4 minutes (including 1 minute preparation time)	TF9
Part 3 Two-way discussion	The examiner invites you to take part in a discussion of a more abstract nature, based on questions thematically linked to the Part 2 topic.	4–5 minutes	TF9

1 Communicate!

Unit topic	Communication
1.1	
Test skills	Reading (AC/GT):
	True/False/Not given
	Short-answer questions
	Speaking Part 1
Vocabulary	Paraphrase
	Ways of communicating
1.2	
Test skills	Listening: Note completion
	Writing extra (AC/GT): Spelling
	errors
Grammar	The passive
Pronunciation	Spelling and numbers
Workbook contents	
1, 2, 3	Reading
4, 5, 6	Grammar: the passive
7	Vocabulary

1.1 SB pages 8–9

1 Encourage the class to talk at length in this first lesson so that, if the class is new to you, you can gauge their language ability. The discussion can take place in pairs or small groups, with a class round-up at the end. Write on the board any useful vocabulary that comes up.

The pictures show the following types of communication:

a mobile phone call
b email
c a postcard
d a letter
e face to face
f a text message
g whistling

> **Possible answers**
> I prefer to speak to someone face to face rather than on the phone.
> I never send postcards when I'm on holiday. They're a waste of time.
> I can't remember the last time I wrote a letter.
> I find it really hard to whistle.

2 Explain to the class that they will probably need to improve their reading speed so that they can cope with the 2,000 to 2,750 words they will have to read in the test. The passage in this unit is about 500 words long, much shorter than the ones (apart from GT Part 1) they will get in the test. Ask the class to read the passage as quickly as possible and time how long it takes them. A native

speaker would take about a minute and a half. While they are reading, they should think about what type of text this is: for example, would they find it in a novel, a textbook or a newspaper? Elicit reasons for their answer.

> **Answer**
> This is a newspaper report about something that is happening around now. It also contains quotes from the different people involved.

3 Students should read through the questions and then scan the passage for the answers. Give them a maximum of a couple of minutes for this activity.

> **Answers**
> 1 1999
> 2 Venezuela, Cuba and Texas
> 3 Atlas Mountains of North Africa

4 Explain that this exercise is similar to the ones found in the Reading Modules. In the test, each reading passage will have a mixture of task types. In the first few units of the Student's Book, there are shorter reading passages with only one task type. Students find the Not given questions the most difficult to do. For advice on how to tackle this type of question, see Test folder 1 (SB page 12). The answer section gives line numbers in the text to help students to find where the answers are.

> **Answers**
> 1 TRUE *With the opening of the island to tourism and the arrival of the telephone, Silbo Gomero had started to die out.* (lines 9–10)
> 2 NOT GIVEN No mention is made of how the children feel about learning Silbo Gomero.
> 3 FALSE *students spend 25 minutes a week learning it* (lines 14–15)
> 4 NOT GIVEN The text doesn't tell us how well Darias teaches.
> 5 TRUE *An important step towards saving the language was the First International Congress of Whistled Languages, which was held in La Gomera in 2003.* (lines 29–31)
> 6 FALSE *If we spoke English, we'd use an English structure for whistling.* (lines 55–56)

5 Explain to students what is meant by a *paraphrase* and how an answer in the Reading Modules often depends on a paraphrase of a word or phrase in the text. Encourage them to use the *Cambridge Advanced Learner's Dictionary* in class and at home.

6 Encourage students to expand their answers. Some of the following language could be put on the board:

My family consists of ...
There are X of us in my family ...
I am an only child.
I come from a large/small family.
I prefer to confide in ...
I find it easy/difficult to say what I want in another language.

Extension activity

1 Ask students to bring in photographs of people who are close to them. In pairs or small groups, get them to talk about the photos. Put up any vocabulary that arises on the board.

2 Other questions can be added to the ones in exercise 6 to encourage students to talk about themselves and their families, for example:
   1 Is there anyone in your family you're sometimes not on speaking terms with?
   2 What do you generally chat about with your friends?
   3 Have you ever had to give a talk to a room of people? If not, would you like to?

Useful language
I don't get on with my ... because ...
I enjoy chatting to friends about ...
I would be embarrassed about / enjoy giving a talk because ...

1.2 SB pages 10–11

1 Ask the class to look at sentences **a** and **b**. Sentence **a**, in the passive, is more impersonal and formal than **b**. Remind students that they will often need to use the passive in the Writing Modules and that Academic Writing is both formal and impersonal.

2 Allow students a few minutes to look at the examples from the reading passage. Refer students to the Grammar folder (SB page 138) if they are unsure about how the passive is formed and used.

3 Ask students to work in pairs to talk about the five inventions.

4 Ask students to look at the picture. Encourage them to talk about their own mobile phone (if they have one) – where it was made, when they bought it, what features it has, etc. Then do the first two questions in class to make sure that students can see the difference between active and passive. The exercise can be done either in class or for homework.

5 This exercise gives practice in forming the passive. It can be done orally in class and then set for homework.

6 These words come from the *Cambridge Learner Corpus*, a database of candidates' scripts from past sessions of Cambridge exams, including IELTS. While writing this course, we have made extensive use of both this and the *Cambridge International Corpus*. Reference to the scripts in the *Learner Corpus* has given us a much fuller picture of what IELTS candidates can and cannot do. This exercise focuses on typical spelling mistakes that IELTS candidates make.

7 Explain to students that names which are spelt out in the Listening Module must be spelt correctly. Elicit all the letters of the alphabet and put them on the board, checking that they are pronounced correctly. Ask students to work in pairs to spell out the names of the inventors and then listen to the recording to check pronunciation.

Recording script

1 Johannes Gutenberg: J-O-H-A-double N-E-S, G-U-T-E-N-B-E-R-G
2 Thomas Edison: T-H-O-M-A-S, E-D-I-S-O-N
3 Vladimir Kosma Zworykin: V-L-A-D-I-M-I-R, K-O-S-M-A, Z-W-O-R-Y-K-I-N
4 William Caxton: W-I-double L-I-A-M, C-A-X-T-O-N
5 Philo T. Farnsworth: P-H-I-L-O, T, F-A-R-N-S-W-O-R-T-H
6 Q

8 Check that students are familiar with the pronunciation of numbers 1–100. Then ask them to listen to the recording and write down the numbers they hear.

Recording script and answers

1 01993 548333
   oh, one, double nine, three – five, four, eight, treble three
2 0° centigrade
   zero degrees centigrade
3 14th March, 2004
   the fourteenth of March, two thousand and four
4 30th November, 1918
   the thirtieth of November, nineteen eighteen
5 5,432 kilos
   five thousand, four hundred and thirty-two kilos
6 £1,500
   fifteen hundred pounds *or*
   one thousand, five hundred pounds
7 £3.12
   three pounds and twelve p *or*
   three pounds and twelve pence
8 £4.50
   four pounds fifty
9 2.5 centimetres
   two point five centimetres
10 70 metres
   seventy metres

---

9 Write on the board some numbers and dates which are important for you. Ask the class to ask you questions about the numbers and dates. Then ask students to work in pairs to do the same. Circulate to monitor their pronunciation.

10 This listening is similar to what is heard in Part 1 of the Listening Module. Ask students to read through the task and get them to discuss in pairs what sort of information could go in the spaces. In the test, the listening is only heard once. At this stage, it is up to you how many times you feel the class needs to hear it played.

Answers (see underlined text in script)
1 home (and) office   2 (from £)80 (to £)250   3 i/I 860
4 8.30 / eight thirty / half past eight   5 Park Lane
6 opposite (the) cinema   7 supermarket   8 cash (only)
9 Stanway   10 (on the) third/3rd

Recording script

Man: Good morning. Computer Solutions.
Woman: Oh, hello. My printer's broken, and I need to get a new one. Someone gave me your number, and I was wondering whether you could help me.
Man: No problem. We stock printers suitable for both <u>home and office</u>.
Woman: Well, I'm a student. I just need one for my coursework. How much do they cost?
Man: An inkjet printer will probably be good enough for what you want – it'll do text and pictures. <u>They start at £80 and go up to £250</u>.
Woman: Mm. Quite a good price range, then. I can spend about £150. Can I get a good one for that?
Man: Yes. <u>I'd go for the Trion i860</u>. It had good reviews, and we've had no complaints about it.
Woman: The i860. I'll come in and have a look. What time are you open to?
Man: Normally we close at 5.30, but today, being Saturday, it's <u>8.30</u>.
Woman: And where exactly are you?
Man: In Hollowridge – 15 <u>Park Lane</u>.
Woman: Fifteen Park Lane, got that. Is that in the town centre?
Man: Yes, <u>opposite the cinema</u>.
Woman: OK, and is it easy to park? If I buy the printer, I'd want to take it home with me today.
Man: No problem. There's a car park quite near, just at the back of the <u>supermarket</u>.
Woman: OK. Oh, one more thing – do you take credit cards?
Man: <u>Cash only</u>, I'm afraid. Will that be all right?
Woman: Yes, but I mustn't forget to go to the bank before I come! Oh, by the way, what's your name?
Man: Jack <u>Stanway</u>. That's <u>S-T-A-N-W-A-Y</u>. There are two Jacks here, so when you ask for me, give my surname, too.
Woman: OK, I will.
Man: I work in the office, but you need to go to the <u>third floor, where the printers are</u>. Just ask for me there, and I'll come out and see what I can do to help. See you later.
Woman: The third floor. Great – thanks for your help. Bye.

Photocopiable recording script activity
(P ⋯→ **page 133)**

Hand out copies of the recording script. Ask the class to read it through to see where the answers are. This should reassure weaker students who may be having difficulty with listening. Students can also take it in turns to read the dialogue aloud in pairs.

Test folder 1

SB pages 12–13
Yes / No / Not given and
True / False / Not given

Make sure students fully understand the notes and advice. It would probably be most useful to go through the task in class: for each question, ask students to identify the relevant part of the passage and then to decide on the correct answer.

Evidence for the answers is given on the right. Students should not write this in the test.

Answers

1	YES	*the answer that most of us would give … this must surely be the most widely recognized function of language* (paragraph 2)
2	NO	*There are several other functions where the communication of ideas is irrelevant.* (paragraph 2)
3	YES	*It cannot be 'communication of ideas', for there is no one else in the room.* (paragraph 3)
4	NOT GIVEN	*Here we have one of the commonest uses of language.* (paragraph 4) The writer doesn't say that we are becoming more aware of it.
5	NOT GIVEN	The writer refers to *the semi-linguistic noises often called interjections (such as 'Wow' and 'Ouch')* (paragraph 5), but not to languages other than English.
6	NOT GIVEN	The writer refers to *the use of such phrases as 'Good morning'* (paragraph 6) to maintain a comfortable relationship between people, but doesn't mention other feelings the phrases might express.
7	NO	*The weather is not as universal a conversation-filler as English people might like to think!* (paragraph 8)
8	YES	*the enjoyment … applies to all age groups.* (paragraph 9)

A healthy diet

Unit topic	Food and drink
1.1	
Test skills	Listening: Note completion
	Speaking Part 1
Pronunciation	Weak and strong forms
Vocabulary	Adjectives describing food
1.2	
Test skills	Writing extra (AC/GT): Using
	appropriate language
	Speaking Part 3
Grammar	Comparing things or talking
	about similarities and differences
	Adverbs of degree

Workbook contents

1, 2	Reading
3, 4, 5	Grammar: comparatives and
	superlatives
6, 7	Vocabulary

2.1 SB pages 14–15

1 Draw students' attention to the pictures, which are of two food pyramids showing the basic diets of people in Asia and people in Latin America. Ask the class to discuss the two diets in pairs. *Staple foods* are ones that the people eat every day.

Possible answers
- The staples for Asia are based on cereals. The staples for Latin America are grains, beans, nuts and tubers, together with fruit and vegetables.
- Latin Americans eat more meat than Asians. Both diets are rich in fruit and vegetables. Asians drink more tea than Latin Americans. They both eat the same amount of sweets and eggs.
- Fruit and vegetables are better for you than sweets and too much meat.
- **a** carbohydrate: rice, wheat, potatoes, corn
  b protein: meat, fish, beans, eggs, poultry
  c fat: dairy, plant oils

2 Ask students to read the information in the Test spot and check they understand. More information on this type of question can be found in Test folder 3 of the Student's Book.

Explain that it is always a good idea to read through the questions before listening to the recording to get an idea of what they are going to listen for.

Answers (see underlined text in script)
1 5,000 2 550 million 3 103 4 clothes 5 March 1994
6 Tuesday 7 first/1st 8 ads/adverts/advertisements
9 8/eight 10 45 minutes

Recording script

Today on the food programme, I'm going to be telling you about two interesting websites which give you information about two very important foods – rice and noodles. First of all, let's look at the Pagewise website. This site will tell you all about the history of rice, about the rice harvest, the different types of rice, how to cook it and what else you can do with it. For example, did you know that rice belongs to the grass family and <u>was first grown about 5,000 years ago</u> in India? It was introduced into Europe about 700 years ago and arrived in the USA in 1726. Nowadays, <u>more than 550 million tonnes is produced around the world each year</u>, 92% of that being produced in Asia.

Rice is the staple food for the majority of the world's population – that is, far more meals are based on rice than on anything else. It is naturally fat- and sodium-free, and <u>one serving has only 103 calories</u>, so it's very good for you. Interestingly, although rice isn't as rich in vitamin C as the potato, for example, it is less fattening. Now, I always find rice difficult to cook, but the best way, apparently, is to keep the lid on the pan when you boil it – this will keep the steam in and produce perfect rice every time. One interesting thing to note is that European and American rice, which is grown in dry fields, absorbs a lot more water than Asian rice, which is grown in flooded fields. Now, other things you can do with rice besides eat it: you can make drinks from it, glue to stick paper together with and also <u>you can make clothes from it</u>!

Moving on now to the Japanese Food Page. There you can find out about the history of the noodle at the Yokohama Noodle Museum site. Noodles can be made from rice or wheat and are the fast food of Japan. There are more noodle shops in Japan than any other kind of restaurant. According to this website, noodles make one of the quickest and least expensive meals – much quicker than a rice dish, for example.

The museum, <u>which opened in March 1994</u>, sounds like it's well worth a visit if you go to Japan. It's more than just an ordinary museum – it's part theme park and part restaurant. And it stays open later than most museums – from 11.00 a.m. to 11.00 p.m., with the last admission being 10.00 p.m. The museum is <u>open every day except for Tuesday</u>, with Sunday being the busiest day and Thursday being the least busy.

<u>The first floor of the museum</u> has a souvenir shop, and you can buy noodle-related objects online as well. It sells bowls for eating noodles out of, equipment for making noodles – even curtains with pictures of noodles on them! There are empty noodle packets on the walls for decoration, and <u>overhead TVs show adverts</u> for noodles from the past 25 years. You can see a display showing how noodles are made and also one giving the history of the noodle.

On two underground levels, there is a historical theme park with shops, houses and restaurants from the year 1958. There are also eight different noodle shops serving ten different types of noodle. If you want to go, you can get there by train. The museum is only a three-minute walk from JR Shin-Yokohama railway station. Shin-Yokohama is about 45 minutes from Tokyo.

On the programme next week, we'll be …

3 Ask students to look at the menu and check that they understand the vocabulary items. Before they listen to the conversation, write up the first sentence of the dialogue on the board and explain that they have to identify the kinds of words which are stressed. These tend to be words such as nouns, verbs, adjectives and adverbs – that is, words that carry content.

Example: *I'll have soup to start with, please.*

Students should then listen to the conversation and mark the stressed words.

Recording script

Man: I'll have soup to start with, please.
Waiter: And for the main course?
Man: Steak, please.
Waiter: With chips and salad or with vegetables?
Man: I'll have some vegetables, please.
Waiter: Mm-hm. And to drink?
Man: Just a glass of water.
Waiter: OK, right away, sir.

Waiter: Would you like a dessert?
Man: Yes, some raspberries and cream, please. And a cup of coffee.

4 Explain that sometimes it is necessary to stress a short word. Usually this happens when:
- it ends a sequence: *How much is it?*
- it contrasts with another word: *I sent it to her, not him.*

Ask students to listen to the example so they can hear the second stressed *and*. Ask them to work with a partner and to look at conversations 1–4, saying whether the underlined words are weak or strong. They should then listen to the recording to check their answers.

Answers and recording script
Listen to the example: I ordered raspberries and cream <u>and</u> ice cream.
Now do the exercise.
1 <u>Do</u> you like chocolate? *weak*
   Yes, I <u>do</u>. *strong*
2 Where's <u>the</u> waiter? *weak*
   That's him, by the bar. *strong*
3 What <u>do you</u> want with the raspberries, cream or ice cream? *weak*
   I'd like cream <u>and</u> ice cream – they're lovely together! *strong*
4 I'm eating <u>at the</u> Savoy Hotel tonight. *weak*
   Not <u>the</u> Savoy Hotel in London? *strong*

Extension activity

Ask students which words they heard in the listening and the pronunciation recordings that are containers for food or drink.
Answers: *bowl, glass, cup, packet* and *pan*.

Elicit from students what other things they would need to use to prepare and serve food and drink.

Example answers:
Crockery: plate, dish, saucer
Cutlery: knife, fork, spoon
Containers: box (cereal), carton (milk), jar (marmalade), bottle (ketchup), packet (biscuits)

5

Answers
1 rotten 2 spicy 3 ripe 4 sour 5 stale 6 bland
7 burnt 8 fresh

6 Refer students to the Useful language box. This will enable them to vary their responses to the questions.

Possible answers
1 I really like noodles and any type of fish.
2 I can't stand meat – I'm a vegetarian.
3 Well, to start with, I'm very keen on melon or prawns. Then, for the main course, I like steak and salad. For dessert, I like any type of fruit or cheese.
4 I like to go out to eat on special occasions. I like French and Italian food.
5 I can only cook pasta, but I'm really good at making lasagne.

2.2 SB pages 16–17

1 You should make sure that students really understand how to compare and contrast, as they will have to do this fairly often in the IELTS Test, especially in the Speaking and Writing Modules. Ask students to read through the information and do the exercise individually, and then to check their answers in pairs.

Answers
1 -er 2 i 3 -er 4 more 5 -est 6 i 7 -est
8 (the) most 9 as 10 than 11 (the) least

2

Answers
1 the best 2 worse 3 the most expensive 4 easiest
5 sweeter 6 cheaper 7 nicer 8 healthier
9 not as expensive 10 the least expensive

5 The exercise gives examples from the *Cambridge Learner Corpus* of inappropriate language.

> **Answers**
> 1 Some people **become angry** when they find that they do not have enough water to grow their crops.
> 2 **Children** are the ones who suffer most during food shortages.
> 3 Many children eat junk food **because** they see their **friends** buying it.
> 4 The **manager** of the supermarket told us to put the **goods** on the shelves.
> 5 There were some **men** planting rice in the field.
> 6 Men eat **a great deal** more meat than **women**. (*A lot more* is also acceptable, but *a great deal more* is more appropriate in a formal report, for example.)
> 7 **Regarding** the food you ordered for your party, could you please confirm the date on which it is required?
> 8 Many **people** in the world do not have enough to eat.

6 Refer the class to the Test spot and Useful language box. Ask students to discuss the questions with a partner. Monitor the pairs and check that they are using a range of language and give them additional vocabulary as required.

> **Possible answers**
> 1 I think that factory farming should be banned because it is cruel and unnatural. I always try to buy organic food, even if it is sometimes more expensive.
> 2 In my opinion, all children should be taught to cook at school. The second point I'd like to make is that if children learned what a healthy diet is at school, then there wouldn't be as much obesity as there is now.
> 3 I believe that fast food plays too great a role in my country. Let me explain. Fifty years ago, everyone used to sit down as a family to eat dinner. Nowadays, they prefer to sit in front of the TV, eating a hamburger.

Extension activity

For homework, ask the class to find out about and draw two diet pyramids – one for their country and one for another country (or continent). They should then report back to the class, comparing the two countries (or continents).

3 Draw students' attention to the box containing information about adverbs of degree at the bottom of page 16. Students should then look at the chart on page 17 which compares the consumption of rice, sugar and tea in five different countries. Go through the examples about rice and then ask the class to give you similar sentences from the sugar column and put them on the board – or ask individual students to come up and put their own examples on the board. Students can then write down six sentences for both sugar and tea.

> **Possible answers**
> India consumes by far the most sugar.
> China consumes nearly as much sugar as Brazil.
> Japan consumes the least sugar.
> Brazil consumes considerably / a lot / much / a good deal more sugar than Indonesia.
> Brazil consumes slightly / a little / a bit more sugar than China.
> India consumes the most tea.
> Japan consumes by far the least tea.
> Japan consumes considerably/far/much/less tea than China (does).
> India consumes considerably / a good/great deal / a lot / much more tea than Japan (does).

4 Write a list of what you eat and drink in a day on the board. Only a few things are really necessary – possibly six items of food and two types of drink. Then ask students to do the same individually. They should walk around the class, or form small groups, and find out what other members of the class usually eat and drink in one day. They then write sentences and report back to the whole class. Put some of the sentences on the board under either formal or informal headings. Check that the class understands the difference. Refer them to the Writing extra box which gives more information on writing academic English.

Writing folder 1

SB pages 18–19
Academic Writing Task 1: Describing processes

In the Academic Writing Module, candidates may be asked to describe a process or explain how something works for Task 1. The input may be in the form of a diagram or other graphic data. Refer students to the Advice box and check that they understand the information. It gives useful advice on how to approach the task.

1   It is important that any answer to a Task 1 question begins with a summary sentence. This should never be copied from the rubric, but should still give the main details of what the diagram or table shows. One way of doing this is to paraphrase the rubric.
    Students should read through a, b and c and then look carefully at the diagram of the human digestive system. Check they understand the vocabulary. Ask them to decide which is the best summary sentence.

> **Answer**
> a

2   Students will receive more marks in the test if they make appropriate use of sequencing words and also make sure the information they give is in the right sequence.

> **Answers**
> c First of all
> a then
> f Next
> g
> e
> b After
> d Finally

3   Both the present simple active and passive are used in this description. The present simple is used to describe a process.
    See the highlighted verbs in the suggested answer to exercise 4 (**bold** = active; *italic* = passive).

4   Paragraphing is very important in both Task 1 and Task 2; students should do a plan before they start writing their answer.

> **Suggested answer**
> The diagram **shows** the human digestive process.
> First of all, food in the mouth *is broken down* by the process of chewing with the back teeth and then by the action of enzymes. The resulting mass *is* then *swallowed* and *is passed* through the throat into the oesophagus. The oesophagus **is** a long tube which **connects** the throat with the stomach. It **uses** muscle action to send the food mass to the stomach.
>
> Next, the food mass **mixes** in the stomach with gastric acid, which **breaks down** the food further and **helps** digestion. From the stomach, the partly digested food **goes** into the small intestine. Here it *is mixed* with a chemical called bile, which *is produced* in the liver.
>
> After passing through the small intestine, the food **enters** the large intestine, where water *is removed* and there **are** bacteria to help in the digestion process. Finally, waste material *is excreted*.

5   Ask students to look at the pictures, which show how chocolate is made, and check that they understand the vocabulary.

6   It is a good idea for students to keep their written homework. It can be very useful for them to work on a second draft following your marking and feedback on the first attempt, as they will learn from earlier mistakes and better understand how to improve their writing.

> **Sample answer**
> The diagram shows the stages in the process of making chocolate.
>
> Chocolate comes from the cacao tree, which is grown in parts of South America, Africa and Indonesia. The tree produces large red pods, which contain white cocoa beans. Firstly, when the pods are ripe, they are harvested, the beans are removed and they are fermented for several days in large wooden boxes. During the fermenting process, the beans turn brown.
>
> Next, the brown beans are spread in the sun to dry. They are then put in large sacks and transported by train or lorry. After this, the beans are taken to a chocolate factory where they are roasted in an oven at temperatures of between 250 and 350 degrees Celsius.
>
> After being roasted, the beans are crushed and the outer shell is removed. This part is not needed for making chocolate. Finally, the inner part of the bean is pressed and liquid chocolate is produced.
>
> (153 words)

3 City attractions

Unit topic	Leisure in the city
3.1	
Test skills	Speaking Part 1
	Reading (GT): Multiple matching
Grammar	Cause, purpose and result
3.2	
Test skills	Listening: Note completion
Vocabulary	Descriptive adjectives
	Adjectives ending in -ing and -ed
Pronunciation	Word stress in related words
Workbook contents	
1, 2, 3	Reading
4, 5	Vocabulary
6	Grammar: cause, purpose and result

3.1 SB pages 20–21

1 It would be useful to have a map of the world. Ask students for examples of cities and ask them to point to them on the map (e.g. London, New York, Shanghai, Delhi, Buenos Aires). Ask for differences between *city*, *town* and *village*. (In British English, a city is generally large with many shops and other facilities, a town is smaller and a village is very small, with few facilities. In American English, *city* is sometimes used of towns and villages, too.)

Ask students to discuss the questions in pairs. Encourage them to expand their answers, particularly by giving reasons. The questions are similar to Part 1 of the Speaking Module.

Go through the questions with the whole class, asking for two or three answers to each.

2 Ask students where Edinburgh is on the map and what they know about the city (pronounced /ˈedɪnbərə/ or /ˈedɪnbrə/).

Background information
Edinburgh
- Capital of Scotland (and was before Scotland became part of the UK in 1707)
- Well-known constructions: Edinburgh Castle, Holyrood House, Forth Railway Bridge
- Well-known events: Edinburgh Festival and military tattoo every August
- Population: 450,000 (smaller than Glasgow)
- Nearer the North Pole than most cities in the world, except those in Scandinavia, Latvia, Estonia and northern Russia

- Mary, Queen of Scots (16th-century Queen of Scotland) lived there
- On the Firth of Forth (the Forth = name of river; *firth* = Scottish word for an arm of the sea reaching into land)

Ask students to read the first paragraph, encouraging them to read quickly and to focus on the main points. They don't need to understand every word. Then ask them why Edinburgh Castle is popular.

Then ask them to read each of the other paragraphs in turn and discuss with a partner why the attraction is popular, using the phrases that are given.

Refer students to the Test spot on page 21. Point out that this type of matching task is used in GT Reading and is similar to matching in Academic Reading.

Possible answers
The castle appeals to people who are interested in history. It's also a good place to go if you want to see the whole city.

Our Dynamic Earth attracts people who want to learn about the planet.

The Forth Railway Bridge is an interesting and unusual engineering structure, so it particularly appeals to engineers.

Deep Sea World is a good place to go if you want to see sharks, piranhas and other fish face to face. And if you're in good health, you can go scuba diving among the sharks!

3 Ask students to read the example and the underlined part of the passage. Ask for the phrase in the passage that means 'in the city centre' (**Answer:** *in the heart of the city*). Point out that the statements normally *paraphrase* the passage.

Ask students to reread each paragraph and, after each one, to look for the statement(s) that match it. This could be done in pairs or small groups.

Answers
1 C *This was very time-consuming. The solution was to construct the Forth Railway Bridge*
2 B *a striking, purpose-built tented structure*
3 D *You must be at least 16*
4 C *It was opened in 1890, and has been in continuous use ever since.*
5 A *The Military Tattoo ... takes place at Edinburgh Castle every August*
6 D *we can help the children in your class to improve their scientific skills.*
7 B *explores the extremes of our planet Earth.*

4 Ask students if they would like to go to Edinburgh. Write on the board one or two answers that give a reason. Ask why the Forth Railway Bridge was constructed. Write on the board answers that give reasons or purposes, for example:

Cause or reason:

It was built because the ferry crossing took a long time.

Purpose or intention:

It was built to shorten the ferry crossing.

It was built so that trains could cross the water.

Make sure students understand purpose: the hoped-for outcome of an action which may not actually happen. Point out the need to explain cause, purpose or result, both in academic and everyday English. Ask students to do the exercise, perhaps in pairs. Check the answers.

Answers

1 d 2 b 3 f 4 g 5 c 6 e

5 Explain the example and which sentences in exercise 4 follow that pattern (3f and 4g). Ask for the answers to the two questions.

Answers

1 cause; noun phrase 2 purpose; clause

Ask students for the sentences in exercise 4 that follow each pattern.

Answers

1 sentences 1d and 6e 2 sentences 2b and 5c

6 Ask for the difference between the two sentences.

Answers

1 *So* gives the purpose or intention. *So that* is also possible.
2 *So* gives the result, the actual outcome of the situation. It may not have been intended. *So that* isn't possible.

Ask students to read questions 3–7 and decide whether *so* is indicating purpose/intention or result in each one.

Refer students to Grammar folder (SB pages 138–139) for further information and examples. The picture shows an exhibit at Our Dynamic Earth.

Answers

3 purpose (*so that* is possible)
4 result (*so that* isn't possible)
5 either purpose or result
6 result (*so that* isn't possible)
7 either purpose or result

7 Ask students to talk in pairs, developing their answers and using grammar and vocabulary that they have learnt during the lesson.

Possible answers
Living in a city is good for young people because of the wide range of facilities. However, it can be bad because of the pollution.
A lot of people move to cities so that they can get a well-paid job.
Cities can be exciting because there is so much to do.

Extension activity

Students could be asked to write a brochure to attract tourists to their own or another town (perhaps doing research on the Internet).

3.2 SB pages 22–23

1 Ask students if they can identify what's shown in the pictures. Write on the board vocabulary that will occur in the listening passage, particularly *harbour, bridge, opera house, boat, café, restaurant*. Tell students that the subjects of the pictures are all mentioned in the listening passage.

Answers
top left: Sydney Harbour Bridge and Opera House
bottom left: a dragon boat
right: the Rocks area of Sydney

2 Ask students to read the rubric. Stress the importance of keeping within the maximum number of words (in this case, three). Point out that the notes follow the order of the passage and that words must be spelt correctly. Play the recording once and ask students to complete the notes. (NB: 'Robin' is a girl's name in Australia and the USA, and a boy's name in the UK.)

Ask students to predict possible answers and word classes that would fit each space.

Suggested answers
What kind of information is needed
1 noun phrase: a building, structure or area (e.g. *road, harbour, hotel*)
2 noun phrase: a building, structure or area (e.g. *hilltop, tower*)
3 noun phrase: period of time (e.g. *two hours* – but not *a year*)
4 noun phrase: an area that could be part of the Opera House (e.g. *reception area, car park*)
5 adjective, possibly a superlative, or noun used adjectivally (e.g. *most popular, most crowded, tourist, business*)
6 noun phrases: things in a district (e.g. *shops, cinemas, street performers*)
7 number (e.g. *500, 1,000* – but not *10*)
8 noun phrases: activities (e.g. *swimming, music*)

Play the recording again, stopping it to check each answer.

Recording script

Robin: Hello?

Jerry: Hi, Robin, it's Jerry.

Robin: Jerry! Nice to hear from you. How're you doing?

Jerry: Fine, thanks. Guess what? I'm going on holiday to Australia next month!

Robin: Wow, that's great!

Jerry: I thought you might be able to give me some ideas about what to do while I'm in Sydney. That's where you come from, isn't it?

Robin: That's right. And I wish I was there now, instead of here in the cold.

Jerry: What's the temperature likely to be there?

Robin: Oh, next month it'll be around 25 degrees. If you went during the British summer, and the Australian winter, it would only be about 16 degrees.

Jerry: I'm looking forward to some warm weather.

Robin: So how long are you staying in Sydney?

Jerry: Only a couple of days. I'm going to spend a month touring Australia.

Robin: Sounds good. Well, you'll need at least a morning exploring the harbour area – it's fascinating. I really like the Pylon Lookout: the entrance is on the bridge. It's got an interesting display on how the bridge was built, and the panorama of the harbour from the observation area is spectacular.

Jerry: Right, I'll do that.

Robin: And of course you can see the Opera House – that and the bridge are Sydney's most famous sights.

Jerry: Do you know if there are any tours of the Opera House?

Robin: Yes, there are. As far as I remember, there's one every 30 minutes, and you spend around an hour exploring different parts of the building, depending which tour it is.

Jerry: Uh-huh. Do I need to book tickets in advance?

Robin: No, just buy them at the Opera House, from the Guided Tours office. You'll see the signs to point you in the right direction.

Jerry: Right, I'll do that. It'll be interesting to find out how the Opera House is run.

Robin: Then I reckon you should walk round the Rocks. It's the oldest part of the city, and always crowded with tourists of all nationalities, as well as local people. The cafés and restaurants keep very busy. Whenever I go back to Sydney, I enjoy sitting outdoors with a cup of coffee, watching the people passing by.

Jerry: Yes, that sounds like a good idea.

Robin: Oh, and I almost forgot – it's the Dragon Festival next month. You should arrange to be in Sydney that weekend. You'll have a great time.

Jerry: What is it?

Robin: You don't know the Dragon Festival? It's to celebrate the Chinese New Year. There are races between lots of traditional wooden boats, decorated with dragons' heads and tails. Each boat has something like 20 people rowing it, and over 2,000 people take part altogether.

Jerry: Mm.

Robin: Crowds of people go to watch. The opening ceremony is pretty exciting, too, with drums and dancing. Why don't you check the dates on the Internet?

Jerry: I will. It sounds great. Well, thanks for the suggestions, Robin. I'm looking forward to my holiday.

Robin: Have a good trip and call me when you get back to the UK. Bye.

Jerry: Bye.

Photocopiable recording script activity (P ⋯⟩ page 134)

Give each student a copy of the recording script. Ask them to find words that would make sense in the notes, but are wrong, for example *Temperature: 16*.

Possible wrong answers
1 harbour, observation area
2 bridge, Opera House
3 30 minutes
4 office (*this isn't enough to identify the correct part of the Opera House*)
5 crowded
6 tourists, local people, coffee
7 20
8 crowds of people, opening ceremony

Students can also take it in turns to read the dialogue aloud in pairs.

3 This exercise will help students to broaden their vocabulary. Encourage them to record vocabulary in notebooks, arranged by topic, with synonyms together, and in phrases. Check that students know what the words in the box mean, then ask them to do the exercise, perhaps in small groups. *Crowded* isn't used; after checking answers, ask students to use it in a sentence, e.g. *The beach was so crowded there was nowhere to sit.*

Answers
1 massive 2 thrilling 3 striking 4 spectacular
5 famous 6 beautiful 7 fascinating 8 terrifying

Ask students for examples of other objects or places that might be described by the words in the box.

4 Write *an exciting experience* and *interesting museums* (from exercise 3, items 2 and 7) on the board, plus *excited* and *interested*. Ask students for phrases containing those two words and write correct ones on the board. Ask for the difference between the *-ing* adjectives and the *-ed* adjectives. (The former have an active meaning, the latter are passive.) Ask for examples using *terrifying*, *terrified*, *fascinating*, *fascinated*. Ask students to read the box at the top of SB page 23.

Ask students to complete the table. When checking answers, make sure the spelling is correct.

Answers

verb	'active' adjective, -ing	'passive' adjective, -ed
to amaze	amazing	amazed
to astonish	astonishing	astonished
to excite	exciting	excited
to fascinate	fascinating	fascinated
to frighten	frightening	frightened
to interest	interesting	interested
to surprise	surprising	surprised
to terrify	terrifying	terrified
to thrill	thrilling	thrilled

5   Ask for the answers.

Answers
1 fascinating 2 interesting 3 astonished 4 fascinated
5 interested 6 amazing

6   Ask one or two students to complete the first sentence,
    then ask students to talk in pairs, completing the
    sentences in a suitable way.

Possible answers
1 I think Sydney is a very exciting city, because there are
  people from all over the world.
2 Some visitors to Shanghai are amazed that there are so
  many tall buildings.
3 It's surprising that Oslo doesn't have more visitors in the
  winter, because it has lots of indoor activities.
4 Most people who visit Cape Town for the first time are
  thrilled when they see Table Mountain.
5 It's astonishing that Cairo is so crowded.

7   Point out the importance of stressing words in the right
    place (it can be very difficult to recognise words that are
    stressed wrongly). Write two or three students' names (of
    two or more syllables) on the board and ask which
    syllable is stressed. Put ' in front of each stressed syllable.
    (If students' names are all monosyllabic or have equal
    stress, use 'Sydney, Au'stralia and 'London). NB Every
    syllable must have a vowel sound; consonants are less
    important, so Au'stralia, Aus'tralia, Aust'ralia and
    Austr'alia are all acceptable.

    Ask students to read the exercise and do it in pairs. When
    they've had enough time, play the recording so they can
    check their answers.

Recording script and answers
1 in'form   in.for'ma.tion
2 ob'serve   ob.ser'va.tion
3 solve   so'lu.tion
4 'ac.tive   ac'ti.vi.ty
5 'lo.cal   lo'ca.li.ty
6 'na.tion   na.tio'na.li.ty
7 a'ca.de.my   a.ca'de.mic
8 'sci.ence   sci.en'ti.fic

8   Ask students to work out from the second column in
    exercise 7 which endings are immediately preceded by
    the stressed syllable.

Answer
-tion; -ity; -ic

Write ex'plain, 'fascinate, 'curious, ob'jective, 'strategy and
'allergy on the board in a column and ask for related
words ending in -tion, -ity or -ic. Write them beside the
related word and ask which syllable is stressed, following
the rule. Mark it (expla'nation, fasci'nation, curi'osity,
objec'tivity, stra'tegic, a'llergic).

9   Write the phonemic spelling of activity on the board
    (/æk'tɪ.vɪ.tɪ/), explaining that each symbol always
    represents the same sound. Ask students (in pairs) to try
    and read the words in the exercise. When checking the
    answers, make sure the correct syllables are stressed.

Answers
1 famous 2 attractive 3 striking 4 historical
5 beautiful 6 magnificent

Encourage students to look up new words in an English-
English dictionary that shows pronunciation and stress
(e.g. Cambridge Advanced Learner's Dictionary). Remind
them that it's useful to write new words in a notebook,
marking stress and saying the word aloud a few times, to
help them remember it.

Test folder 2

SB pages 24–25
Matching

Make sure students understand the information and advice.

1 Ask students if they recognise the place in the picture (Manhattan, New York). Tell them they are going to listen to a guide talking to some visitors to New York.

Ask students to look at the box of options and to give examples of words that would suggest each one.

> **Possible answers (excluding ones used as clues in the passage)**
> A art: *museum, painting, sculpture*
> B shipping: *boat, ferry, dock, quay*
> C famous people: *well-known, celebrity, celebrated* and personal names
> D former amusements: *film/movie, entertainment, leisure* and indications that they are no longer popular
> E geography of the city: *north, island, layout*
> F old homes: *home, house* and indications of past time
> G the range of museums: *history, archaeology, opening hours*
> H transportation: *car/auto, airport, bus station*
> I visiting local people: *home, way of life, call on somebody*
> J wildlife: *animals, zoo, insects*

Allow students time to listen to the talk and answer the questions.

> **Answers (see underlined text in script)**
> 1 E 2 F 3 H 4 D 5 J

Recording script

You will hear the leader of a study programme about New York City talking to the participants.

First, you have some time to look at questions 1 to 5. (*pause*)

Now listen carefully and answer questions 1 to 5.

Well, good morning, ladies and gentlemen, and welcome to New York City and our study program about the city. I know that, for some of you, this is your very first visit to the United States, so I'd particularly like to welcome you and say I just know you're gonna have a great time. First, let me outline this week's program of activities.

Tomorrow morning, Monday, we'll take the Circle Line cruise along the Hudson, East and Harlem rivers, so you can <u>orientate yourselves</u>. It's a fantastic way to see Manhattan Island, the heart of New York, and to <u>bring the map to life</u>. The cruise lasts three hours, and along the way you'll see some of the famous and most impressive sites of the city, like the Statue of Liberty, Battery Park and Brooklyn Bridge.

Then on Tuesday, I want to give you some insight into New York City's fascinating history, created by the millions of immigrants who have come here by sea or by land from all corners of the world, in the hope of finding a better life. But many of them arrived only to <u>live in poverty and terrible, crowded conditions</u>. We'll visit the Lower East Side <u>Tenement</u> Museum, located in a <u>building</u> where 7,000 people were <u>resident</u> between 1863 and 1935, with large families crammed into <u>one- or two-room apartments</u>. On Wednesday morning, we'll go to Grand Central <u>Terminal</u> for a tour of the very impressive <u>station</u>, and a speaker will tell us how New York City's <u>mass transit system</u> has developed, including its <u>subways, railroads, buses and ferries</u>. Over 150,000 people <u>commute</u> to Grand Central daily from their homes outside the city, and the <u>subway system</u> alone carries over seven million <u>passengers</u> each day. And that takes us to Thursday. I'm sure many of you will visit the city's major museums and art galleries, like the Metropolitan Museum of Art, with its hundreds of world-famous masterpieces. But you need to take your own time in places like those, so instead, I'll show you something rather different: a small but very interesting museum dedicated to the <u>fairgrounds</u> of Coney Island, where millions of New Yorkers <u>used to go for a day out</u>, to enjoy <u>rides like the Cyclone Rollercoaster, the Wonder Wheel and the Parachute Jump</u>.

Friday's outing is to somewhere you might not expect to find within the limits of New York City – an area in and around Jamaica Bay that's been set aside as a refuge for a wide range of <u>birds, butterflies, reptiles and rare flowers</u>. Its <u>habitats</u> include <u>salt marsh, fields and woods, several ponds and an open expanse of bay and islands</u>. Although it's close to JFK Airport, this is a good place to escape from the crowds and noise of the city.

OK, now the next thing we need to do is …

2 Go through the example and one or two questions in class: for each question, ask students to identify both the relevant paragraph (A–E) and the relevant part of the paragraph.

Evidence for the answers is given below. Students should not write this in the test.

> **Answers**
> 1 B *streets with familiar names like Savile Row, famous for its men's suits*
> 2 A *listen as we recite parts of his novels*
> 3 D *the former power generating station has been transformed into Tate Modern art gallery*
> 4 C *the original termination of the New River, constructed to bring water to London*
> 5 E *buildings, some of which can only be visited by special arrangement.*
> 6 D *Borough Market, where you'll find it hard to choose among all the fine food and other goods on sale.*
> 7 B *For more than 250 years Mayfair has been the most upmarket district in London*
> 8 D *the new Globe, a replica of Shakespeare's theatre*
> 9 E *you'll discover how Stinking Lane and Turnagain Lane got their names*

4 Ways of learning

Unit topic	Education

4.1
Test skills
	Speaking Part 3
	Listening: Multiple choice
	  Multiple choice with multiple
	  answers
	Reading (GT): Reading effectively

Vocabulary	Words used in academic writing
4.2 Grammar	Review of present tenses
Pronunciation	Word stress

Workbook contents	
1, 2	Grammar: present tenses
3, 4	Grammar: prepositions
5, 6	Reading

4.1 SB pages 26–27

1 Ask students what they think of the two types of lesson in the pictures. Ask if anyone has had one-to-one (also called *one-on-one*) lessons and, if so, what their experience was. Ask students to discuss the questions in small groups.

> **Suggested answers**
> Possible advantages of one-to-one lessons: having the teacher's attention all the time; studying at a speed that suits you; having to think for yourself, not having other students doing the work
>
> Possible disadvantages: not being able to learn from other students; not having the possibility of developing ideas together; not having a chance to relax

2 The recording is fairly similar to Section 3 of the Listening Module. Ask students to read the Test spot, then the rubric, the example (0) and the explanation. NB Morag is a traditional Scottish girl's name. Play the first section of the recording. Check that students understand why C is the correct answer.

Ask students to read the rubric and questions 1–4. Play the second section of the recording.

> **Answers** (see underlined text in script)
> 1 C 2 A 3 B 4 A

Ask students to read the rubric and questions 5 and 6. For question 5, there is only one mark for all three answers, and for question 6, only one mark for both answers. When there is one mark for each answer, each

question is numbered separately. Play the third section of the recording. Remind students to choose only the stated number of answers and to write only A, B, etc.

> **Answers** (see underlined text in script)
> 5 B, D, E (*in any order*)
> 6 B, E (*in either order*)

Recording script

Listen to the example.

Interviewer: Good morning. Now, in this programme, we've been looking at different forms of education for children up to the age of 16. And this week, I've invited Morag to come and tell us what it's like having lessons at home. Morag, have you ever been to school?

Morag: Oh yes, I started at infants' school when I was four, and when I turned seven, I went on to junior school. <u>I left when I was eight,</u> and my mother's been teaching me at home ever since – she's a qualified teacher.

****

Questions 1–4

Interviewer: Why did you leave?

Morag: Well, my family moved to a remote island in Scotland, and <u>there wasn't a school nearby.</u> My parents thought I was quick at learning and could cope with being taught at home instead – the alternative was to live away from home. I enjoyed school, so at first I was quite unhappy about leaving and I missed my friends. But now I prefer it.

Interviewer: Is there anything you don't like about having lessons at home?

Morag: Most of the time, it's great. We start around nine o'clock, five days a week, and work for about six hours a day, which I enjoy. The only difficulty is that <u>I'm the centre of attention – if I feel bored or don't understand something, I can't hide it,</u> as I'm the only student! Some people think I must be lonely, but I enjoy doing things on my own, and anyway I spend most weekends with other people.

Interviewer: Do you work with your mother all day long?

Morag: No, I do a lot of projects on particular topics, and after we've planned one, I do most of the work on my own. So I sometimes spend quite a long time finding information on the Internet or in books. At the moment, I'm doing research into the island where we live. I've talked to a lot of the people who live here, and that was very interesting. <u>I really learn a lot from projects,</u> because you have to look at the topic from different angles and try to make sense of it all.

Interviewer: What do you think is the hardest part of doing projects?

Morag: Mmm, the first stage isn't too difficult. That's when my mother and I talk about what exactly the project should cover. With the one about the island, we decided that I should focus on what jobs were available and why. Then I have to search for material, which is why I use the Internet a lot. Though with most projects, I also interview people or do experiments. <u>After that, I have to write a report on what I've found out and I find that quite hard.</u>

****

Questions 5 and 6

Interviewer: Apart from working on projects, what subjects do you study?

Morag: Well, there's history – I'm not very keen on that, though – it seems to be mostly about fighting. Um, <u>geography's much more fun</u>, because you learn about the world and how things like mountains or the climate affect the way we live. And I know English is necessary, but I don't really look forward to the lessons. Then there's <u>biology, which is one of my favourite subjects. Um, I didn't like economics at first, but after a while I really took to it.</u> We're going to start Spanish soon, but I don't know how much I'll enjoy that – I find the pronunciation of foreign languages quite difficult, and I can't seem to remember the vocabulary!

Interviewer: And what about when you finish your education? Have you thought much about that?

Morag: I haven't really made up my mind yet. I used to want to be a tennis player, but I'm not good enough to be professional, so I'll go on playing just for pleasure. I think photography is fascinating, because there are so many things you can do when you take photographs. So <u>I might go into film-making</u> – I'd like to do something creative. My father wants me to become a musician, like him, but it really doesn't appeal to me. And of course my mother's a teacher, though I think one in the family is enough! <u>I'm thinking seriously about becoming a doctor,</u> even though it would mean a lot of studying.

Interviewer: OK, well, good luck …

3 Ask students to comment on the questions. Encourage them to give reasons for their answers.

4 Ask students about their experience of reading, both in English and in their own language, e.g. what types of documents are easy or hard to read. Ask why they read different types of texts (e.g. textbooks, emails, magazine articles – remind them of discussion of this topic in 1.1, SB page 8) – and whether they read everything at the same speed.

Exercises 4 and 5 will help students with reading in the test. Exercise 5 is similar to a True/False task. It will also help them to read more effectively – both in English and in their own language.

Ask students to discuss the value of the advice in exercise 4 in small groups.

Possible answers

1 Yes: *why* you're reading affects *how* you read it.
2 No: it depends why you're reading the text. For instance, if you're looking for specific information, such as the time that a TV programme starts, you can stop reading as soon as you've found it.
3 Yes: the title may show what aspect of the topic is dealt with and whether the text contains the information you want.
4 Maybe, depending on what the topic is, why you're reading about it and who you ask. It's likely to be more useful *after* you've read a text, though.
5 No: the main information is much more likely to come near the beginning of each paragraph.
6 No: if you need to remember important parts of the text, it's more effective to summarise them in your own words.

---

5 Ask students to read the rubric and passage and do the exercise.

Answers
Advice in exercise 4
1 ✓ (lines 3–4)   2 ✗   3 ✓ (line 12)   4 ✗   5 ✗   6 ✗

---

6 Point out that exercise 6 contains informal paraphrases of slightly more academic words in the reading passage. Ask students to find the words.

Answers
1 comprehension (title)   2 purpose (line 4)
3 method (line 5)   4 specific (line 6)   5 relevant (lines 8, 17)
6 title (line 12)   7 relates (line 21)

---

7 Point out that using words is the best way to remember them. Ask students to complete the exercise.

Answers
1 method   2 title   3 specific   4 purpose
5 Comprehension

---

8 Ask students to form small groups and discuss how best to study and learn effectively. After five or ten minutes, ask each group for some points that they have agreed on, and write them on the board.

Possible answers
- It's usually easier to learn effectively in a group of four or five than in a group of 40 or 50.
- Some teachers are good at making students want to learn. Some know a lot about their subject, but may not be so good at explaining it to students.
- Lessons are more interesting if there is a variety of activities.
- Equipment and facilities, such as CD players and language labs, can be helpful, because they add to the variety of activities.
- It may be more effective to study with other people whose knowledge of the subject is similar to your own. On the other hand, explaining something to someone who knows less than you can help you to understand better.

Extension activity

Ask groups of students either to write advice to other students on how to study and learn effectively (based on their discussion of exercise 8), or to write a description of the ideal learning situation, with a title such as 'The best way to learn'.

4.2 SB pages 28–29

1 Ask students to look at the picture and comment on how and where the person is studying. (She is sitting in a park.) Ask them how easy it is to study in that situation. Then, in pairs, ask them to discuss the questions. They are similar to those in Part 1 of the Speaking Module.

2 Ask students why the present simple is used in the first question of exercise 1 (**Do** you usually **study** …?) and the present continuous in the last (What **are** you **studying** …?). The first is concerned with how often an action is carried out, the second with something temporary.

Ask students to work through exercise 2, perhaps in pairs.

> **Answers**
> **1** b **2** a ('m doing); c (live) **3** b **4** c **5** a **6** c
> **a** present continuous
> **b** present simple
> **c** present simple

If necessary, remind students how the present simple and continuous are formed:

- Present simple: one word only, the same as the form used in dictionaries (except to be), but third person singular ends in -s.

- Present continuous: present simple of to be + present participle (-ing form) of main verb. The present continuous has specific meanings and is used less than the present simple.

3 Ask students to read the rubric, then ask for the correct alternative in 1 (are studying) and which meaning it has from the box in exercise 2 (a). Ask students to complete 2–7. Draw attention to the shaded box.

> **Answers**
> **1** are studying (a) **2** understand (c) **3** am having (a)
> **4** do you work (b) **5** is thinking (a) **6** think (c)
> **7** never spend (b)

4 Ask students to correct the errors.

> **Answers**
> **1** How much time I spend doing homework **depends** on what else I want to do. (relationship verb)
> **2** Please stop talking – I**'m listening** to the teacher. ((a) in exercise 2)
> **3** Most people **feel** tired when they've worked hard all day. ((c) in exercise 2)
> **4** This week we**'re having** lessons in the library because our classroom is being decorated. ((a) in exercise 2)

5 Ask a student how long he/she has lived in his/her present home. Write the answer on the board as a complete sentence, e.g. X has lived in her present home all her life. Draw a timeline to illustrate it:

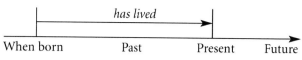

Explain that X started living there in the past, and still does.

Ask another student Have you ever listened to songs in English? (or something else where the answer is likely to be 'yes'). Write Y has listened to songs in English and draw a timeline:

Point out that this means Y listened to songs in the past, but it doesn't say when.

Write on the board I can't go home because I've lost my keys, and draw a timeline:

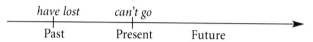

Point out that the action happened at some time in the past, which isn't mentioned, and the sentence focuses on the result in the present.

Ask students to read a–c in exercise 5, which correspond to the three meanings shown in the timelines above (in the same order), then to do exercise 5.

If necessary, remind students how the present perfect is formed (present tense of to have + past participle of main verb).

> **Answers**
> **1** a **2** c **3** b **4** b **5** c **6** a

6 Ask a student how long he/she has been studying English (or another activity which is likely to continue). Write the answer on the board.

Explain that, like the present perfect simple, the present perfect continuous relates a past action to the present. Point out that it generally emphasises a length of time. Remind students how it is formed: present perfect tense of to be + present participle (-ing form) of the main verb.

Ask students to read the rubric, then ask which meaning – a or b – matches each example.

> **Answers**
> **1** b **2** a **3** b **4** a

Refer students to the Grammar folder (SB page 139) for further information.

7 Ask two or three students what they've done since the last lesson, encouraging them to use present perfect tenses. Write examples of what they say on the board, using both present perfect tenses. Then ask students to do exercise 7 in pairs.

Extension activity

Students could be given a short magazine article, extract from a novel or other passage containing a variety of present tenses, and asked to explain the choice of tense in each case.

8 Remind students of the work they did on word stress in 3.2 (SB page 23). Remind them that words that are stressed wrongly can be difficult to understand. Ask them to do exercise 8 in pairs. Then play the recording so they can check their answers. The sentences come from the listening passage.

Recording script

Example: Now in this programme we've been looking at different forms of education for children up to the age of 16.
1 But now I prefer it.
2 The only difficulty is that I'm the centre of attention.
3 After that I have to write a report on what I've found out.
4 What subjects do you study?
5 I do a lot of projects on particular topics.
6 We learn how the climate affects the way we live.
7 I find the pronunciation of foreign languages quite difficult.
8 I can't seem to remember the vocabulary!
9 I think photography is fascinating.
10 There are so many things you can do when you take photographs.

> **Answers**
> 1 pre'fer 2 'di.ffi.cul.ty 3 re'port 4 'stu.dy
> 5 par'ti.cu.lar 6 'cli.mate 7 pro.nun.ci'a.tion
> 8 vo'ca.bu.la.ry 9 pho'to.gra.phy 10 'pho.to.graphs

9 Point out the most useful stress patterns to remember:
  a words with certain suffixes *always* have the stress immediately before the suffix (pattern 1)
  b two-syllable words generally stress the first syllable (pattern 3)
  c longer words generally have two unstressed syllables after the stressed one (pattern 4)

Ask students to read the rubric. Ask them to find words from exercise 8 that end in any of the suffixes in pattern 1, and to mark the stressed syllables. Check answers, then ask students to work in pairs and write answers to the other four questions, marking the stress in each word.

> **Answers**
> (Students should mark stress, but not necessarily divide the syllables):
> 1 e.du'ca.tion, pro.nun.ci'a.tion, pho'to.gra.phy
> 2 pre'fer, re'port
> 3 'stu.dy, 'cli.mate
> 4 par'ti.cu.lar, 'pho.to.graphs
> 5 'di.ffi.cul.ty, vo'ca.bu.la.ry

Ask if anyone's name matches any of the stress patterns, and if so, which one. Suggest students write the names by the appropriate pattern.

Ask students to read the words (+ names) in pairs, each checking the other has the stress on the correct syllable.

Encourage students to mark stress when they write down new words they've learnt.

10 Ask students to discuss the topic in pairs. Encourage them to develop their answers.

Writing folder 2

SB pages 30–31
Academic Writing Task 1: Handling data 1 – line graphs

Refer the students to the Advice box.

1 Check that students know the terminology for talking about line graphs/charts. Line graphs compare two variables. Each variable is plotted along an axis. A line graph has a vertical axis (y) and a horizontal axis (x). Line graphs are good at showing specific values of data and trends in data clearly.

Ask the class to look at chart 1 and decide which is a better summary, a or b. You should point out the title of the chart and the x and y axes.

> **Answer**
> b (This is both more informative and more precise.)

2 Refer students to the Useful language box on SB page 31. Check they understand the vocabulary. A good way to do this is for every member of the class to give an oral example of how one of the words is used. Students then complete 1–10 using the vocabulary from the box to describe what is happening in chart 2.

> **Answers**
> 1 slight fluctuation
> 2 gradual/steady rise/increase
> 3 sharp/steep fall/decline
> 4 gradual/steady fall/decline
> 5 went up / rose / increased sharply/steeply
> 6 reached a peak
> 7 remained/held steady *or* was stable *or* remained constant *or* levelled off
> 8 reached a peak
> 9 fell/decreased/declined steeply/sharply
> 10 went up / rose / increased slightly/gradually

3   Students should complete the task. Each question has a clue as to the type of word(s) needed.

Answers
1 between 2 From 3 increase/rise 4 had risen to
5 fall/decrease/decline 6 rose gradually/steadily
7 sharp/steep/dramatic rise/increase 8 rise/increase
9 rise

Units 1–4 Revision

SB pages 32–33

The aim of this revision unit is to focus on the language covered in units 1–4. Students can do exercises 2–7 in class as a test or for homework.

Topic review

1   The aim of this section is to encourage students to speak, using the grammar and vocabulary they have learned in the previous four units. They should say if the statements are true for them and expand on their answers as much as possible. This is useful practice because in the Speaking Module, they also need to give opinions and expand on what they say.

Possible answers
1 Yes that's true. I also send at least 50 a day – mainly to my friends.
2 True – I wouldn't want it, as I would always be worried I would lose it or it would be stolen.
3 True – I really love reading books and I can't imagine reading a book on a computer screen.
4 No, I think my diet is about the same as my friends' diets.
5 I try not to buy fast food, but sometimes I like to have a pizza.
6 No, my mother is the best cook in my family.
7 I like city *and* beach holidays. One day sightseeing and the next on the beach, sunbathing.
8 No, I can study in my country, too, but I need to learn English.
9 Yes, that's very true. I'd love to go to Sydney and see the Opera House and famous harbour bridge.
10 I hate all the traffic in the city. It would be better if only pedestrians and cyclists were allowed in urban areas.

Grammar

2

Answers
1 originated 2 have been found 3 was always made
4 blew 5 made 6 became 7 was praised
8 were forbidden 9 gave 10 are usually made
11 are mixed 12 is heated 13 melts 14 becomes
15 is removed 16 is blown

3

Answers
1 have been living / have lived 2 believes 3 *correct*
4 *correct* 5 never understands 6 has been waiting
7 I've been / I went 8 *correct* 9 I've known
10 freezes 11 has known 12 are you doing; I'm reading
13 *correct* 14 *correct*

4

Possible answers
1 Las Vegas has a smaller number of high-rise buildings than Osaka, even though it has a slightly larger area.
2 São Paolo has the largest population of the seven cities.
3 Beijing has a much larger area than Durban.
4 Las Vegas has the smallest population.
5 Although New York has a smaller area than Hong Kong, it has fewer high-rise buildings.
6 Osaka has nearly the same area as Las Vegas.

5

Answers
1 of 2 on 3 on 4 on; by 5 at 6 to 7 at 8 on

Vocabulary

6

Answers
1 boring 2 surprised 3 exciting 4 astonished
5 interesting

7   Ask students to justify their answers. The picture is of high-rise buildings in Hong Kong.

Answers
1 crowded – all the others are positive adjectives
2 spectacular – all the others are negative feelings
3 fresh – all the others are negative ways of describing food
4 spicy – all the others are negative ways of describing food

Progress Test 1

Listening

Questions 1–5

Complete the notes below.

Write **NO MORE THAN ONE WORD AND/OR A NUMBER** for each answer.

Example:	Answer:
Social Organiser	Paul .....URQUHART.....

Weekend trips
June
Name of trip to Bath: **1** '............................. and Shopping'

July
London visit to: The National Gallery
Name of London day-trip: **2** 'Shopping and ....,'

Cost
Weekend trip: **3** around £ ....
Day-trip: £30

Time: departure – **4** .... a.m.
                               return – around 5.30 p.m.

To reserve a seat: Sign notice in **5** .... a week in advance

Questions 6–10

Complete the sentences below.

Write **NO MORE THAN TWO WORDS AND/OR A NUMBER** for each answer.

Trip to Bath

6 Take .... and good footwear.

7 A good place to have lunch is in the .... in Bath.

8 There is a .... held outdoors in Bath during the weekend.

9 Maybe hire a .... for a couple of hours.

10 Don't forget to pack a ....

Reading

A SHORT HISTORY OF MEXICO CITY

Although the central region of Mexico's high plateau has been inhabited for at least 20,000 years, Mexico City only dates back to the 14th century. The Aztecs, or Mexica, had reached this area in the previous century, eventually settling on an island in Lake Texcoco. Here, in 1325, the city of Tenochtitlán began to take shape.

5 The lake was shallow, and during the nearly 200 years until 1519, the Aztecs expanded the inhabited area by land refill and the creation of artificial islands. Canals were dug for the transportation of goods and people. Aqueducts were constructed to bring drinking water from natural springs outside the city, dams to protect it against floods, and causeways and bridges to connect the city with the shore. There were many houses,
10 palaces, temples, squares, markets and even a zoo. Perhaps the most striking construction of this period is the Templo Mayor, a double pyramid which still survives. As the capital of an empire stretching from Texas to Honduras, Tenochtitlán was a magnificent and important city. When the Spanish arrived, they called it the 'Venice of the New World'.

The Spanish began their conquest of Mexico in 1519 and came close to Tenochtitlán the
15 same year. In 1521, they took control of it, after fierce fighting that destroyed most of the city. A new capital, with a new name, was built on the ruins, using Spanish architectural styles. One part of the lake was filled in to join the island to the shore, and Mexico City became the capital of the wealthiest colony in the Americas, the centre of trade between Spain and China.

20 By the beginning of the 17th century, it was a busy, lively city, with some residents leading a splendid and luxurious way of life. Not everything went well, though: heavy rain in 1629 caused a great deal of destruction, in which many people died, and thousands lost their homes. A large part of the city had to be rebuilt. For much of the century, the residents suffered from social and economic pressures, including serious food
25 shortages, which erupted in riots in 1692.

In the 18th century, too, many new buildings were constructed. It was a prosperous period, when the new aristocracy paid for splendid buildings, banquets and balls, not to mention the latest fashions from Europe.

The rise of Napoleon in the early 19th century led to political changes throughout
30 Europe. An uprising took place in Mexico in 1810, with the aim of ending rule from Spain. This goal was finally achieved in 1821, when Mexico City briefly became the capital of the Mexican Empire. Since 1823, it has been the capital of the Republic of Mexico, apart from a short period, from 1863 to 1867, when the country was again an empire.

In the first few decades of the 20th century, plans were drawn up for the urbanisation of
35 Mexico City; slum-clearance and housing development programmes were introduced, and factories spread through the city. During the 20th century, the population grew fast, and the city is now one of the largest in the world. It has changed a great deal since it was founded nearly 700 years ago.

Questions 1–10

Do the following statements agree with the information in the reading passage? Write

TRUE   *if the statement agrees with the information*

FALSE   *if the statement contradicts the information*

NOT GIVEN *if there is no information on this*

1 Mexico City and the central region of the high plateau have been inhabited for the same length of time.

2 The Aztecs generally preferred to live on islands.

3 The area where people lived was artificially increased between 1325 and 1519.

4 The Spanish had heard of Tenochtitlán before they reached Mexico.

5 The Aztec inhabitants of Tenochtitlán left when the city was conquered.

6 Rain destroyed the whole of Mexico City in 1629.

7 In the 18th century, some residents of Mexico City bought European goods.

8 Spanish rule of Mexico ended in 1810.

9 Since 1823, Mexico has always been a republic.

10 Industrialisation of Mexico City took place in the early part of the 20th century.

Writing

Writing Task 1 (AC)

You should spend about 20 minutes on this task.

> *The charts below give information about mobile phone possession and use in the town of Eden Hills.*
>
> *Summarise the information by selecting and reporting the main features, and make comparisons where relevant.*

Write at least 150 words.

Percentage of people possessing a mobile phone by sex and age in Eden Hills (2002)

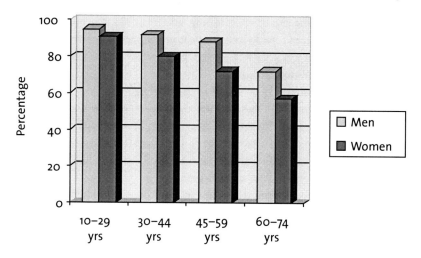

Text messaging by age and gender of mobile phone owners in Eden Hills (2002) in percentages

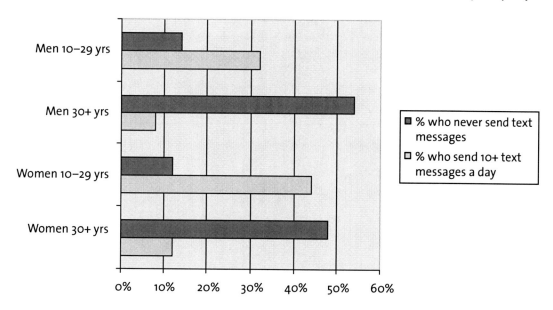

© Cambridge University Press, 2006

Progress Test 1 Key

Listening

1 Fashion   2 Theatre/Theater   3 (£)160   4 seven/7/7.00
5 reception   6 (a) camera   7 park   8 film festival
9 boat   10 swim(-)suit

Recording script

You will hear a student asking about trips from her college. First, you have some time to look at questions 1 to 5.

Now listen carefully and answer questions 1 to 5.
Woman: Hello.
Man: Hi – can I help you?
Woman: Yes, I was looking for the social organiser. I'm sorry, I don't know his name.
Man: He's not here at the moment, but I can probably help you. He's called Paul Urquhart, that's <u>U-R-Q-U-H-A-R-T</u>. My name's Will.
Woman: Oh, OK. I was wondering about trips this term.
Man: We've got three – one in June and two in July.
Woman: Great – where are they to?
Man: The first one's to Bath – we call this the '<u>Fashion</u> and Shopping' weekend because we visit the Costume Museum. The second one is to the National Gallery in London to see their Renoir exhibition and then free time on the Sunday. I'm sure that's going to be very popular with everyone.
Woman: Mm. And the other trip?
Man: That's to London, too. This is only a day trip. It's called 'Shopping and <u>Theatre</u>'. You do your shopping in the morning and in the afternoon see a play. Not sure which one yet, though, but there's always something good on at that time of year in the West End.
Woman: How much are the trips?
Man: I haven't worked out a final price yet for the weekend trips, but last year they were £150. I guess we'll be charging <u>about £160</u> this year – that's actually very good value. The day trip will obviously be much cheaper – £30.
Woman: Is it a very early start?
Man: All trips leave here at <u>seven</u> in the morning. Some people think they can turn up at 7.15, but I'm afraid we don't wait around. We aim to get back at about five-thirty in the evening.
Woman: OK. And when do I need to decide whether I'm going or not?
Man: I'll put a notice up about a week before the trip leaves, and you'll need to sign your name to say you're interested. It'll be in <u>reception</u> rather than the common room, where the other notices are.
Woman: OK, thanks. I'll think it over.
****

Before you hear the rest of the conversation, you have some time to look at questions 6 to 10.

Now listen and answer questions 6 to 10.
Woman: Can you tell me a bit more about the trip to Bath? I've never been there.
Man: Sure. There's loads to see and do – you'll definitely need to bring good walking shoes with you – oh, and a <u>camera</u>, of course. No need for a map, as we'll give you one.
Woman: Uh-huh. Now, I know we're going to a museum and have some free time to go shopping, but what else can we do?
Man: OK, well, on the Sunday, you could take a bus tour of the city in the morning, and if the weather's nice, I'd buy some sandwiches and eat in the <u>park</u> rather than queuing up to get a seat for lunch in one of the cafés. They're always crowded.
Woman: What about in the evening?
Man: Well, there are the usual things to do – nightclubs and so on. But there's a <u>film festival</u> in one of the museum gardens while we are in Bath, and that should be great – you can sit under the stars and be entertained.
Woman: Sounds wonderful.
Man: It should be – as long as it doesn't rain, of course. Anyway, another idea for a sunny day is to get a <u>boat</u> and go on the river for a couple of hours. You can hire bicycles, too, but I think that would be too tiring if it's hot.
Woman: What about the hotel? I forgot to ask about that.
Man: Sure – it's called the Regent and it's modern. There's a restaurant, and I think they're building a gym, but it won't be ready when we go. However, what they do have is a small indoor swimming pool, so remember to take a <u>swimsuit</u> with you!
Woman: It all sounds great – I'll definitely go. Thanks a lot, Will.

Reading

1 FALSE   *Although the central region of Mexico's high plateau has been inhabited for at least 20,000 years, Mexico City only dates back to the 14th century.* (lines 1–2)

2 NOT GIVEN We are told that the Aztecs settled on the island, but nothing about how often they chose islands.

3 TRUE   *during the nearly 200 years until 1519, the Aztecs expanded the inhabited area by land refill and the creation of artificial islands.* (lines 5–6)

4 NOT GIVEN We are told that *Tenochtitlán was a magnificent and important city* (lines 12–13), but there is no indication of whether the Spanish had heard of it before reaching Mexico.

5 NOT GIVEN We are told that most of the city was destroyed, but not what happened to the Aztec inhabitants.

6 FALSE   *heavy rain in 1629 caused a great deal of destruction, in which many people died, and thousands lost their homes. A large part of the city had to be rebuilt.* (lines 21–23)

7 TRUE   *the new aristocracy paid for splendid buildings, banquets and balls, not to mention the latest fashions from Europe.* (lines 27–28)

8 FALSE   *An uprising took place in Mexico in 1810, with the aim of ending rule from Spain. This goal was finally achieved in 1821* (lines 30–31)

9 FALSE   *Since 1823, it has been the capital of the Republic of Mexico, apart from a short period, from 1863 to 1867, when the country was again an empire.* (lines 32–33)

10 TRUE   *In the first few decades of the 20th century, ... factories spread through the city.* (lines 34–36)

Writing

Sample answer

According to the charts, in 2002 among all age groups in the town of Eden Hills, more men possessed a mobile phone than women, and although there was a steady decline in mobile phone ownership with age, more than 50% of each age group possessed a mobile phone. Mobile phone possession was greatest among the 10–29 age group (90% and over, compared with just over 70% for men and about 57% for women in the 60–74 age group).

Both men and women sent text messages, but the 10–29-year-olds had a greater tendency to send more than ten text messages a day – over 30% for men and over 40% for women. In contrast, only around 10% of men and women over 30 sent more than ten text messages a day. Over 40% of women and over 50% of men in the over-30-year-old category never sent text messages at all.

(153 words)

5 Discovering the past

<table>
<tr><td colspan="2">Unit topic   History</td></tr>
</table>

5.1	
Test skills	Reading (AC/GT):
	True/False/Not given
	Multiple choice
	Note completion
	Speaking Part 3
Vocabulary	Types of building
	Collocations related to research
5.2	
Test skills	Listening: labelling
	Writing extra (AC):
	Task 1: A description of a place
Grammar	Review of past tenses

Workbook contents

1, 2, 3, 4	Vocabulary
5, 6	Grammar: past tenses and
	sequencing

5.1 SB pages 34–35

1 It would be useful to take a map of the world into the classroom so that students can point to where the places are. The exercise can be done as a whole-class activity or in pairs or small groups.

> **Answers**
> 1 B The Great Wall, China   a system of defence
> 2 A The Moai, Easter Island   sculptures
> 3 D The Parthenon, Greece   a temple
> 4 C The Pyramids, Egypt   tombs or burial chambers

> **Background information**
> - The Pyramids: 4th-dynasty stone monuments on the Giza plateau on the south-west outskirts of modern Cairo. The Great Pyramid of Cheops (c. 2589–2566 BC) is 146m high and 230m square and is made up of 2.5 million limestone blocks.
> - The Great Wall of China stretches 4,100km across northern China from the Yellow Sea to the Central Asian desert. It was begun in 221 BC. It is 7.6m high and 3.7m wide, made of earth and stone, with a facing of bricks.
> - The Parthenon is made of marble. It was built between 447 and 433 BC on the Athenian Acropolis.

2 The article gives background information on the Moai. Ask students to scan the text to find the answers to the two questions. It is important that students do not worry about the five missing words or any words they are

unsure of. Tell them not to use a dictionary or ask about vocabulary at this stage. The text is about 700 words, and students should take about three minutes to read it.

> **Answers**
> 1 In the Pacific Ocean between Chile and Tahiti.
> 2 They were built by the Rapa Nui people for religious reasons.

3 Ask students to work in pairs to match the words with their meanings. These words are all nouns and are quite specialised. If students find this exercise difficult, then allow them to use a dictionary.

> **Answers**
> a 5   b 3   c 4   d 1   e 2

When students know what the words mean, they should try to find where they go in the text.

> **Answers**
> 1 e extinct   2 c remains   3 d field   4 b sites   5 a clan

4 Ask the class to refer to the Test spot. Explain that, up to now, students have had reading passages with only one task type. The article in this unit has three different types of task and, as a result, is similar to one of the readings they will meet in the actual test. Students should work through the questions. They should try to avoid using a dictionary, as one will not be allowed in the test.

> **Answers**
> 1 TRUE   *He co-ordinated a team of experts (line 16)*
> 2 FALSE   *Scientists once believed ... in the 5th century. (lines 21–25)*
> 3 NOT GIVEN   We know that the number and size of the Moai varied from clan to clan, but not the burial chambers themselves.
> 4 NOT GIVEN   There is no mention of how long the Moai took to build.
> 5 TRUE   *The building of Moai ... until the 16th century. (lines 53–54)*
> 6 FALSE   *they weren't spending ... were hunted to extinction (lines 59–60)*
> 7 A (line 25) and E (line 67)
> 8 (Rano Rarku) volcano (lines 44–45)
> 9 33m (tall) (line 45)
> 10 rollers (line 61)

5 The collocations in this exercise are all common in Academic English. Explain that *collocations* are words which are often found together. There are many collocations, and being aware of which words go together

will enable students to demonstrate to the examiner a wide range of vocabulary and thus gain higher marks. In this exercise, students need to decide which verb *can't* be used with the specified noun.

> **Answers**
> 1 to get   2 to find   3 to do   4 to make

6 The aim of this exercise is to make students aware that they have to expand their answers during the Speaking Module.

> **Answers**
> a Too short and doesn't show the examiner what the candidate knows
> b A good answer, relevant and showing a range of language
> c An expanded answer, but fails to answer the question and includes irrelevancy

Students should then work through the three questions orally, trying to use some of the language in the Useful language box.

> **Possible answers**
> 1 Personally, I think that it is a subject that really needs a teacher who is imaginative and has a real interest in history. Let me give you an example of how *not* to teach history: if a teacher just reads out a list of dates, then it can become very boring and the class will be totally unmotivated.
> 2 For one thing, a teacher could take you to places of historical interest and really make you understand what was happening at the time. For another, he or she could show you films of famous people or battles to make the subject more alive.
> 3 Yes, there are so many periods of history that are interesting – for example, the Egyptian civilisation or the Romans; the Ming dynasty in China or the history of the Ottoman Empire. I think I would choose to study more modern history – American Independence, for example.

Extension activity

Divide the class into groups and ask each group to do a homework project on a particular aspect of history that interests them – possibly the history of their school, their town/country, etc. or the history of another country or famous person. They should give a presentation to the rest of the class about their subject and also prepare a poster to display in the classroom.

5.2 SB pages 36–37

1 Ask students to give an example of a sentence using each of the past tenses reviewed here, to ensure that everyone understands the terminology and how each tense is formed, and write them on the board. Allow students to work through the exercise. If they are still unsure, refer them to the Grammar folder (SB page 139).

Note that each example 1–4 contains various past tenses (see verbs in italics).

> **Answers**
> PS – c – 1 (*invited*), 2 (*believed*), 4 (*found*)
> PC – a – 3 (*were building, weren't spending*), 4 (*were carrying out*)
> PPS – b – 2 (*had come*), 4 (*had occurred*)

2 Students should work through the exercises in pairs orally in class, and then write the answers for homework.

> **Answers**
> 1 When did the Berlin Wall fall? It fell in 1989.
> 2 When did the Pharaohs build the Pyramids? They built the pyramids around 2600 BC.
> 3 When did cavemen do the wall paintings at Lascaux? They did the wall paintings at Lascaux approximately 15,000 years ago.
> 4 When did Mao Zedong govern China? He governed China from 1949 to 1976.
> 5 When did the USA become independent? It became independent in the late 1700s.

3 It might be useful to draw a timeline on the board so that students can see how this tense is often used to show an interrupted action.

> **Answers**
> 1 was digging; saw   2 was giving; went off
> 3 were looking; heard   4 dropped; was putting

4 Write on the board the prompt *Before Europeans arrived on Easter Island …* This will help to focus students' minds on why the past perfect is used.

> **Answers**
> 1 The people had built large sculptures called Moai.
> 2 They had used volcanic rock to build them.
> 3 They had carved pictures on some of the Moai.
> 4 They had cut down the forest.
> 5 They had stopped fishing.

5 Sometimes it is not necessary to use the past perfect unless the fact that an event actually happened before another event needs to be emphasised. If this isn't the case and the narrative is simply about something that happened in the past, the past simple is used.

> **Answers**
> 1 was working   2 discovered   3 contained   4 had spent
> 5 hadn't/had not had   6 was   7 began / had begun
> 8 were digging   9 found / had found   10 led / had led
> 11 had broken into   12 were

6   Refer students to the Test spot and Test folder 10 if they require more information about this task. Tell students about a museum you have visited and encourage them to ask you questions about it. Then ask them to describe to their partner a museum they have been to. Encourage students to use the language from the Useful language box.

7   Ask students to look at the task for this exercise. They are going to listen to a guide describing where things are in a museum. Check they understand *right* and *left, middle, back, opposite*, etc. by asking questions about the classroom. Check also that students understand that they should write the letter(s) next to 1–5. Students should try to get used to hearing the recording only once, as in the examination.

Answers (see underlined text in script)
1 AA   2 L   3 B   4 ER   5 GS

Recording script

Good morning, ladies and gentlemen. Now, before I tell you a little bit about the history of the museum, let's make sure you can find your way around. There are three floors to the museum, and we have a lot of very interesting things for you to see. You are now standing in the hall after entering through the Main Entrance.

I know you are all particularly interested in <u>Australian art, and you'll find examples of this if you go up the steps in front of you and go through the door immediately on your left</u>. There are also other displays of Australian and Native American objects on the second floor – <u>you'll find the lift in the corner of the room off the Australian art gallery</u>.

You may find it useful to go into the <u>bookshop before you begin the tour of the museum. It's here, as you can see, straight ahead of you, up the main steps</u>. The cloakroom and toilets are both in the basement – you can take the stairs next to the main entrance or use the lift.

If you'd like to become a member of the museum, you can apply at the museum office. Membership is £30 a year, and this entitles you to free entry. <u>The museum office is on this floor, up the steps and to your right. And opposite the museum office, also on your right, is the Egyptian room</u>. There, you'll find a selection of mummies and wall paintings – some over 3,000 years old.

At present, I'm sorry to tell you there are two galleries which are closed. The first one – <u>to your right between the main steps and the steps to the basement – is our Greek sculpture gallery</u>. The other one, the African paintings gallery, is on the first floor and is undergoing decoration. Both will be re-opening in March. Now, if you'd like to follow me up the main ...

The pictures are of an Egyptian sarcophagus, the philosopher Epicurus and an Aboriginal boomerang.

Extension activity

Orally, students should take it in turns to give exact instructions to their partner as to how to reach various places in the college. For example: how to get to the Principal's office; how to get to the library.

8   This exercise is to give practice in the use of prepositions of location, which is useful for possible questions in Task 1 of both AC and GT Writing.

Sample answer

My first school was in the middle of the village where I lived. It was built in the 1960s and had large, airy classrooms and, next to it, some excellent playing fields. When you went into the building, there was a large hall on the left where we had our daily gym class, morning assembly and our lunch.

On the right was where the Headteacher had her own room at the front of the school, next to the Reception. The classrooms were off two long corridors, and there were also toilets on each corridor. The building was only one storey and had a flat roof.

Each classroom was identical. The teacher sat behind a large desk at the front of the class. Behind her was the blackboard. Opposite her were six or seven rows of desks, which is where we sat. No changes were made to the building when I was there.

(153 words)

Test folder 3

SB pages 38–39
Sentence and note completion

Make sure students fully understand the notes and advice.

1   Ask students to read the rubric and sentences, and think about what might fit each space, considering both meaning and grammar. Point out that they'll hear the example before question 1. Stress the importance of writing no more than three words for each answer. Play the recording.

> **Answers (see underlined text in script)**
> **1** capital **2** houses of rock **3** 12th/twelfth **4** royal
> **5** Agriculture **6** Gold **7** trading centre/center
> **8** salt **9** 1600

Recording script

You will hear part of a lecture about the ancient African city of Great Zimbabwe.

First, you have some time to look at questions 1 to 9. (*pause*)

Now listen carefully and answer questions 1 to 9.

One of the most impressive structures of southern Africa is Great Zimbabwe, a ruined city surrounded by a massive stone wall reaching a height of ten metres. This wall and the stone buildings within the city have survived, but unfortunately not the houses of the majority of people, which were of mud. Great Zimbabwe was part of a state which covered much of the interior of south-east Africa, and may well have been the capital. There's disagreement over the precise meaning of the name 'Zimbabwe': one interpretation is 'houses of rock', as this material was used for the most important buildings. Because of the historical significance of the Great Zimbabwe site, the name was adopted by the present country on independence in 1980.

Not very much is known about the people who constructed Great Zimbabwe, as they had no written language, and their oral traditions haven't survived. They were probably Shona-speaking people who moved into the area around the sixth century, and began building the stone walls – using granite quarried from nearby hills – in the twelfth. The walls were followed by the stone structures within them. One of these, the Great Enclosure, is likely to have been a royal residence, and it's the largest ancient structure south of the Sahara.

It's unclear why that particular site was chosen for Great Zimbabwe. Although the grasslands of the area were ideal for cattle grazing, the soil may not have supported agriculture to the extent required to feed so many people. Grain and other staples may have had to be brought in from elsewhere. It used to be thought that the site was chosen for the city because of the gold found in the district, but it now seems that this wasn't exploited until a century after Great Zimbabwe was founded. At least for part of the time that the city existed, its wealth seems to have come from its role as a trading centre. Ivory and, later, gold were traded through East African ports for cloth and other goods from Arabia and further east. This was probably the main source of Great Zimbabwe's power and wealth.

By the middle of the 15th century, however, the city was in decline. Trade had moved further north. Local resources had apparently been overused, and salt was scarce. Possibly for these reasons, although we may never know for certain, Great Zimbabwe was abandoned by about 1600. At the height of its prosperity, the city was probably home to 18,000 people, perhaps more, but now it simply consists of ruins.

2   Ask students to read the words in the box. Point out that words in boxes usually *paraphrase* words or phrases in listening and reading passages. Ask for synonyms of the following:

aim	objective, goal, end
catalogue	list
district	area, region
questions	queries
record	file
society	club, group

Make sure students understand these terms:
- cross-reference: a note in a book or other document that tells you to look somewhere else in the same document for more information;
- source document: a book, letter or other written text that information has been taken from.

> **Answers (see underlined text in script)**
> **1** books **2** aim **3** record **4** questions
> **5** source documents [*NB: three sections are underlined*]
> **6** daily life **7** software **8** cross-references **9** society

Recording script

You will hear two friends discussing how to carry out research into family history.

First, you have some time to look at questions 1 to 9. (*pause*)

Now listen carefully and answer questions 1 to 9.

Martin: Jo, you're doing research into your family history, aren't you? Can you give me some advice?
Jo: I'd be glad to. Are you thinking of doing the same?
Martin: Yes, I might. My grandfather's just given me a box of old family photos, and I'd like to find out about the people in them. But I need to know more about how to set about it, before I make up my mind.
Jo: Well, the first thing is find out more about the different things you could do. It's worth going to the library and reading one or two introductions to the subject. It'll give you an idea of what the possibilities are and what's involved.
Martin: Right.
Jo: Then you should work out what you're trying to get out of it. I mean, do you just want to discover the direct line of your ancestors, or *all* your relations, for instance? You can't really carry out the research efficiently unless you've decided that.
Martin: Uh-huh.

Jo: Then you should <u>sit down at your computer and get down all the information you already have</u>. Start with yourself, then your parents, then work through all the members of your family that you're interested in. Anything you can think of concerning names, dates, where they lived, and so on. And you need a system to keep track of anything you're not sure of, so you can try and find out later.

Martin: Right.

Jo: Once you've got that far, you should think about all your living relations, and maybe close friends of theirs, and arrange to talk to them. It's a good idea to put down <u>a list of things you want to ask them</u> first, but don't limit yourself to those. Encourage your relatives to talk about the family in a more unstructured way, too. You never know what might come up.

Martin: What about things like, um, <u>birth certificates, photographs</u> and so on? How useful are they?

Jo: Oh, they're essential. They're <u>the primary evidence</u> that you need. Ask your relations if they've got anything that would be useful. There might be some real treasures tucked away somewhere.

Martin: At the back of a drawer, maybe.

Jo: Right. They can give you a real opening into history, particularly if there are any old <u>letters or diaries</u>. Just a casual mention of visiting Auntie Mary, for example, can tell you about people you hadn't heard of, or where someone lived. I think that what you'll enjoy most is finding out as much as possible about your ancestors – <u>where they lived and worked, how much money they had, how they spent their free time</u> – all that sort of thing. That's much more interesting than simply knowing a person's name and when they were born and died.

Martin: Yeah, I agree. How should I organise all the material, do you think?

Jo: Well, <u>there are special computer programs available</u> for doing family history. It's easiest if you use one of those. I can give you details of what I used – it was very good.

Martin: Oh, thanks.

Jo: One way it helps is by making it easy to group information together in various ways. For instance, <u>if you've got a file about a person, you need to be able to see that some of the information there also relates to a different file, say about a particular year</u>.

Martin: It must have been hard to keep track of everything in the days before computers.

Jo: Yes. I think I'd have given up pretty soon! And it's worth <u>becoming a member of a family history organisation</u> – I got so many good ideas from the other members, and it was very helpful to be able to talk about what I was doing with people doing the same thing.

Martin: Mm, good idea. OK, well, thanks, Jo. That's given me a lot to think about.

Jo: Let me know how it goes.

Martin: Oh, don't worry – I'll be on the phone asking you for help!

3 This is a difficult passage and task, so students should be given a great deal of help. It may be best to do the exercise as a class activity. Remind students that sentences 1–5 follow the order of the passage.

Answers

1 G *the history of a nation (or other group) is a story that gives meaning to the members of that nation living today.* (paragraph 1)

2 C *Historians try to combine an understanding of social, economic, political and cultural activity into a general story, explaining how these have affected each other to shape the general course of human events.* (paragraph 2)

3 E *the historian must develop a theory ... the more evidence it can satisfactorily account for, the better the theory.* (paragraph 3)

4 A *historians largely rely on developing new methods of analysis ... that show the relevance of evidence that was previously ignored.* (paragraph 4)

5 F *No historical theory can be proved beyond all doubt, because there is room for interpretation in any human activity.* (paragraph 5)

---

6 What is job satisfaction?

Unit topic	Work
6.1	
Test skills	Listening:
	Flow-chart completion
	Sentence completion
	Labelling a diagram
	Table completion
	Multiple choice
Vocabulary	Work
	Collocations with *money*
6.2	
Test skills	Writing extra (GT):
	Task 1: Letter of application
	Speaking Part 2
Grammar	Past simple or present perfect?
Workbook contents	
1, 2, 3	Reading
4, 5	Grammar: past simple or present perfect?
6	Vocabulary

6.1 SB pages 40–41

1 The pictures are of a man working hard in the office and a woman playing with some paper clips, looking very bored. Ask students to look at the pictures and describe how they think the people are feeling. Suggested adjectives:
   - *motivated, interested, ambitious, driven, challenged*
   - *unmotivated, bored, fed up, tired, apathetic, uninterested, unchallenged*

Ask students to work with a partner to discuss the two charts. Ask them what conclusions can be drawn from the charts.

> **Suggested answers**
> UK workers are working longer hours than in the past.
> People who work long hours are more likely to do so because they are inspired by their bosses.
> People who work shorter hours probably do not feel inspired by their bosses.

2 Students should work with a partner or in small groups for this exercise. Monitor the pairs or groups and help with any vocabulary difficulties.

3 Refer the class to the Test spot. The recording should be stopped after each stage to allow students to read through

the questions carefully and give them time to ask any questions about vocabulary. Point out that, in the test itself, the recording is played all the way through without stopping. Make sure that everyone is aware of the rubric – no more than two words or a number for each answer.

> **Background information**
> Abraham Maslow was an American behavioural psychologist who worked both in academia and industry. He published a number of Human Relations books until the early 70s, but it was his first book, *Motivation and Personality*, published in 1943, that set out his idea of the hierarchy of human needs.

> **Answers (see underlined text in script)**
> 1 behaviour 2 job satisfaction 3 19th/nineteenth 4 money 5 in teams 6 basic/Basic 7 status/Status 8 55% 9 40% 10 B

Recording script

Questions 1 and 2

My lecture today is on motivation at work. If managers are to improve the running of their organisation, it's important for them to understand what motivates the workforce – to know how to satisfy both the high flyers and those who have lower ambitions or ability.

First of all, let's look at the model of how motivation works. You will see that every member of the workforce has needs or expectations, and these needs and expectations will <u>affect each person's behaviour.</u> For example, they will work harder if they know that they will be rewarded – that is, if they can achieve their goals of higher pay or promotion. <u>The achievement of these goals will, in turn, lead to job satisfaction.</u> This then feeds back into the worker's needs or expectations.

****

Questions 3–5

Over the years, the development of different theories of management and different approaches to organisation has affected the way we view motivation. In the <u>19th century</u>, the writer Frederick <u>Taylor put forward the theory that workers were only interested in making money</u>. In contrast, in the early 20th century, researchers found that people went to work to satisfy a *range* of different needs, and not simply for financial reward. One need, in particular, was emphasised – the social need. An early study done on a coal-mining company, for instance, showed that <u>people generally were happier and worked more productively if they were able to work in teams.</u>

****

Questions 6 and 7

One important 20th-century theory of motivation was that put forward by Maslow in 1943. Maslow identified five important needs which he placed in a triangle: <u>at the bottom of the triangle, he put what he called 'basic needs'</u>: good pay and pleasant working conditions. Then, above the basic needs, he put 'security needs' – safe working conditions and job security. His third need he called 'social' – the need to have friends at work and get on with the boss. <u>Fourth were 'status</u> needs' – a job title and social recognition. Finally, at the top of the triangle, Maslow identified the need for advancement – to have a challenging job with opportunities for promotion. His theory isn't perfect, but it's a convenient framework for viewing the different needs and expectations of work that people have, and, what's more, I believe it's still valid today.

✳✳

Questions 8–10

During an early 21st-century survey of full-time employees, when asked what gave them job satisfaction, 72% said having an inspirational leader. <u>Fifty-five per cent of those questioned found satisfaction in the challenging nature of their work</u>, 50% by being paid well, and <u>40% said flexible working hours</u>. Consequently, we can see that this indicates that today, an employee's opinion of the quality of the leadership in their workplace is an important factor influencing belief in the company as a good place to work.

Motivation varies over a person's working life and also according to where they live. Studies show that people have different goals in different countries. For example, a good lifestyle would appear to be more important in Spain than it is in Sweden. Financial security is more important in the US than in the UK. Social contact at work is important to workers in both Germany and in Australia, <u>but not of top importance in Britain</u> and Italy. As to high status, this is more important in the USA than to Europeans. These results indicate clear differences between countries, but I think they shouldn't be taken too seriously.

There have been many theories which have attempted to explain the nature of motivation. These theories are all partially true, and by and large all help to explain the behaviour of certain people at certain times. However, none really provide all the answers. The best a company can do is to provide people with the right environment to be self-motivated. If they are self-motivated, they will perform well.

Photocopiable recording script activity
(P ⋯➔ page 135)

If students have found this piece particularly difficult, give out the recording script, so they can read the text to find the answers.

4   Students should spend ten to 15 minutes on this task, either in class or for homework. Encourage them to use an English-English dictionary.

> **Answers**
> 1 waste   2 left   3 spent / has spent / spends   4 change
> 5 pay   6 lend   7 gave   8 invest   9 saved / has saved / saves   10 made / has made / makes

5   Students should discuss the questions.

Extension activity

Ask students to look at the recording script and explain what a *high flyer* is. Put the following on the board and ask them to work through the expressions, explaining what they mean.

1   a blue-collar worker
2   a white-collar worker
3   a shift worker
4   a striker
5   a workaholic
6   someone on flexitime
7   someone who has been laid off
8   someone who has been fired/sacked

> **Answers**
> Someone who ...
> 1   works in a factory.
> 2   works in an office.
> 3   sometimes works days, sometimes nights.
> 4   is refusing to work because of an industrial dispute.
> 5   works all the time.
> 6   can begin work late/early and leave early/late.
> 7   has been make redundant.
> 8   has lost their job because they have done something wrong.

6.2 SB pages 42–43

1   Units 4 and 5 have covered both past and present tenses, so students should be familiar with the form and function of these tenses. However, there is often confusion about how and when they are used. Ask the class to work through this exercise.

> **Answers**
> 1 PS   2 PP   3 PS   4 PP

2   Ask students if they have heard of the entrepreneur Richard Branson. Put any information they have on the board. Students should then read through the article about Richard Branson to get an idea of who he is and do the exercise, deciding which tense is appropriate.

> **Answers**
> 1 grew up   2 went   3 started   4 left   5 went
> 6 didn't graduate   7 founded   8 opened
> 9 have expanded   10 started   11 founded
> 12 exceeded   13 has spent   14 hasn't only spent
> 15 has tried   16 crossed   17 broke

3 This exercise should take ten to 15 minutes.

> **Answers**
> 1 Have you ever had/taken
> 2 Did you learn/take/have
> 3 Have you ever thought
> 4 Have you ever spent / Did you spend (when you were at school)
> 5 Did you want
> 6 Have you ever had
> 7 Did you take
> 8 Have you ever seen

4 Writing a job-application letter requires specialised, formulaic language. Ask students to read through the letter and decide which of the words in the box complete the sentences. This could be done for homework.

> **Answers**
> 1 post   2 manager   3 Department   4 experience / skills
> 5 qualified   6 CV   7 skills / (experience)   8 salary
> 9 closing   10 interview

5 Draw students' attention to the mind map and explain how doing one will help them to prepare their talk. Ask them to match the points in the task with the points on the mind map. The last point is usually the one which is expanded on the most.

> **Suggested answers**
> - Who they are: A teacher at my secondary school
> - What was special about this person: Had worked in advertising. Knew about the business world.
> - What other people say about this person: Liked by most students. Not traditional enough, said parents.
> - Why this person has motivated you: Friendly, gave me confidence, extra help with exams. Helped with university application. Made me interested in business studies.

Ask students to do the task for themselves, using a mind map and then giving the talk to a partner. They should time themselves so they have an idea of how long one to two minutes actually is.

Extension activity

Students should prepare a talk for the class (one to two minutes long) on their job of choice. They should talk about the advantages and disadvantages of the job; the qualifications and qualities needed; and the role this job has in society. They should make sure that the talk is well organised and based on notes.

Writing folder 3

SB pages 44–45
Task 2: Understanding the question and planning your writing

1 Refer students to the Advice box. Tell them that it is a good idea to use a highlighter pen to highlight the important parts of the question. They also need to practise writing 250 words so they get to have some idea of what that number of words looks like on the page. This will stop them worrying in the test about how much they have written. Another reason for practising Task 2 is that timing is important, and students may never have tried to write a timed essay. They should always time themselves when they start writing so they can see how long it takes them.

Students should work through the questions.

> **Answers**
> 1 appropriate
> 2 may be appropriate, if this is your only knowledge and experience and you make that clear
> 3 probably irrelevant
> 4 appropriate
> 5 appropriate
> 6 appropriate if it's relevant, for example if your argument is that managers are paid more and therefore are expected to work longer
> 7 inappropriate: irrelevant
> 8 appropriate if it is relevant
> 9 inappropriate: irrelevant
> 10 may be appropriate if your arguments in the main body of the essay support this

2 Ask students to read through A, B and C.

> **Suggested answers**
> - A is inappropriate because:
>   – it repeats the question;
>   – it is too strongly worded for an introduction (they are usually more general);
>   – it contains irrelevant personal information.
> - B is fine – general but to the point.
> - C is possibly best as a paragraph after the introduction. It is going on to talk about different situations in different countries, and this would make a good paragraph for the body of the essay.

3 Draw the class's attention to the Useful language boxes. Students should then think of good examples to give in a task such as this one.

4

> **Answers**
> The two parts are:
> 1 Working hours today are too long.
> 2 People are not spending as much time as they should with their families or on leisure activities.

> **Sample answer**
> In the 20th century, people believed that life in the future would be easier and that they would have more leisure time and spend less time at work. However, now we are in the 21st century, we can see that this is not the case. In fact, people in most countries need to work even harder today than they did in the past.
>
> This can affect families particularly badly. It is often necessary for both parents to work in order to earn enough money to pay the bills. Not only that, it is very unusual for them to work just nine to five. My parents are both professional people. My father is a lawyer, and my mother is a marketing manager. Both of them leave the house well before eight o'clock in the morning and usually get home about seven thirty.
>
> As a consequence, our family, consisting of three children, has always had a nanny or au pair to look after us. However, my family is still a close family, despite my parents going out to work. I do not think it is a big problem if my parents are not constantly at home with us. I think it is more important if they spend quality time with us – that is, time when we are all happy together.
>
> In conclusion, I would like to say that working long hours nowadays is a fact of life. It is up to the individual to try to work out a credible work-life balance so that they can spend quality time with their family and still pursue their work goals.
>
> (266 words)

Unit topic	Advertising
7.1 Test skills	Speaking Parts 1 and 3 Reading (AC/GT): Multiple choice Headings
Vocabulary	Word formation
7.2 Test skills	Listening: Sentence completion Matching
Pronunciation	Sentence stress
Grammar	Relative clauses
Vocabulary	Advertising

Workbook contents

1	Reading
2, 3, 4, 5	Grammar: relative clauses
6	Vocabulary

7.1 SB pages 46–47

Ask students what points they think the pictures exemplify (e.g. companies can become well known for one type of product (such as cola) and then make another (such as T-shirts); people provide free advertising for companies).

1 Point out to students that this activity will help them to develop their answers in the Speaking Module, particularly Parts 1 and 3. Ask them to read the exercise and, in pairs, to expand the answers (1–3) by choosing from a–e.

Answers
1 a,e   2 c   3 b,d

Ask students to discuss the three bullet points, expanding their answers and using the phrases in bold in a–e.

Possible answers
- I do occasionally, for instance if I've bought something and been very disappointed with it.
- I'm not sure. Maybe it does, because wherever you go, you see or hear ads.
- I suppose it does occasionally. I once bought a very expensive mobile phone because I thought it looked good in the ads. I didn't need it, since I already had a mobile.

2 This activity will help students with both multiple-choice and headings tasks in the Reading Modules. Ask them if they know what a *viral* is. If not, encourage them to find out when they read the passage. The passage is typical of Section 3 of General Training Reading. Multiple-choice and headings tasks are used in both Reading Modules.

Background information
A *viral* is a very short film, used for advertising, and sent to people's computers.

Toby Young is a British journalist whose work includes articles, plays, books and reviews.

Ask students to read the example question, the first paragraph and the explanation of the answer. Then ask them to read question 1 and the second paragraph, then question 2 and the third paragraph. These three questions focus on the main point of each paragraph, as preparation for the headings task.

Answers
1 C   *the Viral Factory was making a 20-second film to promote my recently published book.*
2 A   *Viral marketing ... probably dates back to 1996, when it was used to advertise a free email service. Every time a customer used the service, the company's website address was automatically included at the end.*

Ask students to read the Test spot, then to read paragraphs 3–6, choosing the best heading (A–F) for each one.

Answers
3 E   *Today, viral marketing is a lot more sophisticated.*
4 B   *But if a viral arrives in your email inbox from a friend, you'll be curious and click on it.*
5 C   *if the clip is too obviously designed to advertise a particular product, people won't pass it on ... On the other hand, nobody will buy the product if they don't know what it is.*
6 F   *traffic to my website increased dramatically*

3 Ask students to complete the table, making sure they understand all the words. Encourage them to learn and record word families, marking stressed syllables. Draw attention to the change in stressed syllable between *'curious* and *curi'osity*.

Answers

verbs	nouns	adjectives
	'virus *and* 'viral *when referring to a viral advertisement*	'viral
pro'mote	pro'motion, pro'moter	pro'motional
'advertise	'advertising, 'advertiser, ad'vertisement (UK), 'adver'tisement (USA), 'advert, ad	
'memorise	'memory	'memorable
a'ttend	a'ttention	a'ttentive
	curi'osity	'curious
suc'ceed	suc'cess	suc'cessful

4 Using words from exercise 3 will help students to remember them.

5 Ask students for their opinions.

Extension activity

Students could be asked to carry out a survey in the street of people's opinions of different forms of advertising (e.g. commercials on TV, film and radio, Internet pop-ups, posters on hoardings (billboards), plastic bags, brand names on clothing, virals).

7.2 SB pages 48–49

1 Ask students to form small groups and interpret and comment on the three opinions. Ask each group to summarise their opinions of advertising and briefly present them to the class.

2 Check that students know what an advertising agency is (**Answer**: a company that plans and designs advertising campaigns on behalf of other companies). Tell students they are going to listen to the head of an agency. First, he gives a brief history of advertising. Ask students to read questions 1–6 and decide what class of word is required in each space (**Answer**: all the spaces require a noun). Play the first part of the recording.

Questions 7–11: ask students to read the rubric, and check they understand everything in the questions and box (NB *celebrity endorsement* = using a well-known person, as him/herself, to advertise a product). Point out that the words in the box are unlikely to be the same as ones in the recording. Play the second part of the recording.

Recording script

Questions 1–6

Interviewer: My guest this evening is advertising expert Gary Phillips, who's going to tell us how advertising works. Welcome to the programme.

Gary: Thank you.

Interviewer: How did it all start?

Gary: When everyone lived in small communities and knew the local farmer who grew and sold vegetables, advertising was unnecessary. But in a larger community, it's a different situation. In fact, advertising dates back well over 2,000 years, and <u>for centuries, adverts simply gave information</u>: one of the earliest surviving ones is a sign painted on a wall in ancient Rome showing property to let. Later, they announce that books, say, are available, and where they can be bought.

Interviewer: So, when did advertising become more persuasive?

Gary: The big change occurred in the late 19th century. Technological developments had made mass production possible, which meant firms could make products in large numbers, of roughly the same quality, and at roughly the same price. <u>Companies then found they had to stimulate demand in order to sell these products.</u> At the same time, in some countries, there were plenty of people with money to spend on <u>luxuries and other inessential goods. This created opportunities for companies to make and sell these at a much greater profit</u>. So a lot of advertising focused on luxury goods. Another reason for the change in the nature of advertising was that more and more businesses were set up, making similar products, and <u>in the face of this competition, manufacturers needed to advertise in order to survive</u>. This was really the beginning of advertising designed to *persuade* people to buy. And when Freud's theories about our subconscious began to be applied in the advertising industry in the 1920s, advertising became very effective.

Interviewer: How does persuasive advertising work?

Gary: It tries to make people want a certain item, let's say a car. If we only bought goods for practical reasons, manufacturers would soon go out of business. <u>So they appeal to our emotions</u> in their advertising, to make us believe that if we buy that particular car, we'll feel good, we'll be in the fashion, people will admire us. Instead of focusing on the car's mechanical properties, the <u>advertising is about the benefits</u> that we hope to gain.

****

Questions 7–11

Interviewer: Gary, tell us about some of the techniques that manufacturers use to persuade us.

Gary: Let's start with one of the most important aspects of advertising, the name given to a product. Sometimes there's a symbol, too. Imagine a company which makes children's clothing. <u>It can spend a fortune on making the name well known, and giving it a particular image, so that when consumers see the name, or the logo, they associate it with particular qualities</u> – style, value for money, fun, fashion, whatever. And they're more likely to buy that particular make.

Another very powerful, and very old, technique is to make it almost impossible for consumers to avoid the advertising. <u>You keep seeing a TV commercial for running shoes, perhaps several times in an evening, see adverts for them in newspapers and magazines, you see posters in the street.</u> That helps to fix the product in your mind, so next time you buy some running shoes, and you see a whole row of different products, the chances are you'll buy the shoes whose name you remember.

Of course, with many products – <u>furniture for instance – advertisers attract us with special offers or the chance of winning a holiday. And words like *bargain* and *sale* are used very frequently</u> to encourage shoppers to buy.

Interviewer: But surely consumers realise that advertisements are simply trying to sell products?

Gary: They do, of course. So agencies often produce advertisements that are entertaining. <u>A certain washing powder used to run an advertising campaign that appeared to be saying to the consumer, 'Look, you know and we know that we're trying to get you to buy our product, but at least we'll give you a laugh.'</u> It was very effective, because the manufacturer seemed to be on the same side as the consumer.

Another technique is to use <u>a famous person to promote a product, even if there's no real connection, like showing an athlete eating snacks.</u> This can work, because we learn by imitating people who are important to us. So advertisers use film stars, pop singers – even cartoon characters, particularly if the product is targeted at children.

Language is an important aspect of advertising, and here's just one example. <u>A TV commercial for engine oil</u> showed a man washing his hands in the oil. Of course, car engines and hands are made of different materials, so he can't tell us the oil will work equally well in an engine. Instead, <u>he tries to get the viewer to reach that conclusion without stating any facts</u>: he says, 'Think how it'll work in your car.' He's *implied* the oil is good for car engines without *saying* so.

Interviewer: OK, now if we go on to another question …

---

3   Ask two or three students to read the sentence as marked. Point out that it is difficult both to say and to understand. Play the recording, then ask individuals or the whole class to repeat it with the stress on the correct words. Ask for the difference between the underlined words on page 48 and those stressed in the recording.

> **Suggested answer**
> Words that are stressed tend to be 'content' words, that is, those that convey most meaning: mostly nouns and main verbs. 'Grammatical' words, such as pronouns and auxiliary verbs, are usually unstressed.

Recording script

My <u>guest</u> this <u>evening</u> is <u>advertising</u> <u>expert</u> <u>Gary</u> <u>Phillips</u>, who's <u>going</u> to <u>tell</u> us how <u>advertising</u> <u>works</u>.

4   Ask students to underline the content words, then play the recording so that they can check. The stressed words are underlined in the script below.

Recording script

Interviewer: <u>Welcome</u> to the <u>programme</u>.
Gary: <u>Thank</u> you.
Interviewer: <u>How</u> did it all <u>start</u>?
Gary: When <u>everyone</u> <u>lived</u> in <u>small</u> <u>communities</u> and <u>knew</u> the <u>local</u> <u>farmer</u> who <u>grew</u> and <u>sold</u> <u>vegetables</u>, <u>advertising</u> was <u>unnecessary</u>. But in a <u>larger</u> <u>community</u>, it's a <u>different</u> <u>situation</u>.

5   Ask students for examples of the various word classes, and write these on the board if necessary. Then ask students to write the word classes under the appropriate heading, with examples if required.

> **Answers (with possible examples)**
> Content words: adjectives (e.g. *local*, *larger*), adverbs (e.g. *locally*, *largely*), nouns (e.g. *farmer*, *vegetable*), main verbs (e.g. *start*, *lived*)
>
> Grammatical words: auxiliary verbs (e.g. *will*, *have*), conjunctions (e.g. *when*, *and*), prepositions (e.g. *in*, *by*).

6   Read sentence 1, giving *larger* particular emphasis. Ask students why it needs extra stress (**Answer:** it forms a contrast with *small*). Ask one or two students to read the sentence aloud. Do the same with sentence 2 (**Answer:** *persuade* contrasts with *gave information*).

Read sentence 3, ensuring that *advertising* is not heavily stressed. Ask why it isn't (**Answer:** the word has already been used, so it doesn't provide new information). Ask one or two students to read the sentence aloud. Similarly with sentence 4 (**Answer:** *inessential goods* refers to an idea that has already been mentioned – *luxuries*). Play the recording, then ask students to work in pairs and read the four sentences aloud, paying particular attention to stress and checking each other.

Recording script

1 When everyone lived in small communities, advertising wasn't necessary. But in a larger community, it's a different situation.
2 For centuries, adverts simply gave information. The big change occurred in the late 19th century. This was really the beginning of advertising designed to persuade people to buy.
3 My guest today is advertising expert Gary Phillips. Gary, have we always had advertising?
4 At the same time, in some countries there were plenty of people with money to spend on luxuries and other inessential goods.

7 Write on the board two or three examples of sentences including relative clauses, for example:

*Ads **that use humour** tend to be popular.*
*Mass production, **which became possible in the 19th century**, meant that a lot of goods had to be sold.*

Ask students to identify the relative clauses. Make sure they understand that the relative clauses add information about the noun or noun phrase preceding them (*ads, mass production*). Ask for the difference between the two relative clauses. Explain that essential information is given in defining relative clauses, and extra information in non-defining relative clauses.

> **Suggested answers**
> Relative clauses are shown in bold above.
>
> The first is essential, as it helps to define what is being talked about. *Ads tend to be popular* means something different because it refers to all ads, and not only those which use humour.
>
> The second one gives extra information: *Mass production* is enough to define what is being talked about.

Ask students to do exercise 7.

> **Answers**
> 1 non-defining   2 defining

8 Ask students for the relative pronouns in the sentences on the board (*that* and *which* in the above examples) and in exercise 7 (*who* and *which*). Make sure students understand why the examples in this exercise contain defining and non-defining relative clauses, respectively.

> **Suggested answers**
> If *who are important to us* is omitted, *people* refers to people in general, which changes the meaning of the sentence. If the relative clause is omitted from the second sentence, it is still clear who is referred to.

Ask students to do exercise 8.

> **Answers**
> 1 A great deal of advertising is about the benefits that we hope to gain. *defining*
> 2 Ordinary people who appear in advertisements are usually intended to make the viewer or reader identify with them. *defining*
> 3 Jewellery and perfume, which are luxury goods, are usually very profitable for the manufacturer. *non-defining*
> 4 Consumers that see the same advertisements many times are likely to remember the name of the product. *defining*

Ask students to complete the table, based on the sentences in exercises 7 and 8, and to answer the question that follows it.

> **Answers**
>
> | | defining | non-defining |
> |---|---|---|
> | people | *who* or *that* | *who* |
> | things | *which* or *that* | *which* |
>
> Non-defining relative clauses need commas.

If students require further information, refer them to the Grammar folder (SB pages 139–140).

9 Ask students if they have seen the forms of advertising in the pictures, then ask them to form groups of three and do exercise 9.

> **Answers**
> 1 e   2 f   3 b   4 a   5 d   6 c

Ask the groups to define the forms of advertising, using relative clauses.

> **Suggested answers**
> These are small advertisements that people put in a newspaper or magazine, usually because they want to buy or sell something. (small ads)
>
> This is an advertisement which is broadcast on TV or the radio. It usually lasts 30 seconds or a minute. (a commercial)
>
> This is an advert on a long piece of cloth which is attached to a building. It can also be an advert which appears on a web page, usually across the top. (a banner)
>
> This is an advert which appears on a computer screen when you're on the Internet and open a new window. (a pop-up)
>
> This is an advert made up of several large pieces of paper, which are pasted to a very large board – a hoarding or billboard – outdoors. (poster on a hoarding)

Extension activity

Students could be asked to analyse advertisements (e.g. on TV or in magazines), according to the techniques of persuasion that they use. The advertisements could be in their own language or in English, if available. The list A–H at the bottom of page 48 could be used as a starting point for the analysis.

Test folder 4

Headings

Make sure students fully understand the notes and advice.

1   Ask students to read the rubric, example and paragraph
    A. Make sure they understand why x is the best heading.
    Ask them to complete the exercise.

Answers

Example   x   *that's what more and more retailers are giving us*

1   vii   *In between news clips, recipe tips and beauty advice, the screens show advertisements*
2   iii   *the early years of in-store TV ... sometimes left a lot to be desired. This has been changing, though, as advertisers get more sophisticated at using in-store TV.*
3   xi   *In-store ads have to be particularly attention-grabbing*
4   viii   *Ads that communicate facts ... work better than the more emotional ... Shoppers ... want the ad to tell them specifically about a brand and what it is going to do for them.*
5   xii   *content is tightly tailored to particular store areas*
6   iv   *A minority of customers feel that, rather than wasting money on in-store TV, the retailer should lower prices, or at least invest in more useful services. The biggest turn-off, though, for both customers and staff on the shop floor, is noise.*
7   v   *it has become more difficult for manufacturers and others to reach a mass audience on regular television. Through in-store TV, they can reach the large numbers of people*
8   i   *the majority of customers feel that in-store TV improves their overall shopping experience.*

2   This exercise forces students to consider a large number
    of options, all of which relate in some way to the
    paragraph.

Answer
v   *a healthy buyer–seller relationship results in interdependencies between the two parties.*

8 Time to waste?

8.1 SB pages 52–53

1 Ask students what they think about the leisure activities shown in the pictures (dancing, playing the guitar, pottery): are they a waste of time or worth doing? Ask students for examples of active and passive activities, and ask if they think one type is more worthwhile than the other. NB *Leisure* is pronounced with a short 'e' (/e/) in British English, and with a long 'ee' (/iː/) in American English.

> **Possible answers**
> I think it's a good idea to spend your leisure time actively, particularly if you don't get much exercise while you're studying or working.
>
> Sometimes you need to relax and use your brain rather than do anything active.

2 Ask students if they know of any arts centres that organise a variety of cultural activities. If so, ask for examples of the activities. Ask students to read the rubric and Test spot. Point out that although the format is slightly different, completing a table is essentially the same as note-taking. Ask students to note the headings of the table, and to read about Jake Duff in the text. Make sure they see why *comedy* is the answer to the example. Ask them to complete the table.

> **Answers**
> 1 rural life   2 best newcomer   3 talk   4 booklet   5 play
> 6 growing up   7 actors   8 photographic exhibition
> 9 everyday objects   10 polished metal

3 Explain that there are a number of ways of talking about the future in English, and usually the speaker/writer has a choice of more than one: it isn't the case that one is right and all others are wrong. Five ways are listed in a–e. Make sure students know what they mean.

> **Answers**
> 1 c   2 e   3 c   4 d   5 a   6 b   7 a   8 d
> a *will*
> b *will*
> c present continuous / *be going to*
> d *be going to*
> e present simple

For more information about the future, refer students to the Grammar folder (SB page 140).

4 Often, when talking about a future event, the speaker/writer gives their opinion of how likely it is to happen. This grammatical exercise is in the form of an IELTS classifying task.

> **Answers**
> 1 a   2 c   3 a   4 a   5 b   6 c   7 b   8 a   9 a   10 b

Extension exercise

Draw three columns on the board, headed *likely, not sure* and *unlikely*. Ask students for examples of phrases that express these probabilities, both from exercise 4 and from what they know. Write appropriate answers in the columns.

Possible answers
likely
be likely/certain/sure/bound to
it promises to
I'm convinced/sure/certain/positive
probably
I have no doubt
It is probable/likely that
may well

not sure
may/might/could
there's a chance/possibility/likelihood that
maybe/perhaps/possibly
it is possible that

unlikely
to be unlikely to
it is unlikely that
there's little chance/possibility/likelihood
I doubt / don't think

5 Ask students to form pairs and talk about the events, using the phrases given.

> **Possible answers**
> 1 I'm convinced I'll enjoy the show, because I've always wanted to see her perform.
> 2 I may enjoy myself, but there's a chance the audience will be disappointed.
> 3 I'm sure I'll hate the film just as much the second time.
> 4 Maybe I'll be able to learn the rules quickly, but there's a chance I'll spoil the game for the other players.

8.2 SB pages 54–55

1 Ask students what they think of the activities in the pictures (paragliding, rock climbing, painting), and why they think people choose to do them. Make sure they understand the five categories ('relaxation', etc.) and the activities given. Ask for further examples that might give similar experiences. Ask what leisure activities students do, and why.

> **Background information**
> • Paragliding: the sport of jumping out of an aircraft with a special parachute that allows you to travel a long horizontal distance before you land
> • Scuba diving: the sport of swimming under water with special breathing apparatus. *Scuba* is originally an acronym, formed from the initial letters of *self-contained underwater breathing apparatus*.

> **Possible answers**
> *relaxation*: yoga, collecting stamps
> *excitement*: watching or playing football, dancing
> *communion with nature*: walking in the countryside, angling
> *companionship*: playing in an orchestra, going out with friends
> *creative expression*: painting, singing in a choir

2 Ask students to read the rubric, Test spot, example and questions 1–9 for the listing task. Play the first part of the recording, drawing students' attention to the examples when they hear them.

> **Answers (see underlined text in script)**
> 1 rock climbing   2 paragliding
> 3 chess (1–3 in any order) 4 music
> 5 football (4–5 in either order) 6 surfing
> 7 bird-watching (6–7 in either order)
> 8 painting   9 drama (8–9 in either order)

Questions 10–14: ask students to read the rubric, Test spot, example and questions. Play the second part of the recording.

> **Answers (see underlined text in script)**
> 10 (a) full experience   11 (to) socialise/socialize
> 12 retail therapy   13 entertainment   14 life

Recording script

Example

Leisure activities are as varied as crossing the Arctic, or collecting foreign coins, or a visit to a museum. Research into people's experience of leisure has revealed that people get a number of different kinds of enjoyment from leisure, some of which I'll briefly talk about now. But bear in mind that most activities will provide several types of experience.

We often talk about leisure as giving the opportunity for relaxation. <u>Yoga is generally relaxing</u>, both physically and mentally, <u>as is stamp collecting</u>. Relaxation tends to be associated with undemanding activities, but many leisure activities are far from relaxing.

Questions 1–9

At the opposite end of the spectrum is '<u>flow</u>', the name given to a very intense experience, where you're completely absorbed in what you're doing and lose track of time. This often comes from activities where people set themselves challenges to test and improve their skills, as in <u>rock climbing</u>. Many activities that provide flow carry a considerable physical risk, which is likely to add to the experience – <u>paragliding</u> is just one example. But the same intensely emotional experience may occur in a very different activity, like <u>chess</u>. It isn't the activity alone which provides the experience, but also what the participant brings to it.

Another feature of many leisure activities is the introduction to a whole new social network, <u>providing companionship</u> with other like-minded people. <u>New friends can be made through joining a music club</u>, for instance. And <u>social relationships can be strengthened through a shared interest in football</u>. The media open up this experience to everyone who wants to participate, even if they don't play.

Then there's the pleasure that some people get from being in <u>communion with nature</u>, either alone or with companions. <u>Surfing, for example, is likely to focus your entire attention on the sea</u>, while <u>one of the more relaxing ways of relating to the natural world is bird-watching</u>.

Leisure activities can also provide an opportunity to <u>express creativity</u>. Again, these can be solitary or companionable. <u>Painting</u> is often done alone, although many people join a club that can give them encouragement and tips for improvement, while <u>drama</u> is normally a combined effort, with a performance as its goal.

* *

Questions 10–14

<u>An essential aspect of leisure</u> is that we can pick hobbies to suit our personality, our needs and our wallet, and we can drop them at any time. <u>This control is crucial</u>, as people benefit from feeling that they're making their own decisions. That's one reason why children need to choose their own hobbies, instead of having them imposed by their parents.

With large numbers of people wishing to spend time on leisure activities, there's a growing <u>demand for the organiser</u> – whether it's a cinema or a dance class – <u>to ensure that participants have a full experience</u>. It isn't enough just to show a film: customers want to be able to find out in advance what's on, travel to the cinema easily, feel welcome when they arrive and have the chance to buy popcorn to eat during the film.

People may enjoy an activity – a dance class, for instance – but drop it because these other parts of the experience have been overlooked. They're likely to enjoy themselves much more if they're made to feel welcome and there's an opportunity to socialise when the dancing ends.

Like cinemas, the retail sector is making efforts to package a variety of experiences. Many people go shopping for pleasure and spend far longer comparing and discussing products than they do actually buying. This has even gained a name in recent years – 'retail therapy' – reflecting the view that it makes people feel better.

Shopping used to be purely practical: we bought what we needed. But that's no longer enough. Many shopping centres now ensure shoppers are provided with entertainment as well. This is good for business, as it attracts more customers, who stay longer and spend more.

And is leisure good for us, or simply a waste of time? According to psychologists, participating in leisure activities makes us healthier, both physically and mentally, and increases the pleasure we gain from life. So we've got good reason to carry on with our hobbies!

Photocopiable recording script activity
(P ⋯⋗ **page 136)**

Pairs of students could choose five leisure activities that are mentioned and design a leaflet to attract people to them. The information could include what is in the recording script, what other students say about the activities and what they find on the Internet.

3 Explain that vowel sounds fall into three main categories: short, long and diphthongs. Point out that spelling is not a helpful guide to pronunciation. Give examples from the students' language of the three categories, if appropriate.

NB The name of each vowel, *a, e, i, o* and *u*, is the same as its main long or diphthong pronunciation. Ask students to read exercise 3 and categorise the underlined vowels.

Answers	
short vowels:	full /ʊ/, instead /e/, skills /ɪ/, study /ʌ/, hobby /ɒ/
long vowels:	far /ɑː/, more /ɔː/, music /uː/, bird /ɜː/, people /iː/
diphthongs:	about /aʊ/, goal /əʊ/, time /aɪ/, there /eə/, year /ɪə/

Ask students to listen to each word and repeat it as a group. The words are in the same order as above the table. Then ask students to form pairs and take turns to read the words, checking each other's pronunciation.

Recording script

Listen and repeat.

full	far	about	instead	goal
time	more	there	music	bird
skills	year	study	people	hobby

4 This activity will help students to anticipate the types of questions they might be asked in Part 3 of the Speaking Module, and to evaluate answers. Ask them to form groups of three, read the example questions and complete the set of four questions about one or more of the activities – either the ones in exercise 4 or another activity. Draw attention to the activities in the cartoons (playing computer games, collecting autographs). As they finish, individuals should question someone from another group. After a while, ask the class how easy it was to reply to the questions, and how well people answered the questions.

Possible answers
Watching television
Why do you think some people enjoy watching TV?
What sorts of programmes are the most educational?
Playing computer games
How is playing computer games different from playing other games?
Can playing computer games a lot affect relationships with other people?
Collecting autographs of famous people
What expenses might be involved in collecting autographs?
Do you think it's a good idea to buy autographs from other collectors? Why / Why not?
Reading
Is it more useful to read books or read material on the Internet? Why?
Do you think free libraries, where people can borrow books, are a good idea?
Why do you think some people never read for pleasure?
What are the disadvantages of reading? Why?

Writing folder 4

SB pages 56–57
General Training Writing Task 1: Writing a letter

Refer students to the introduction and Advice box. This unit aims to take students through the expressions and layout required in a letter. Students often find it hard to know how to begin a letter, and the Useful language box contains suggestions for letter purpose, which should be of help.

1

> **Answer**
> The letter is to the local council.

2

> **Answer**
> C is correct here because you don't know the name of the person you are writing to. A is informal to a friend, and B is to someone you have met/know the name of and is semi-formal.

3

> **Answer**
> A is better, as there is an explanation of who is writing and a clear reason for writing is given.
> B is too abrupt and gives the reader no idea of who is writing. It is also very rude – implying something about the council which may or may not be true, but which in any case is unlikely to receive a positive response.

4

> **Answer**
> It only deals with one suggestion – the question asked for 'suggestions'. Also it talks about how to find money for the facility, which was not asked for. And it contains some further irrelevancy towards the end. The reader wouldn't be interested in the personal information given.

5

> **Answer**
> This is too informal. A better ending would be something like:
> *I do hope you will consider my suggestions and ideas. Please get in touch with me if you would like to discuss them further. I look forward to hearing from you in the near future.*

6

> **Suggested answers**
> 1 Too abrupt: *I would like to work in your cinema if you have a vacancy in the near future.*
> 2 Too informal: *I hope that you will consider my application favourably.*
> 3 Too flowery: *I saw your job advertisement in the paper last week.*
> 4 Too rude: *I would appreciate it if you could reply as soon as possible.*
> 5 Too rude: *I'm afraid that I will be unable to attend the interview next week. I hope it will be possible to arrange another date.*
> 6 Too rude: *I'm afraid that I haven't yet received an application form.*
> 7 Too formal: *I'm sorry to say that I do not think you have adequately answered my question.*
> 8 Too informal: *I enclose my CV.*
> 9 Too informal: *Please do not hesitate to get in touch if you have any questions about my application.*
> 10 Too formal: *You will see from my CV that I am very well qualified for the position.*

7 This letter is not an exact correction of the one in the Student's Book, but is politer and more agreeable in tone.

> **Possible answer**
> Dear Sir/Madam,
> I am a 20-year-old student and I am studying physical education at Pulteney College. I have been studying there for the past two years. I am writing to ask if there are any part-time job vacancies at your sports centre.
> I really enjoy sport, and my areas of particular interest and expertise are running, tennis, judo and basketball. I have had some experience of coaching for these sports during the time I have been at the college. Last year, I worked in the holidays at a sports centre in my own country. I will be able to provide references from this summer job and also from my teachers at the college. I qualify as a sports teacher in two years' time.
> I would prefer to work in the evenings and at weekends, as I have classes during the daytime, and I can start from the beginning of October.
> I look forward to hearing from you in the near future.
> Yours faithfully,
> (159 words, not including opening and closing phrases)

Units 5–8 Revision

SB pages 58–59

The aim of this revision unit is to focus on the language covered in units 5–8. Exercises 2–6 can be done as a test in class or for homework.

Topic review

1

> **Possible answers**
> 1 Well, in fact, I do sometimes, because sometimes the advert is for something I really need.
> 2 Absolutely true! There's nothing I like more than going to museums and places of historical interest.
> 3 Well, they have been saying this for years, and all I can say is that people are working harder than ever.
> 4 If you don't work hard, it's unlikely you will ever have any money – unless of course you win the lottery.
> 5 It is probably easier to get a job in the first place if you have qualifications.
> 6 Yes, that's true, but only because it is very expensive to go to the theatre.
> 7 No, I don't think this is true. I think more people than ever are interested in history – you only have to look at TV scheduling and the number of Hollywood films that are based on historical characters.
> 8 Both are very important to me – I need long holidays, but I also need to have enough money to go somewhere nice.
> 9 Yes, I already have a job organised in the local supermarket.
> 10 No, I think my dad works the hardest. He's a lawyer and doesn't come home till late most nights.

Grammar

2

> **Answers**
> 1 levelled off 2 has dropped back 3 has changed
> 4 declined 5 was 6 was 7 experienced
> 8 continued

3

> **Answers**
> 1 My colleague is always late for work, which makes my boss really angry.
> 2 The archaeologists have found the tomb of the king who/that ruled the country in 4500 BC.
> 3 We went to see the film which/that won an Oscar this year.
> 4 I am writing a book review which/that might upset the author.
> 5 Archaeologists are people who often have to work in difficult conditions.
> 6 I don't like advertisements which/that don't tell the truth.
> 7 What was the name of the company which/that gave all its workers a bonus last year?

4

> **Answers**
> 1 My wife, who lives in New York, works in advertising.
> 2 The Dorchester Hotel, which is near Hyde Park, is very comfortable.
> 3 I know a lot of people who are archaeologists.
> 4 The boy who played the part of Peter in the play goes to my college.
> 5 The people who built the Pyramids must have worked long and hard.
> 6 My manager, who is very strict about punctuality, has been with the company for years.

5

> **Answers**
> 1 site 2 research 3 tomb 4 salary 5 promotion
> 6 motivation 7 manager 8 earn 9 spend 10 waste
> 11 save 12 pay 13 play 14 exhibition 15 dancing
> 16 performance 17 relaxation 18 activity
> a manager b earn c performance d research
> e exhibition

6

> **Answers**
> 1 carries out / does 2 reached 3 analysed 4 support
> 5 carrying out / doing; lead

Progress Test 2

Listening

Questions 1–5

Complete the sentences below.

Write **NO MORE THAN TWO WORDS AND/OR A NUMBER** *for each answer.*

1 Coppersmith Engineering was founded in ....

2 It has recently developed engines for certain types of ....

3 Since starting a joint venture, there has been an increase in ....

4 The building that is under construction is to be a new ....

5 The company recently won an award as the .... in the city.

Questions 6–10

Which activity will each trainee learn about?

*Choose your answers from the box and write the letters **A–H** next to questions 6–10.*

A	domestic sales
B	export sales
C	marketing
D	purchasing
E	recruitment
F	salaries and wages
G	training
H	warehouse

6 Carol ....

7 Frank ....

8 Philip ....

9 Stephanie ....

10 Minh ....

Reading

Questions 1–7

The reading passage has seven paragraphs **A–G**.

Choose the correct heading for each paragraph from the list of headings below.

*Write the correct number **i–x** by each question.*

List of Headings
i   How advertising reached the majority of consumers
ii   An uncertain future
iii   Not everyone wants to see advertisements
iv   Changing preferences in television programmes
v   The rising cost of television advertising
vi   Advertisers' difficulties are nothing new – but they're getting worse
vii   Using consumers to do the advertising
viii More television stations, but fewer people watch each one
ix   How advertisers plan their spending
x   Strong sales don't require most of the spending on advertising to go to TV

1 Paragraph A ....
2 Paragraph B ....
3 Paragraph C ....
4 Paragraph D ....
5 Paragraph E ....
6 Paragraph F ....
7 Paragraph G ....

Questions 8–13

Do the following statements reflect the claims of the writer in the reading passage? Write

    YES   *if the statement reflects the claims of the writer*

    NO   *if the statement contradicts the claims of the writer*

    NOT GIVEN *if it is impossible to say what the writer thinks about this*

8   The percentage of spending on advertising that is wasted is falling.

9   Internet advertising leads to higher sales than newspaper advertising.

10   Changes in the number of television stations available has affected advertisers.

11   Most people believe that the quality of advertising has become worse.

12   A number of people were surprised by the level of sales of Prilosec.

13   Advertising is likely to return to what it was in the 20th century.

The crisis in advertising

A Advertisers have known for a long time that half the money they spent was wasted: their problem was that they didn't know which half. But now they're facing bigger challenges than ever before, and as a result, they're probably wasting even more of their advertising budget.

B For years, the main media used for advertising in the USA were newspapers – now affected by a fall in the number of readers – magazines, television, radio, cinema and outdoor (that is, posters on billboards in the street). These have now been joined by the Internet. The most effective medium was television: when there were only two or three channels in each country, TV commercials were seen by maybe 90% of consumers, and advertisers from banks to airlines to car manufacturers spent vast amounts on television advertising.

C Now, though, with the growth of satellite and cable TV, the number of channels has multiplied, so audiences are much smaller than in the past. Because of this, and the popularity of the Internet, advertisers may find they are reaching no more than a third of the public.

D Another problem for advertisers is a change in attitudes. As the average American sees around 3,000 advertisements of various sorts every day, the findings of some recent surveys are hardly surprising: two-thirds of Americans would like to avoid advertising altogether – particularly on TV. Consumers are buying personal video recorders, not least because they make it possible to see TV programmes without watching the commercials.

E To deal with these challenges, companies are changing their approach to marketing. Procter & Gamble, manufacturer of many of the household goods found in millions of homes, is the world's biggest advertiser, spending $4 billion a year. In the 1990s, 90 per cent of that was spent on TV commercials, but now the percentage is much lower, and sales remain strong. In 2003, the company launched a non-prescription medicine, Prilosec. Only about a quarter of the marketing budget was spent on TV, while the rest went to other forms of marketing, and many in the advertising industry expected the launch to fail as a result. Instead, the product sold very well.

F Some companies are experimenting with different ways of reaching consumers, such as 'viral' marketing, an electronic version of word-of-mouth advertising. Procter & Gamble – which helped to launch TV soap operas as a new way to market goods in the 1940s – is once again looking for fresh approaches to advertising. In 2001, it started an ambitious programme involving several hundred thousand US teenagers. It uses them to discuss ideas about new products and to encourage their friends to buy the items. In return, the teenagers get to hear about and use new things before most other people.

G It's hard to predict what advertising will be like in a few years' time, but it's sure to be far more varied than it was in the last century. It has always been the job of the advertising industry to be inventive. Now it isn't just a question of inventing new ads – advertisers are having to invent new ways of persuading consumers to buy.

Writing

Writing Task 1 (GT)

You should spend about 20 minutes on this task.

You were hurt in a minor accident at a local swimming pool and you wish to complain to the swimming pool management.

Write a letter to the manager of the swimming pool. In your letter

- *say who you are*
- *give details of the accident*
- *suggest how the swimming pool management could prevent similar accidents.*

Write at least 150 words.

You do **NOT** need to write any addresses.

Begin your letter as follows:

Dear Sir or Madam,

Progress Test 2 Key

Listening

1 1934 2 boats 3 turnover / (sales) 4 office (block)
5 best employer 6 F 7 D 8 B 9 H 10 E

Recording script

You will hear a manager from an engineering company talking to a group of new trainees. First, you have some time to look at questions 1 to 5.

Now listen carefully and answer questions 1 to 5.

Ah, good morning, everyone. My name's Jeremy Armstrong, and I'm in charge of your training programme here at Coppersmith Engineering, manufacturers of what we like to think are the world's best diesel engines! I'll start by giving you a very brief background to the company.

Right. Now, the founder, John Coppersmith, was born locally in 1910. In 1932, he started making bicycles in a shed at the bottom of his garden. This proved so successful that two years later, he rented a small factory unit and set up Coppersmith Engineering – so <u>we date back to 1934</u>. And since then, we've produced over ten million engines.

As you probably know, the engines we manufacture are not for cars, but for vehicles used in industry and agriculture. <u>In the last few years, we've also made engines that are used to power boats</u>, including police launches and lifeboats.

Another fairly new development is that ten years ago, we set up a joint venture with a Japanese manufacturer and as a result, <u>we're seeing a big rise in turnover</u>, while keeping production costs steady.

Of course, this success gives us great confidence in the future, and so we're currently in the middle of a five-year plan to improve the buildings we have here. We've just completed a new test facility, and as you were coming in, you probably noticed <u>the site where we're constructing an office block</u>. At present, our desk-based staff are in several buildings, and they're all due to move into the new one in six months' time.

Oh, and, er, just one more point I'd like to mention: our goal has always been to achieve top quality in everything we do, so when <u>we received an award</u> last month from the city council, <u>naming us 'best employer'</u>, we were very proud indeed.

* *

Before you hear the rest of what the manager has to say, you have some time to look at questions 6 to 10.

Now listen and answer questions 6 to 10.

OK, now I'll give you an idea of what to expect in the next few days. You'll each be spending today and tomorrow with one of our staff, following him or her around, sitting in on meetings, and generally learning about that particular activity.

Now, this is how I've allocated you. Er, <u>Carol</u>, you said in your interview that you're interested in finance, so I've put you with <u>the person who deals with payments to staff</u>. This is the busiest week in the monthly cycle, as all the <u>overtime</u> has to be calculated before <u>pay day</u>.

Now, <u>Frank</u>, I believe you've already had some training in sales, and you want to look at the process from the other side, so <u>the purchasing section</u> is where you'll start off. You'll be able to find out <u>how we buy goods and services from our suppliers</u>.

Next on the list is <u>Philip</u>. You said you hope to work in advertising, so I *had* arranged for you to work alongside our marketing manager. But I'm afraid she's on sick leave at the moment, so instead you'll be with someone who <u>deals with sales to other countries</u>. As you speak two or three languages, you should find you can use them.

<u>Stephanie</u>, you didn't mention any preference, so <u>I've put you with the warehouse</u> manager. We purchase goods almost every day and have frequent deliveries, so you'll see how we handle all the goods that come in – not to mention the finished products waiting to be despatched to customers.

And lastly, <u>Minh</u>: I understand you've been working in an employment agency and would like to look at the <u>application process</u> from an employer's point of view. We're about to advertise for new training staff to join my section, so you'll be with the person who's <u>responsible for recruiting</u> them. You might have some good ideas for how they should go about it.

OK, now if you'd like to come this way …

Reading

1 vi 2 i 3 viii 4 iii 5 x 6 vii 7 ii

8 NO	*But now … they're probably wasting even more of their advertising budget.* (paragraph A)	
9 NOT GIVEN	*newspapers – now affected by a fall in the number of readers … These have now been joined by the Internet.* (paragraph B) We aren't told whether Internet advertising has become more effective than newspaper advertising.	
10 YES	*the number of channels has multiplied, so audiences are much smaller than in the past. Because of this, … advertisers may find they are reaching no more than a third of the public.* (paragraph C)	
11 NOT GIVEN	*two-thirds of Americans would like to avoid advertising altogether.* (paragraph D) We are told that many people don't like advertising, but not whether they think it has become worse.	
12 YES	*many in the advertising industry expected the launch to fail as a result. Instead, the product sold very well.* (paragraph E)	
13 NO	*it's sure to be far more varied than it was in the last century.* (paragraph G)	

Writing

Sample answer

Dear Sir or Madam,

My name is Suzi Loh and I reported having an accident in your changing room last Wednesday. I am now writing to complain formally about the state of the floor in the women's changing room.

Last week, I attended the Wednesday morning session. When I was getting changed in the women's changing room, I slipped and fell. The floor was very greasy for some reason, probably the result of the cleaning fluid which had been used. Luckily, there were other people in the changing room, and they were able to help me. I only grazed my arm, because someone caught me as I fell. Otherwise, I might have been knocked unconscious when I hit the floor.

I think it is vital that you investigate the type of cleaning products that are being used at the pool and also perhaps consider changing the type of flooring being used before someone is seriously hurt. I look forward to hearing your response.

Yours faithfully,

Suzi Loh

(159 words, not including opening and closing phrases)

9 Climate change

Unit topic	The environment
9.1	
Test skills	Reading (AC): Summary completion
9.2	
Test skills	Speaking Part 3
	Listening: Note and table completion
	Writing extra (AC): Task 1: A diagram
Grammar	Countable and uncountable nouns
Vocabulary	Collocations related to the environment

Workbook contents

1, 2, 3	Reading
4	Grammar: noun-verb agreement
5	Grammar: countable/uncountable nouns
6	Vocabulary

9.1 SB pages 60–61

1 The picture is from the film *The Day after Tomorrow*, which is about what might happen in New York if the climate changes. Doing this quiz will help students prepare for reading the article. Ask them to work through the quiz in small groups and compare answers.

> **Answers**
> 1 A   2 C   3 A   4 B

2 Students should scan the article to find the answer to the question. The article is about 700 words long and should take them about two and a half minutes.

> **Answer**
> Ronald Stouffer

3 Students should read through sentences 1–5 carefully and then read the text again to match the right heading to the right paragraph A–E.

> **Answers**
> 1 C *impact on ecosystems, agriculture* (line 47); *placing animals like polar bears at risk* (line 56)
> 2 E *'You can't say ...' says Stouffer* (lines 74–75); *'Is society aware ...' says Marianne Douglas* (lines 79–81)
> 3 A This paragraph talks about now and in the future.

> 4 D *Greenland's ice sheet* (line 58); *the Maldives* (lines 65–66); *the Nile Delta* (line 67); *Bangladesh* (line 68); *the eastern seaboard of the USA* (line 70)
> 5 B *Most scientists believe ... But some scientists also point to ...* (lines 29–33)

4 Refer the class to the Test spot. This explains the summary task. For more information, go to Test folder 5. For this summary, remind students that they must only use words which are in the article.

> **Answers**
> 1 average   2 (coral) reefs   3 heat   4 habitats
> 5 ice sheet/cap   6 populated   7 seven/7   8 fossil fuels
> 9 sources of energy

Extension activity

Students should look back at the text and find the following words. They should work in small groups to explain the meaning of the words/phrases and use an English-English dictionary to help them.

1 massive (line 13)
2 catastrophic (line 14)
3 still being disputed (line 29)
4 to impact (line 47)
5 partial (line 63)
6 devastating (line 65)
7 doomsday scenarios (lines 71–72)
8 has gone unchecked (lines 78–79)

> **Answers**
> 1 very large   2 terrible   3 still being argued about
> 4 to have a powerful effect on a situation or person
> 5 not complete   6 destructive   7 a time when death and destruction will happen   8 has not been stopped

9.2 SB pages 62–63

1 Countable and uncountable nouns often cause students problems in the Writing Module. It is important that they learn to recognise whether a noun is countable or uncountable so that they can make appropriate changes to the grammar in the rest of the sentence. Students should read through the four sentences and, using the information contained in them, fill in the rules in a and b.

> **Answers**
> a *research; information; much; amount;* singular
> b *scientists; countries; many; number*

Refer the class to the table giving a list of which words can be used with which type of noun, to the notes below it and to the Grammar folder (SB pages 140–141) if more information is needed.

2 This is an example of a dictionary entry so that students who have little experience of dictionaries can learn where to look to find out if a noun is countable or uncountable.

Answers

countable	uncountable
university	pollution
country	information
activity	news
job	weather
scientist	accommodation
meal	advice
	knowledge
	research
	climate
	work

3 Warn students that some nouns – for example ones which refer to groups of people like *company, family, staff, government* – can be used with either singular or plural verbs and pronouns.

Suggested answers
1 Global warming is happening / happens faster than (many/most) people think.
2 Information about ecology courses at universities is hard to find.
3 A lot of people are studying mathematics at my college this year.
4 Are/Is the company going to put new equipment in the computer lab next year?
5 The news this morning isn't good.
6 My work on climate change is being / is going to be published next week.

4 Students can improve their writing skills by using more formal words in essays.

Suggested answers
1 **A number of / Many** people **think** that **much of** the information about climate change **has** been wrong. **Much / A great/good deal of** research **has** taken place into whether it **has** been more influenced by natural occurrences such as volcanoes.
2 **Many / A number of** gases trap the sun's heat in the atmosphere and **cause** a gradual warming of the Earth.
3 **A good/great deal of** research **has** found that all people **need** to do **is** use **less** fossil fuel.
4 There **is** evidence that a car **emits** as **much** carbon dioxide a year as an entire house. **Much / A large amount of** energy can be saved by driving more smoothly and keeping the tyres inflated.

Extension activity

For homework, ask students to find out the difference between the following (ask them to look in CALD):
1 paper / a paper
2 coffee / a coffee
3 experience / an experience
4 damage / damages
5 hair / a hair
6 work / a work
7 glass / a glass
8 travel / travels
9 iron / an iron
10 room / a room

Answers
These are the most commonly confused meanings, but there are others – see CALD.
1 paper = to write on
  a paper = a newspaper, an academic thesis
2 coffee = the plant/substance
  a coffee = a cup of coffee
3 experience = in general
  an experience = one experience
4 damage = destruction
  damages = compensation
5 hair = lots of hairs together, generally on your head
  a hair = one single strand on your head/leg/arm, etc.
6 work = your job
  a work = e.g. of art
7 glass = the substance
  a glass = a container for drinking out of
8 travel = used mainly as an adjective, e.g. travel agency (although can also be an abstract noun)
  travels = the travels of Marco Polo
9 iron = the substance
  an iron = what you use to make your clothes smooth
10 room = space to move
  a room = a place

5 This exercise is similar to a Part 3 Speaking Module. It also acts as a warm-up to the listening in exercise 6. Have students work in pairs and ask and answer the questions on recycling. The pictures show someone taking a shower, cycling to work and a computer which has been unplugged. Refer students also to the Useful language box and monitor them to make sure they use some of this language.

6 Ask the class to read through the notes and predict what sort of answer is required for each gap. Play the recording as many times as is necessary, but remember that it is heard only once in the test.

Answers (see underlined text in script)
1 (US$)2,000 2 conserving energy 3 light bulb(s)
4 refrigerator/fridge 5 (the) water 6 8/eight minutes
7 TV/television 8 ($)24 9 beef 10 bulk

Recording script

Good morning and welcome to the programme. Did you know that today is Earth Day? Well, in case you didn't, I'm here to tell you what you can do to save the planet. According to a new book published recently, called *51 Easy Ways to Save the Planet*, each household in the USA could save as much as $2,000 on annual bills and help the Earth at the same time. Most people seem to think that there's nothing they can do on a local level – that it's something for governments to tackle. Well, according to the authors of this book, they couldn't be more wrong. And those of you who don't live in the USA, stay with us – there's plenty you can do, too!

The book focuses on conserving energy, and the authors say that if 35 per cent of the US population can be persuaded to follow their suggestions, US carbon-dioxide emissions can be reduced to the level targeted in the Kyoto Protocol, signed by a number of countries, but not the USA, in 2001.

Did you know, for example, that making a contribution to reducing the use of fossil fuels can be as simple as changing the type of light bulb you use? The new kind of bulb lasts ten times longer, uses one-fourth of the energy and produces more light per watt than the old type. Although they initially cost more, they quickly pay for themselves and will save you money in the long term.

Another way the authors suggest you can save the planet is to place your refrigerator somewhere out of the sun and away from the oven or radiator. So simple! Now, do you leave the water running when you clean your teeth? Well, many of us do, and it's wasting precious resources. Apparently, if your faucet is leaky and drips every three seconds, it can waste 29 gallons, or 110 litres, of water a month. Scary or what? Also, if you take an eight-minute shower instead of a ten-minute one, you will save about 290 gallons, or 1,100 litres, of water a month, so start timing yourself today!

Now, do you use the remote control for your TV? Do you realise that, according to the book, one-fourth of the energy consumed each year by the TV is used when it's actually turned off? Most people don't know about this, but the only way to stop wasting energy is to unplug it, not leave it on standby.

Your car is the next target. Your car is responsible for emitting as much carbon dioxide per year as your whole house. So choose your car with care. Tuning your engine will improve its efficiency by 15 to 50% and just pumping up the tyres regularly will save you $24 in gas.

Food next. The average American eats 265 pounds, or 120 kilos, of beef per year. By reducing your intake by just one pound, or half a kilo, each week, you can save $109 over the year. Did you know that the electricity used to water, feed and package just half a kilo of beef is the equivalent of burning one gallon of gas in your car's engine?

Now, finally, when you go shopping, why don't you buy your groceries in bulk rather than in small sizes? This will result in annual savings of up to $293, but, of course the problem is: where to put all those bulk buys? Would you need to build an extra room, buy extra refrigerators and use more electricity, thus defeating the object of saving energy? Well, that's a question I can't answer, but I do think there are some good ideas in this book. Why don't you try some out and let me know how you get on? There'll be a prize for the best email on the subject. So, ...

7

Answers
1 f 2 g 3 a 4 e 5 b 6 c 7 d

8   As a class, read through the diagram, checking to make sure everyone understands the process (see Writing folder 1).

Sample answer
The diagram shows what might happen to the Earth if people continue to burn fossil fuels and cut down forests. The cycle begins when factories use fossil fuels such as coal or gas or wood as a source of energy in manufacturing. These factories emit huge clouds of smoke, which pollute the atmosphere. The smoke is composed of carbon dioxide and other gases. These gases trap heat which would normally escape into space, thus producing the phenomenon we call the 'greenhouse effect'. The warming increases water vapour in the air, and more heat is absorbed into the atmosphere. If carbon dioxide and other greenhouse gases continue to pour into the atmosphere unchecked, the world will warm rapidly. Rising temperatures will melt snow and ice, and sea levels will rise. Many of the Earth's towns and villages are built on the coast, and a rise in sea level will spell disaster for them. (151 words)

Test folder 5

SB pages 64–65
Summary completion

Make sure students fully understand the notes and advice.

1   Ask students to skim the passage, then to read the summary. Check that they understand this. Ask them to read the passage more carefully and complete the summary.

Answers
1 ice melt   2 flooding   3 hail   4 glaciers
5 growing season   6 crops   7 seeds   8 harvests
9 famines   10 malnutrition   11 fungus

2   Ask students to read the summary. Check that they understand it, and ask them to predict possible meanings and word classes that would fit each gap.

Play the recording.

Recording script

You will hear part of a talk about winds high above the earth.

First, you have some time to look at questions 1 to 11. (*pause*)

Now listen carefully and answer questions 1 to 11.

Today I'm going to talk about one of the major influences on the weather – jet streams – and one in particular. Basically, a jet stream is a wind, although it blows much more regularly than most of the winds we experience. It may help to think of it as a narrow, fast-flowing 'river' of air.

The Polar Front Jet Stream, which affects the weather of North America and the British Isles, is between 9 and 13 kilometres above sea level. It flows right round the globe, in sections thousands of kilometres long, and moves much faster than winds at ground level, reaching a maximum during the winter. Then the normal speed is about 400 kilometres an hour, though speeds of over 600 kilometres an hour have been recorded. The stream moves from west to east, because of the rotation of the earth.

The jet stream is formed on the boundary between two blocks of air of different temperatures. To the north, there's the cold air of the North Pole region, and to the south, the sub-tropical air closer to the equator. This, of course, is much warmer. The difference in temperature results in a difference in pressure, and this in turn forces the air to move.

Unlike rain or snow, which we've always known about, jet streams are a relatively recent discovery. In the 1940s, during the Second World War, pilots flying high-altitude planes noticed that they travelled faster when they were going eastwards, helped by strong tailwinds. Modern planes are affected, too. A flight from London to New York takes about 7½ hours, but travelling in the opposite direction takes an hour less. This, of course, means a considerable saving in time and fuel. The drawback is that when planes enter and leave a jet stream, they meet considerable turbulence. So even for highly sophisticated modern aircraft, navigation isn't as easy as you might expect.

As I mentioned, jet streams affect the weather, so weather forecasters need to include them in their calculations. Data about the jet stream and other high-level conditions is fed into computers, making it possible to pick out the areas where depressions may form. In the British Isles, forecasters then calculate whether these depressions are likely to develop into storms, which may cause structural damage as they rush in from the Atlantic, or whether there'll be nothing more serious than showers. In fact, the jet stream has a major influence on the Atlantic depressions that bring rainfall to the British Isles all year round. This is actually a very beneficial climate, although not everyone would agree!

If global warming really starts to accelerate in the second half of this century, as many scientists expect, the area of warm air will be much larger during the summer than it is now. The impact on the jet stream will be that it will be located further north. The British Isles will then become dry, with an almost complete lack of summer rain. So there's a pretty unpleasant change in prospect.

3 Check that students know the meanings of the words in the box. Ask them to read the summary; check that they understand it. Remind students that the words may be paraphrases of the listening passage. Play the recording.

Recording script

You will hear a university teacher talking about the effects of a volcanic eruption on the weather.

First, you have some time to look at questions 1 to 7. (*pause*)

Now listen carefully and answer questions 1 to 7.

One of the most powerful volcanic eruptions ever recorded took place in 1815. In April of that year, Mount Tambora, in what's now Indonesia, erupted with catastrophic violence, ejecting over a million and a half tonnes of ash, which darkened the sky over a radius of 500 kilometres. Much of it reached the upper atmosphere and remained there for the next two years. To a considerable extent, this blocked solar radiation from reaching the earth, significantly lowering temperatures, particularly in the northern hemisphere.

The following year, 1816, became known as 'the year without a summer'. Southern Italy had the unusual experience of seeing snowflakes, and the sun was masked by a cloud of what looked like smoke. During the spring growing season, temperatures were abnormally low, and crops were ruined by hail and rain.

The resulting shortages made food very expensive across Europe, and thousands of people died of starvation. There was social unrest, as the poor took to the streets, and high levels of violence.

In the north-eastern United States, the spring of 1816 arrived late and was exceptionally cold, with rain, frost and snow continuing into June. Crops were destroyed, animals died and tens of thousands of people were forced to move to the richer soil and better growing conditions of the Midwest. So, indirectly, the volcanic eruption contributed to the rapid settlement of this region.

Another side-effect of the eruption was that Mary Shelley wrote her novel *Frankenstein* when the bad weather forced her to stay indoors during a holiday in Switzerland.

A place to work or live in

Unit topic	Buildings
10.1	
Test skills	Speaking Part 1
	Listening: Note completion
	Writing extra (GT):
	Task 1: A letter of complaint
Pronunciation	Polite intonation
Vocabulary	Phrasal verbs and collocations
	with *house* and *home*
10.2	
Test skills	Speaking Part 2
Grammar	*-ing* forms and infinitives (1)
Workbook contents	
1, 2	Reading
3	Vocabulary
4	Grammar: *-ing* forms and
	infinitives

10.1 SB pages 66–67

1   Refer students to the pictures. They show two types of student accommodation: a shared flat and a study bedroom in a hall of residence. Ask students to talk about the advantages and disadvantages of each and encourage them to give opinions and state preferences.

Allow students to work through the questions in pairs, checking to make sure they expand their answers. They should try to use as many of the phrases and expressions from the Useful language box as possible.

2   Ask the class to read through the questions (1–10) and predict the answers. Play the recording.

> **Answers (see underlined text in script)**
> 1 food   2 20 minutes   3 (the) summer (vacation)
> 4 ($)150   5 washing machines   6 27 Whitaker
> 7 volleyball   8 (the) basement   9 no smoking   10 ($)25

Recording script

Woman: Can I help you?
Girl: Yes, please. I'm looking for the accommodation officer. Do you know where she is?
Woman: I don't, I'm afraid. *I* can probably help you. My name is Joanna Swift. Do sit down.
Girl: Thank you. I'd like to move into a college room in October. Can you tell me a bit about what's available?
Woman: Certainly. We have two blocks for women students. The first is Ridgeway House. There are two types of room – an ordinary bedroom with desk, etc., which is $230 a week, <u>that's</u>

<u>with food, of course,</u> but not en-suite facilities, and then there's the bigger study bedroom, which is $270 a week.
Girl: Mm. I think I'm more interested in the cheaper room. But are they very small?
Woman: Well, they're not very big, but there's a large common room with a TV on each floor, so there's somewhere to go and talk to friends or see the news. The university campus is a five-minute bus ride, <u>or 20 if you walk</u>.
Girl: Oh, that's not so far.
Woman: No, but there is something that you may find a problem – I'm afraid Ridgeway House is <u>closed in the summer</u>, but not the winter, <u>vacation</u>.
Girl: Oh, that *is* a problem, actually. I need somewhere for the whole year.
Woman: Mm. International House may suit you better. It's much cheaper – only $130 to share a room or <u>$150 for a single room</u>. Food isn't included in the price, but there's a kitchen on every floor and <u>washing machines on the ground floor</u>.
Girl: That sounds better, but I wouldn't want to share. I'm such a tidy person, you know, I would find sharing difficult. I'd like to have a single room, if one is available.
Woman: There are a few singles still available for next year, but you'll have to make up your mind fairly soon, as it's such a popular hall. Why don't you go and take a look? The address is <u>27 Whitaker</u>, that's spelt W-H-I-T-A-K-E-R, Place.
Girl: Yes, I'll do that.
Woman: There are also quite a few facilities you might be interested in. There's an outdoor swimming pool for the warmer months and <u>an all-weather volleyball court</u>.
Girl: I think I'm probably more interested in having access to a computer.
Woman: No problem – there's a computer room situated <u>in the basement</u>. It's run by volunteers and is always open in the evenings and at weekends. Now, I should tell you that there's really only one rule in International House, and that is that <u>no smoking is permitted anywhere on the premises</u>. They also have an unofficial policy of no noise after ten o'clock at night.
Girl: That won't be a problem. I will go and have a look and then come back. Would I need to pay a deposit today?
Woman: It would be better, and you also need to fill in the application form. <u>The fee is $25, which you pay now</u>, with a further $100 deposit when you get the key. I'm sure you'd enjoy living there – it's a lovely building and was only finished last year.
Girl: It sounds brilliant. Thank you very much for your help.

> ### Photocopiable recording script activity
> (**P** ···> page 137)

- Hand out copies of the recording script and examine the text in detail, eliciting where the answers come from and pointing out distractions.

- Make copies of the recording script with the prepositions blanked out. Give each pair of students a copy and ask them to work together to fill in the prepositions.

3 Play the beginning of the recording from exercise 2 again so students can hear the polite phrases. Then ask the class to repeat, using the same intonation pattern. Ask students to make up dialogues which include the phrases and then perform them for the class.

4 This exercise is designed to make students aware of polite and friendly intonation in English. Play the recording twice – once so that they can build awareness, and the second time so they can make a decision as to whether the exchange is polite and friendly or unfriendly.

Answers
1 U 2 F 3 U 4 U 5 F 6 U 7 F 8 F

Recording script

1 **Man:** Here's your book.
Woman: Thank you.
2 **Woman:** You're a student here, aren't you?
Man: Yes, that's right.
3 **Woman:** I'm here for my tutorial.
Man: Come in.
4 **Man:** Have you seen Peter?
Woman: No, I haven't.
5 **Woman:** Where's the milk?
Man: I'm sorry, I don't know.
6 **Man:** Have you finished with that book?
Woman: Yes, I have.
7 **Man:** What's the time?
Woman: I've no idea, actually.
8 **Woman:** Hello.
Man: Oh, good morning.

5 Encourage students to keep a collocation notebook. Having a good grasp of collocations will improve their test scores.

Answers
1 My house is **semi-detached**.
2 Josh **moved house** eight times when he was a child.
3 Don't worry about finding a hotel – I can **put you up** for the night.
4 After they had children, they decided to **extend** their house.
5 Tania's mother was very upset when Tania **left home**.
6 The council **are pulling down** the old cinema / **are pulling** the old cinema **down**.
7 Dr Thomas is very happy to **rent out** the flat / **rent** the flat **out** to students for a reasonable amount.
8 I live in a **bungalow**.
9 My aunt's house **is very spacious**, but it's (a bit) dilapidated.
10 I have lived in both **terraced** and **detached** houses.

6 This task can be done in class or for homework.

Answers
1 past 2 However 3 attention 4 because 5 Would
6 run 7 limit 8 agree 9 when 10 hearing

7

Sample answer
Dear Mr Smith,

As you know, I have rented 45 Marlborough Road from you for a year from 2nd October. However, I am afraid I will no longer be able to move in on that date, as my plans have had to change because of illness.

During the summer vacation, I was working in a factory as a supervisor. Towards the end of my shift, I slipped on some oil and fell and broke my arm. Luckily, it was a clean break and will mend without problem. However, it is my right arm, and so I am unable to write for the time being.

At present, I am at home in Cape Town until the plaster can be taken off – I think this should be in the first week of November. I will then return to my course in the UK and take up residence at 45 Marlborough Road.

I hope this will not cause you any difficulties.

Yours sincerely,

(154 words, not including opening and closing phrases)

10.2 SB pages 68–69

1 The picture is of the Swiss Re headquarters (30 St Mary Axe) in London. It is nicknamed 'The Gherkin' because of its appearance. It is an office building.

2 Ask students to read through the details on Norman Foster and the Swiss Re building. Check they understand the vocabulary.

3/4 These exercises should make students aware of the different ways the *-ing* and *to* form are used. Refer them to the Grammar folder (SB page 141) if they continue to have problems.

Answers
3 The *-ing* form is used as a noun in sentence 1. In sentence 2, it is a present participle, and in sentence 3, it is an adjective.
4 1 *finished studying* (line 12)
2 *after leaving* (line 5), *before doing* (line 6)
3 *managed to send* (line 3), *was beginning to develop* (line 7), *decided to continue* (line 10), *decided to start* (line 12), *helps to reduce* (line 20)
4 *he went to Manchester University to study architecture* (lines 8–9)
5 *there wasn't enough money to send him* (lines 3–4)
6 *persuaded him to get a job* (lines 4–5), *allows the maximum amount of natural light to come into* (line 19)
7 *makes the people of the city feel very proud* (line 28)

5

6

Answers
1 The architect made the builder ~~to~~ use triangular-shaped glass.
2 You had better ~~to~~ do your essay before **going** out.
3 I gave up **living** with my parents years ago.
4 Have you finished **doing** the cleaning?
5 He suggested **renting** the apartment next year.
6 I object to **paying** such a high rent.
7 I look forward **to hearing** from you in the near future.
8 The college wouldn't let me ~~to~~ move out of the hostel.
9 I'm interested **in going** to see the house tomorrow.
10 The estate agent advertised in the paper to **get** more people **to see** the house.

7   Students should work together.

Suggested answers
1 to have children
2 to feel part of a group
3 to enjoy themselves
4 to look cool
5 to find friends
6 to look more attractive
7 to help the environment

8   Students work in pairs. Monitor their exchanges to make sure they are using the *-ing* forms correctly.

9   The pictures are of Tate Modern art gallery in London and a sculpture titled *Marsyas* by Anish Kapoor, which was exhibited in the Turbine Hall of the gallery.

Play the recording twice – the first time, students should just listen, and the second time, they should try to analyse what was said, using the questions to guide them.

Answers
• The speaker covered all the points. The most important point is the last one, and she spent longest talking about that. The others were covered quite quickly, but that is acceptable.
• Yes, the vocabulary included: *landmark, architects, demolish, exhibition space, a perfect setting, dedicated, artistic movements, floating, exhibits.*
• Everything she said was relevant. However, if she had talked about her favourite painting at length, that would be seen as irrelevant.
• *Huge, vast, enormous, large*

Recording script

The building that I like most is Tate Modern art gallery in London. Um … I first went there with my family a couple of years ago. The gallery got a lot of publicity when it first opened because the building was originally a power station – um, you know, for making electricity. It is a huge brick building, a real landmark, and it's on the south bank of the River Thames. To build the gallery, the architects had to demolish most of the interior of the power station. Er, now, the main hall, called the Turbine Hall, has become a vast exhibition space.

I really like this building for a number of reasons. Firstly, it is light and airy and very modern – a perfect setting for modern art – I really love modern art. The large Turbine Hall means the gallery can exhibit enormous modern art installations, something I think that nowhere else in London can do.

Secondly, I … I like the fact that there are … er, a lot of other large rooms leading off the main Turbine Hall, and these are dedicated to particular artists or artistic movements like Picasso and Art Deco, and things like that. Some of the exhibits are paintings, but there are sculptures and installations, too. There is a … there is a lot of space to see everything clearly, even when there are people in the building.

There are wonderful views from the windows in these rooms – of the river and … and also of Norman Foster's Millennium Bridge – and beyond you can easily see St Paul's Cathedral. You get the feeling you are floating above the river. This is especially true when you go up to the restaurant on the top floor. There are large windows on both sides of the restaurant, and you can … you can see most of London from there.

Finally, just outside the gallery, beside the river, there is a special space for exhibits. I like this because it means you are involved with the exhibits even before you go into the gallery, and I think it makes people want to go inside. I think it's really my favourite building.

Students should then prepare a similar talk. Walk around the class, helping with vocabulary and ideas, if needed. If possible, it would be useful for students to record their talk and then analyse it afterwards. They shouldn't worry if they hesitate – a few *ums* and *ahs* are quite acceptable.

Extension activity

Encourage students to take it in turns to give illustrated talks once a week on a subject of their choice – their town, their hobby, their favourite band. They should come prepared with photos, maps, etc., and each student should prepare a question that they would like to ask.

Writing folder 5

SB pages 70–71
Academic Writing Task 1: Handling data 2 – bar and pie charts and tables

It is important not to add anything which is not shown in the chart or table when answering Task 1. Students should be given practice in writing 150 words in 20 minutes, so they do not worry about the length or the time during the test.

1 Read through the Advice box and then ask the class to work through the statements in exercise 1.

> **Suggested answers**
> 1 In 1991, there were (almost) four times as many detached houses as semi-detached.
> 2 *correct*
> 3 The number of flats in 2001 was less than half the number of semi-detached houses.
> 4 *correct*
> 5 In 2002, the majority of Canadians lived in detached houses.
> 6 In 2002, a higher percentage of Canadians lived in detached houses than in semi-detached ones.
> 7 *correct*

2 Refer the class to the example and the Useful language box.

> **Possible answers**
> It can be seen from the table that in 2000, UK households with children were generally far more likely to possess home-entertainment equipment, such as video games, than those without children.
> According to the table, the number of people with children who have DVD/video is more than double the number who have a PC.
> It can be seen that more people with children have a PC than have satellite TV.
> The number of people without children who have a PC is nearly the same as the number who have satellite TV.

3 Ask students to read through the answer and to look at the words in the box. They need to refer to the chart to make sure they choose the right words to fill the gaps.

> **Answers**
> 1 oldest   2 10–15 (years)   3 younger   4 satellite TV
> 5 most popular   6 television   7 50 per cent
> 8 games console   9 40 per cent   10 a computer
> 11 few   12 children

4 Below is a suggested model chart for students to use to gather their information.

Home Entertainment Equipment

	PC	DVD	Games console	Satellite TV	Internet
Number of women					
Number of men					

11 Animal life

Unit topic	Animals
11.1	
Test skills	Reading (AC):
	Multiple choice
	Multiple choice with multiple
	answers
Vocabulary	Definitions relating to social
	organisation
11.2	
Test skills	Listening:
	Sentence completion
Grammar	Articles
Vocabulary	Compound nouns
Pronunciation	Diphthongs

Workbook contents	
1, 2, 3	Grammar: articles
4, 5, 6	Reading
7	Vocabulary

11.1 SB pages 72–73

Ask students what they know about the lives of the creatures in the pictures (e.g. birds build nests and lay eggs, spiders spin webs to catch insects which they can eat, bees live in large groups and co-operate).

1 Ask students to answer the question. Point out that in this unit, *animal* is used in the sense that includes fish, birds and insects. It can also be used to exclude those categories.

> **Possible answers**
> Some similarities: in general, animals and human beings live in pairs or larger social groups, have a home, and parents bring up their young.
>
> Some differences: animals appear to have very little choice in how they behave, e.g. each species eats certain foods and lives in certain habitats. Human beings have much more choice. Animals generally devote most of their time to survival (e.g. searching for food) and bringing up the next generation. Unlike human beings, very few animals can use tools, and they can communicate only a very small range of messages.

2 Explain that the words and phrases in the box are commonly used in connection with social organisation, and some are used in the reading passage. Ask students to do the exercise.

> **Answers**
> 1 d 2 e (from *nucleus*, meaning the central or most important part of something) 3 c 4 h 5 b (note that *communal* can be stressed on either the first or the second syllable) 6 a, f, g 7 i

Extension activity

Ask students (in groups) to complete a table with the following headings:
1 Activities that are equally likely to be communal or solitary
2 Activities that are usually communal
3 Activities that are usually solitary
4 Parents' responsibilities in bringing up their children
5 Members of an extended family

> **Possible answers (answers may differ, depending on the students' cultural background)**
> 1 eating, watching television, walking, singing
> 2 dancing, going to the cinema, bringing children, working in a shop or hospital
> 3 reading, using a computer, studying
> 4 providing a home and food, teaching them how to look after themselves and how to behave towards other people, making sure they go to school, making sure they are healthy or get medical treatment if necessary
> 5 as well as those in exercise 2, item 3, cousins, grandchildren, etc. May include in-laws, e.g. brother-in-law, sister-in-law, parents-in-law

3 Ask students to read the rubric and the first extract quickly, and to identify the main topic of each paragraph.

> **Suggested answers**
> A animals that live alone
> B animals that live together only while bringing up their young
> C fish and birds that live in large groups
> D animals that live in co-operative groups
> E insects that live in complex, co-operative groups

4 Ask students to read the rubric, questions and Test spot, then to read the passage again carefully and answer the questions.

> **Answers**
> 1 C *Others, such as spiders, are normally solitary, meeting only to mate* (lines 4–5)
> 2 B *European robins raise their chicks in a pair, away from other members of their species, while herring gulls form larger groups ... consisting of many pairs living close together* (lines 9–12)
> 3 C *Hens ... establish a hierarchy ... Those at the top of the 'pecking order' get to eat before the others.* (lines 16–19)

4 **A** *Lions ... usually live in a relatively permanent group ... where some activities ... are social, and others ... are solitary. (lines 21–25)*

5 **A** *Worker bees ... have several jobs in succession, depending on their age. (lines 28–29)*

5 Ask students to consider these questions.

Possible answers
- Bringing up the young: advantages include more adults to look after and feed the young, and protect them from predators; disadvantages include crowding, adults attacking the young that aren't their own.
- Finding food: advantages include more adults to find it and fetch it; disadvantages include more competition if food is scarce.
- Protection against other animals: advantages include safety in numbers – a reduction in the chances of an individual being killed by a predator, more adults deter or resist attack; disadvantages include the size of the group making it prominent and therefore attracting predators, and adults attacking the young that aren't their own.
- Conflict: advantages include mutual protection; disadvantages include conflict arising through competition for food or space.

6 Ask students to skim the passage.

7 Ask students to read the passage carefully and find the five answers.

Answers
C *As an individual predator ... can only consume a finite number of eggs or chicks, each individual is less likely to be eaten. (lines 8–11)*
D *Groups of adult elephants surround all their young, giving each one much greater protection than its parents alone could provide. (lines 11–13)*
E *while learning how to raise their own young in the future. (lines 17–18)*
F *the range of antibodies that different females provide increases their resistance to disease. (lines 20–21)*
G *When one has found food, others may simply join it (lines 23–24)*

11.2 SB pages 74–75

1 Ask students if the cartoons suggest any stories to them (the first shows Aesop's fable 'The Hare and the Tortoise'; the second illustrates Kipling's fable 'How the Camel got his Hump', which is mentioned in the listening passage). Ask students if they can think of examples. Ask why animals are sometimes used.

Possible answers
- traditional stories, fairy stories, animated films
- Animals can be used to make a serious point amusing, so that readers absorb the point without realising it is being made. They can also show the effects of human behaviour on other species.

2 Play the recording and have students complete the sentences.

Answers (see underlined text in script)
1 creation **2** realistic **3** protection **4** moral
5 language **6** political **7** children **8** workload

Recording script

Animals have played a major role in human society for many thousands of years – as food, to help in hunting and to provide companionship – and their importance is reflected in our mythology. Many cultures have myths in which animals play a significant role in the creation of the earth and everything on it: for example, a snake is a major figure in the mythology of the Aboriginal people of Australia.

There's a long tradition of animals appearing in literature and, nowadays, in films, too. Sometimes they appear as themselves, as in 'wild animal stories', a popular literary form in the USA in the first half of the 20th century. These stories aimed to give a realistic view of animals and their lives, although the standpoint was occasionally somewhat romanticised. And many authors have written stories arguing the need to give animals greater protection, often by reducing the amount of pollution human beings create.

In this literary approach, the *actual physical* qualities of a species are presented, but animals are often used *symbolically* in literature, particularly in fables. These are short stories, usually written to make a point about a moral issue, often through satire of how human beings behave. Impossible events take place: most characters are animals that have a command of language, and behave in other respects, too, like human beings, while keeping their own physical shape.

Fables are thought to have originated in the Middle East two to three thousand years ago, and they're also found in the ancient literatures of Iran, India and other cultures. Aesop, who lived in Greece in the sixth century BC, wrote a large number of fables that still retain their popularity, and many other writers have followed in his footsteps. In English literature, a much longer fable is George Orwell's political satire *Animal Farm*, published in 1945.

Animal Farm is unusual in being a fable for adults. Far more often, the target audience is children, and fables provide them with examples of good and bad behaviour. *The Just So Stories*, written by the British author Rudyard Kipling in the late 1890s, are typical of the genre. As in the same author's *Jungle Book*, the stories contain many animal characters. *The Just So Stories* tell of how the Earth began, and of the people and animals who live on it, and they recommend certain ways of behaving.

Let me give you an example. One story, 'How the Camel got his Hump', is set at the time when animals were first domesticated. A dog, a horse and an ox work for a man, but the camel, who lives alone in the middle of the desert, is lazy and refuses to work. As a result, the other three animals have a heavier workload. They complain to the magical creature in charge of all deserts, who tells the camel to work. The camel simply replies 'humph'. So the magical creature punishes him by giving him a hump on his back. This holds enough food for the camel to work for three days without eating, to make up for the time he's missed. The moral of the story is that everyone ought to work, in order to contribute to the common good.

Give students a copy of the recording script, and ask them to underline the sentences or phrases that correspond with the sentences in exercise 2. Remind them that the sentences paraphrase the passage, and ask them to write sentences with a gap, where these words from the passage are the keys: *myths, snake, films, pollution, Aesop, 1945, hump.*

> **Possible answers**
> Animals appear in the .... of many cultures. (myths/mythology)
> An important figure in Aboriginal mythology is a .... (snake)
> Nowadays, animals are often found in literature and .... (films)
> Some stories encourage people to help animals by producing less .... (pollution)
> Many fables were written by the ancient Greek author .... (Aesop)
> *Animal Farm* first appeared in .... (1945)
> The camel's .... contains enough food to keep him working for three days without stopping. (hump)

3 Point out to students that the use of the articles (*a/an, the* and zero) is one of the most complicated areas of English, and that they should concentrate on the four rules given (a–d), as they are among the most important.

Ask students to read the exercise and complete rules a and b.

> **Answers**
> a *a/an*; 1 and 2 b *the*; 3 and 4
> Point out that *The dance* refers indirectly to *a complex series of movements*, as it uses a different word to refer to the same concept.

4 Ask students to complete the exercise, following rules a and b. This incident occurred in 1996.

> **Answers**
> 1 a
> 2 a (according to rule a; there is more than one zoo in Chicago. If there were only one, *the* would be used, to refer to something unique.)
> 3 a 4 the 5 an 6 the 7 The

5 Point out that using no article ('zero article') correctly is just as important for communicating effectively as using *a* and *the*. Ask students to read rules c and d. Ask them which uncountable noun in c and which plural countable noun in d has no article.

> **Answers**
> c Co-operation d Lions

6 Ask students to apply rules a–d to the ten numbered instances of *a/an, the* and no article (zero article).

> **Answers**
> 1 a 2 a 3 a
> 4 b (They have been referred to indirectly by the mention of 'a hospital'; in other words, it means 'the patients in the hospital that has already been mentioned'.)
> 5 b (Also implied by 'the hospital'.)
> 6 c 7 b 8 c 9 d 10 d

For more information about articles, refer students to the Grammar folder (SB page 141).

7 Point out that joining two words to form a new one is one of the most common ways of creating new words in English. Words that are often used together start by being written as two words, then they may be hyphenated and are finally written as a single word.

Ask students to form compound words consisting of *work* + a word from the box. Check that they understand their meanings.

> **Answers**
> workbook: a book used in educational establishments containing text and questions and sometimes having spaces for a student to write answers in
> workforce: the group of people who work in a company, industry, country, etc.
> homework: work which teachers give their students to do at home
> workload: the amount of work to be done, especially by a particular person or machine in a period of time
> workplace: a building or room where people perform their jobs
> worksheet: a piece of paper with questions and exercises for students
> workshop: a room or building where things are made or repaired using machines and/or tools; also a meeting of people to discuss and/or perform practical work in a subject or activity

8 Ask students to complete the exercise.

> **Answers**
> 1 workforce 2 workplace 3 workload 4 worksheet
> 5 workshop 6 Homework

9 Remind students of the difference between diphthongs, and short and long vowels (8.2, page 55). Point out that each diphthong sound can be represented by several spellings. Ask students to work through the exercise in pairs, saying each word aloud and completing the table.

Have students listen to the recording and repeat the words as they hear them.

Recording script

1 day; came   2 my; right   3 how; out   4 ear; year   5 boy; join
6 no; although   7 air; there

Ask individual students to read one of the sets of words with the same diphthong (1–7 in the table). Then ask individuals to read one of the columns of words with various diphthongs in the box in exercise 9.

Test folder 6

SB pages 76–77
Multiple choice

Make sure students fully understand the notes and advice.

1   Ask students to read the rubric and options, then play the recording while they choose the five answers.

Answers (see underlined text in script)
A   *wide-ranging journeys*
B   *the rapid, deep dives that come naturally to sharks*
D   *solitary individuals in search of food*
E   *aggressively chase away or bite smaller individuals of the same species*
G   *a threatening display*

Recording script

You will hear part of a lecture about sharks.

First, you have some time to look at questions 1 to 5. (*pause*)

Now listen carefully and answer questions 1 to 5.

It isn't easy for scientists to study sharks in their natural habitat. There's very little that can limit the movement of these fish, and their streamlined bodies are designed to carry them on <u>wide-ranging journeys</u> each day. Scientists, on the other hand, are able to spend only a few hours at a time in the water and are restricted to relatively short distances. Divers, too, are incapable of <u>the rapid, deep dives that come naturally to sharks</u>. As a result, the information we can gain about the behaviour of sharks is usually limited to brief moments in their daily lives.

Sharks' activities are often closely tied to their feeding routine. Some species spend daylight hours not far off shore, and move in closer to land after dark, presumably to feed. Contrary to popular myths, sharks don't feed on everything that crosses their path. They're carnivores, and different species have different diets, ranging from small shrimps and crabs to dolphins.

Sharks are found in various groupings. For example, the species that live on tropical reefs are often observed swimming together in small groups, apparently engaged in hunting or social activities. But at other times, these same species are seen as <u>solitary individuals in search of food</u>.

Many social interactions are observed within groups of sharks. When they're feeding on dead whales, for example, large white sharks will often <u>aggressively chase away or bite smaller individuals of the same species</u> and will eat most of the food themselves. Dominance hierarchies between species are also common over access to food. Reef whitetip sharks, for instance, are forced to take second place to silvertip sharks.

Perhaps the most spectacular and well-documented social behaviour by the shark is the readiness for combat displayed by the grey reef shark of tropical Pacific reefs. When one of these sharks is approached rapidly by a diver or cornered against the reef, it exhibits <u>a threatening display</u> which increases in intensity as it becomes more agitated. If the shark is pressed further, it will probably attack. This display seems to be unrelated to defence of any specific territory, so it may represent a defence of personal space or a warning to a potential predator.

2   Ask students to skim the passage, then read the example. They should then read and answer each question in turn.

Answers
1   C   *incapable of true suffering*
2   B   *it now seems that something similar is also true of farm animals*
3   C   *showing them pictures of familiar sheep faces reduced all three measurements*
4   A   *Those that learned the task were more likely to experience a sudden increase in heart rate*
5   C   *pigs will avoid the one where they had previously been shut in for several hours after eating*
6   C   *a more general aim of ensuring that the society will function*
7   A   *He claims that these animals therefore deserve basic rights*
8   B   *First for some findings. In 2004, researchers in Cambridge, UK, reported … Donald Broom, professor of animal welfare at the University of Cambridge, says … Other research has shown …*

---

12 Sport: just for fun?

Unit topic	Sport
12.1	
Test skills	Speaking Parts 1 and 3
	Listening: Table completion
Vocabulary	Sport
	Word formation
12.2	
Test skills	Reading (AC/GT): Matching
Grammar	*Should, had better, ought to*
Workbook contents	
1, 2, 3, 4, 5	Reading
6, 7	Grammar: *should, had better, ought to*

12.1 SB pages 78–79

Ask students to comment on the pictures, and say if they have ever tried, or would like to try, those sports.

1 Ask students to discuss the questions in small groups. Encourage them to develop their answers, in particular speculating about why the sports are popular.

Possible answers
Although not many people watch baseball, quite a lot play it so that they can keep fit.

A lot of people watch football on TV. Maybe it's because football is fashionable, and there are plenty of articles about it in the media.

2 Check that students understand the words in the box, then ask them – in pairs – to complete the sentences and define the extra word.

Answers
1 event 2 record (draw students' attention to the stress: *'record* [noun], *re'cord* [verb]) 3 spectator 4 Extreme
5 competitors; runner-up 6 team; score 7 tie
8 amateurs (point out that *amateur* is both an adjective and a noun)

referee: a person who is in charge of a game and who makes certain that the rules are followed

3 Ask students to complete the table with the most common words related to those given.

Answers

verb	noun (person)	noun (activity)	adjective
	athlete	athletics	athletic
to compete	competitor	competition	competitive
to score	scorer	score, scoring	
to win	winner	win, winning	winning

4 Ask students which verb collocates with each activity. Ask which verb is often used before an *-ing* form.

Answers
1 play 2 go 3 play 4 do 5 do 6 go/do 7 do
8 go 9 go 10 play
Before an *-ing* form: often *go* (numbers 2, 6, 8, 9; also *go running/jogging/shopping*)

5 Check that students understand the six headings.

Possible answers
Team sports: sports in which a number of people work together in a group

Winter sports: sports that are done on snow or ice

Spectator sports: sports that people go to watch

Extreme sports: sports that are dangerous and exciting

Athletics: a group of specific competitive sports, including running, jumping and throwing; in the USA called *track and field*

Contact sports: sports in which competitors are allowed to touch each other, e.g. to get the ball

Ask students in small groups to complete the table with sports from the box, and with any others they can think of.

Answers (with some additions to those given in box)
Team sports: basketball, baseball, ice hockey, rugby, soccer (+ American football, cricket)

Winter sports: ice hockey, skiing, snowboarding (+ bobsleigh)

Spectator sports: basketball, baseball, boxing, horseracing, ice hockey, rugby, soccer, sumo wrestling (+ tennis and many others)

Extreme sports: bungee jumping, parachuting, snowboarding, white-water rafting (+ rock climbing)

Athletics: cross-country running, discus, the high jump, triathlon (+ pole vault, hurdling)

Contact sports: boxing, rugby, sumo wrestling (+ wrestling, American football)

6 Ask students to read the rubric and table, and to think about possible answers, considering both grammar and meaning.

Play the recording as students complete the table.

Recording script

Man: Hello, Grayson's Adventure Days. How can I help you?

Woman: Oh, good morning. I want to book an activity day as a birthday present for my father, so could you give me an idea of the sorts of things you organise, please?

Man: What a great present! Do you want the activity to take place in a particular location?

Woman: No, anywhere in the country would be OK.

Man: Right. Well, how about bungee jumping? That's our most popular activity.

Woman: Uh-huh.

Man: After a safety briefing, you're securely fastened to the correct bungee rope for your weight. Then the crane takes you up to a height of 50 metres <u>in a cage</u>, and you jump from it.

Woman: You make it sound so easy!

Man: In fact, some people change their minds at the last moment. But for the really brave, <u>you can also book our special, which is one normal bungee jump and then a backwards one</u>. It's quite an experience!

Woman: I can imagine! Is it available every day?

Man: We do bungee jumping <u>all year round, on over 120 dates</u>, and in various locations, but you should try to book about four weeks in advance, if possible, as it's very popular.

Woman: OK. And are there any age restrictions? It'll be my father's 50th birthday, so I hope he isn't too old.

Man: No, he certainly isn't too old, but <u>we'll require a certificate from a doctor</u>, to confirm that he's in good health.

Woman: Oh, he's very fit, so that won't be a problem. How much is it?

Man: It costs £57 per person for the standard jump, and <u>97 for the special</u>.

Woman: Right. Now, I've heard of something called 'zorbing'. Do you do that, too?

Man: Yes, we do. That's another very popular activity.

Woman: What exactly is it?

Man: Well, you're securely attached in the centre of a zorb, either alone or with another person. <u>A zorb is over three metres high, and it consists of one ball inside another</u>, both made of clear plastic, so you can see out through them.

Woman: And what happens next?

Man: You roll down a hill, at speeds of up to 50 kilometres an hour. You can also choose the hydrozorb experience, where 25 litres of water is thrown inside with you, and <u>you aren't attached</u>, so you slide around in the water while you're rolling.

Woman: Wow! I'm sure my father would enjoy that. What about the dates?

Man: The zorb rides take place <u>between April and October, but just at weekends</u>.

Woman: Are there any restrictions, I mean, for height or weight?

Man: Your father needs to be at least 160cm tall and <u>weigh no more 110 kilos</u>.

Woman: Oh, that's fine. How much does it cost?

Man: Zorbing is £50 per person.

Woman: <u>And is hydrozorbing the same price?</u>

Man: <u>No, that's £65.</u>

Woman: Right, I'd better give my father details of both the bungee jumping and zorbing, and let him choose, and then I'll get back to you.

Man: Fine. We tend to get fully booked, especially at this time of year, so you ought to book well in advance.

Woman: OK, I'll get back to you in the next few days. Thanks very much for your help.

Man: No problem. Bye.

Woman: Bye.

Photocopiable recording script activity
(**P** ⋯⟶ page 139)

Give students a copy of the recording script, and ask them to design a magazine advert or a brochure for Grayson's Adventure Days.

7   Ask students to discuss the questions in small groups. Encourage them to help each other by using the phrases from the Useful language box.

12.2 SB pages 80–81

1   Ask students to revise material and ideas from 12.1 by discussing the question in small groups. Remind them of some ways of expressing a purpose (*to, in order to, so, so that*) and a reason (*because, because of*).

2 Ask students to read the rubric, skim the passage and list the reasons given for doing sport. The picture is of an ancient Greek vase showing a chariot race.

3 Ask students to read the task carefully, find the relevant parts of the text (i.e. references to Ancient Greece, etc.) and decide on the answers. Remind students to answer only according to what is stated in the passage.

Extension activity

Students might be interested in using the Internet to research the history of a specific sport. They could form small groups, choose a sport, carry out research, then write a short report summarising their findings. If these are displayed, students can read each other's reports.

4 Ask students to read the four sentences and answer questions 1 and 2.
Note: *should* and *ought to* are modal verbs; *had better* is a semi-auxiliary because it shares some but not all of the grammatical characteristics of auxiliary verbs.

Draw attention to the use of *to* with *ought* but not the other two, and to the position of *not* in *you'd better not.*

5 Ask students to read the statement and the five pieces of advice that could be given in response. Ask them to answer questions 1–3.

Draw students' attention to the notes. Point out that *ought to* is rather old-fashioned.

6 Ask students to read the rubric and example, then ask them to think of advice to give in each of the situations 1–5. Encourage them to use the range of forms, *should, had better* and *ought to.*

7 Point out that in exercises 4–6, *should* is used to give advice. In exercise 7, it is used to talk about the future. Ask students to read the rubric and examples. Then ask them to do the exercise.

Refer students to the Grammar folder (SB page 141) for more information.

8 Ask students to discuss the question in small groups and to encourage each other.

Writing folder 6

SB pages 82–83
Task 2: Connecting ideas 1

1   Examiners give higher marks to students who use connecting words appropriately. Most students are aware of *and*, *but* and *so*, but they also need to realise the importance of variety in their writing. Ask students to decide which column they should put the connecting words into.

Answers

and	but	so
in addition (to)	though	consequently
also	unfortunately	therefore
what is more	despite (the fact that)	as a result (of)
in fact	however	this means/ meant (that)
	although	

The words aren't all used in the same way, and students should read through the examples to see whether the connector links two clauses or begins a new sentence. Point out that the contraction *What's more* is also acceptable in neutral or information writing.

2   Students should work through the questions.

Answers

1   a   In addition / Also / What is more / In fact
    b   What is more / In addition / In fact
2   a   Though / Although / Despite the fact that
    b   though / although
    c   However / Unfortunately
    d   Despite
    e   Despite
3   a   consequently / therefore / as a result
    b   As a result of
    c   This means that / Consequently, / Therefore, / As a result,

3   Students should read through the letter. Check for understanding.

4

Answers

1 A   2 C   3 B   4 A   5 B   6 A   7 B   8 B   9 C

5

Suggested answers

1   ... I think it's a hard profession; they have to work hard.
2   ... are very dangerous.
3   ... are invaluable for maintaining high standards.
4   ... it is a fairly expensive sport.
5   ... will be deciding which of the national competitions to enter.
6   ... didn't win the national league.
7   ... were then allowed to compete in a higher league.
8   ... celebrated with a party.
9   ... they have won cups for playing football.
10 ... are advised to eat well.

Units 9–12 Revision

SB pages 84–85

The aim of this revision unit is to focus on the language covered in units 9–12. Exercises 2–6 can be done as a test in class or for homework.

Topic review

1 The aim of this section is to encourage students to speak, using the grammar and vocabulary they have learned in the previous four units. They should comment on the statements and expand their answers as much as possible. This is useful practice, because in the Speaking Module, they also need to give opinions and expand on what they say.

Possible answers
1 This doesn't apply to me, because I prefer a temperate climate. Hot weather is great sometimes, but I wouldn't like it all year round.
2 No, I don't agree. For me, it's more important to feel that I'm improving, even if I lose every time.
3 I think you can benefit in lots of ways from having pets; for instance, children can develop a sense of responsibility by looking after them.
4 I don't suppose I make much difference to global warming, but at least I try to reduce the amount of waste I throw away.
5 I don't agree at all. I'd love to live alone and be able to do what I like at home without having to think about how it affects other people.
6 I'm not sure about this. I agree we need to understand human behaviour better, to try and prevent some of the awful things people sometimes do. But I'm not sure whether studying animals is the most effective way of finding out about human beings.
7 No, I'm sure it's far more exciting to play than to watch, because you have to respond very quickly to everything that's going on.
8 Everyone ought to have a home, but if some people were given one free, it might create ill feeling among other people.
9 It's so hard to know the best thing to do. For example, if you buy produce or goods from a developing country on the other side of the world, you're helping people in that country, but the transportation pollutes the environment.
10 I think everyone should have the chance to be independent and learn to look after themselves, so leaving home at 20 seems like a good idea to me.

Grammar

2

Answers (letters refer to rules in 11.2)
1 – (d) 2 – (d) 3 – (c) 4 – (d) 5 a (a) 6 – (d)
7 a (a) 8 The (b) 9 – (d) 10 The (b) 11 the (b)
12 – (d) 13 – (c) 14 – (d)

3

Answers
1 have 2 to move 3 to keep 4 writing 5 studying
6 to be 7 (to) improve 8 having 9 to believe
10 adapting

4

Answers
1 much time 2 many countries 3 many universities
4 much accommodation 5 much research
6 many animals 7 much pollution 8 much work
9 Many people 10 much news

Vocabulary

5

Answers
1 recycling 2 endangered 3 extend 4 extended
5 workshop 6 referee 7 spectators 8 extreme
9 bungalow

6

Answers
1 effects of 2 melting of 3 effect on 4 increase in
5 threat to 6 loss of 7 causes of 8 dependency on

Progress Test 3

Listening

Questions 1–5

Complete the notes below.

Write NO MORE THAN TWO WORDS AND/OR A NUMBER for each answer.

Crocodiles

- largest species: *estuarine or saltwater crocodile*
- maximum weight: *900 kg*
- largest recorded crocodile: **1** .... *metres*
- factors limiting size: *genetics and* **2** ....
- crocodile has been compared to **3** ....
- crocodiles possess powerful **4** ....
- body has a **5** .... similar to a mammal's

Questions 6–8

*Choose the correct letter, **A**, **B** or **C**.*

6 Research has shown that crocodiles

    A recognise other crocodiles.

    B alert each other to danger.

    C are not social creatures.

7 The humans who are the biggest danger to crocodiles are

    A skin collectors.

    B farmers and fishermen.

    C frightened villagers.

8 How do the researchers in the Okavango Delta catch crocodiles?

    A They use drugs.

    B They cover the animal's eyes.

    C They wrap the crocodile's tail in a towel.

Questions 9 and 10

*Choose TWO letters **A–G**.*

*Which **TWO** countries have helped crocodile conservation with the creation of new habitats?*

A Bangladesh

B China

C Madagascar

D Australia

E Honduras

F India

G Zimbabwe

Reading

A review of Nigel Townson's *The British at Play*

An estimated three million Britons take part in some sort of sporting activity every week. Globally, around four billion people – over half the world's entire population – watch at least part of major events like the Olympic Games. Sport is big business. In fact, it is the UK's 11th largest industry, employing over 400,000 people.

But these figures don't get to the heart of the social power and significance of sport in the modern world. It is a powerful social force in Britain, as in many other cultures. Friends and colleagues regularly discuss sport, and it is one of relatively few topics that are acceptable when initiating social interaction with strangers. Expressions from sport have passed into general use: we talk about 'team players' in situations that have nothing to do with sport, and the word 'goal', meaning an objective, probably evolved from its meaning in sport.

Why is sport so important in society? *The British at Play – a Social History of British Sport from 1600 to the Present*, by Nigel Townson, sets out to answer that question by examining the connections between sport and social class, gender, violence, commercialism, race and even our sense of national identity.

The British at Play explains these complex issues simply and straightforwardly. For example, it highlights the way in which sport contributes to the creation of 'in groups', most notably the supporters of particular football teams. Such informal associations define themselves by their loyalty to their own group and opposition to others, the 'out groups', and in an extreme form, this opposition leads to the phenomenon of football hooliganism. The author handles the issue well, showing what is wrong with the well-known stereotypes of soccer hooligans. He argues that media coverage of fan behaviour helps to create a climate in which hooliganism occurs. And when trouble does break out, the media sensationalises and exaggerates it, with the result that an atmosphere of panic builds up in the country.

Several of the topics relate to social changes in Britain in recent decades. Women are entering fields of activity which would have been closed to them just a generation ago – as football commentators, producers of sports programmes for radio and television, editors of sports magazines. This greater visibility of women highlights the weakening of the traditional view that sport is mainly for men.

The worldwide health-and-fitness boom has to some extent been driven by our growing wish to have a 'perfect' body shape. And that desire has been encouraged, if not created, by the emphasis in sport on images of 'ideal' male and female bodies.

Sport fits in well with the global TV world of beautiful and perfectly muscled young people, exercising or playing sports, dressed in the latest fashionable sports gear. Sport images in the media do not depend on the written word, just on strong images, reaching out directly to the emotions of the viewer – the perfect medium for advertisers.

So sport becomes big money, attracting more and more commercial interest and investment. Some international TV companies depend on the popularity of sport for their survival. Football clubs turn themselves into businesses, raising money by selling merchandise and by selling their shares on the stock market.

The British at Play is an excellent work, of great value and interest to a wide range of audiences, but if I have one criticism of it, it is this: despite its title, the book is not about play. It does not ask the most basic question of all – why do people do sport? Why is it so popular? The book did not, for me, go far enough in transmitting the power, the energy, the passion, the emotion and the joy of sport. The social power of sport ultimately rests on this psychological and physical appeal – the way it involves the whole person, the way in which it allows us to play.

Questions 1–8

Complete the summary below.

*Choose **NO MORE THAN TWO WORDS AND/OR A NUMBER** from the passage for each answer.*

Sport is of major importance around the world, with around **1** .... participants in the UK. It has great social significance. Unlike many other subjects, it is sometimes used to start conversations between **2** .... , and it is the source of a number of everyday **3** ....

The writer examines the way in which groups are formed whose members show **4** .... to each other. Their **5** .... to 'out groups' can lead to violence. The writer rejects the common **6** .... that are used to describe football hooligans. Instead, he focuses on **7** .... in the media, and shows how this can create a public sense of **8** ....

Questions 9–13

*Complete each sentence with the correct ending **A–G** from the box below.*

9 The change in personnel in sports activities

10 Growing interest in health and fitness

11 Advertising related to sport

12 The greater role of business in sport

13 The only weakness of *The British at Play*

A is unlikely to continue in the same form.
B lies in how the appeal of sport is explained.
C shows that sport is no longer seen as a mainly masculine activity.
D makes considerable use of pictures of sportsmen and women.
E has resulted in large salaries for players.
F is partly caused by a focus on the physical characteristics of sportsmen and women.
G has led to changes in the activities of some football clubs.

Writing

Writing Task 2 (AC)

You should spend about 40 minutes on this task.

Write about the following topic:

> *Everyone can play a part in helping to stop global warming and the destruction of the planet.*
>
> *To what extent do you agree or disagree with this opinion?*

Give reasons for your answer and include any relevant examples from your own knowledge or experience.

Write at least 250 words.

Progress Test 3 Key

Listening

1 6.2 / six point two (metres)   2 (the) environment
3 a submarine / submarines   4 jaws   5 heart   6 A   7 B
8 B   9/10 D, G (in either order)

Recording script

You will hear a lecture about crocodiles. First, you have some time to look at questions 1 to 5.

Now listen carefully and answer questions 1 to 5.

This week we're going to be looking at some creatures with a ferocious reputation – the crocodile. The largest species of crocodile in the world is the saltwater, or estuarine, crocodile which can be found in south-east Asia, and, more especially, in northern Australia.

This crocodile is the largest living reptile in the world, bar none. It can weigh up to 900 kilos, and as for length – the average maximum size for males is around five metres. However, the largest crocodile ever recorded was <u>six point two</u> metres, and this croc was killed by poachers in Papua New Guinea in 1983.

It used to be thought that crocodiles would grow indefinitely until they died, hence producing very large, very old crocodiles. However, there's some doubt over this now, and it's likely that maximum size is instead influenced by inherited characteristics and by the <u>environment</u>. Few individuals seem predisposed towards very large sizes even if all the conditions are right.

Crocodiles are very sophisticated creatures. They can float or sink at will, finely tuning their buoyancy – in this way they resemble <u>a submarine</u>. The liver is squeezed back to make more room for the expanded lungs. While submerged – they can stay under for up to two hours – a protective membrane closes over their eyes, like swimming goggles.

Crocodiles feed on a large variety of prey, such as small mammals, birds and even domestic livestock. They have very strong <u>jaws</u>, but they don't chew their food; they swallow it in large chunks, and it is broken down in the stomach. Crocodiles can go for long periods without eating. There are in fact numerous examples of the animals not feeding for a whole year. They become extremely thin, but they're still active and are perfectly capable of feeding when food appears. Some species of crocodile can even tolerate freezing temperatures. This is because a crocodile has a very sophisticated circulatory system – with a <u>heart</u> more like a mammal's than a reptile's.

****

Before you hear the next part of the lecture, you have some time to look at questions 6 to 10.

Now listen and answer questions 6 to 10.

Because crocodiles look like logs of wood, people assume, wrongly, that they will behave in the same way. However, studies have shown that crocodiles are quite complex socially. <u>Individuals know other individuals</u> and have long-term relationships with each other. They also learn very rapidly how to avoid dangerous situations. Some species can also become quite tame. One crocodile biologist, Frederico Medem, described a doctor in Colombia who had an Orinoco crocodile. He had raised it from a baby. This crocodile was a female, about three metres long, and it played with the children and the family dog.

Crocodiles of all species are threatened by many human activities. In the past, commercial over-exploitation by skin collectors and indiscriminate killing by frightened villagers have resulted in many species suffering drastic declines in numbers, but no species has become extinct because of human exploitation. However, what is most threatening the crocodile is destruction of its habitat. Because they are quite large animals, they require areas that are both large and diverse, and this brings them into conflict with <u>local farmers and fishermen</u>.

One conservation project which is working well is with Nile crocodiles in the Okavango Delta, in Botswana. Although the Nile crocodile is not listed as endangered, research suggests it should be. The number of nest sites has decreased by a third in the last 15 years. Fishermen destroy the nests, crocodile ranchers take their eggs and also do not return enough juveniles to the wild, and there is now only one small part of the delta left for crocodiles to lay their eggs. To get data on the crocodiles in the area, researchers have measured, tagged and taken blood samples from over 1,500 crocodiles – all without drugging the animals. <u>They catch the crocodile by throwing a wet towel over its head</u> – this is important, as a dry towel will come off too easily, thus allowing the crocodile time to escape – and they tie up its jaw with rubber bands. The animal is then released.

Countries encountering a decrease in their crocodile population include Bangladesh, China and Madagascar. Some other countries, such as <u>Australia</u>, have already taken steps to improve or create new habitats, to positive effect. However, this has not always been the case elsewhere. The creation of dams and a new lake shore has had little effect in Honduras and India because of drought or an increase in water use for agriculture. <u>Zimbabwe</u>, though, has seen an increase in numbers of its crocodiles because of expanded habitat.

Too readily, we have cast crocodiles as ruthless predators, feared them, misunderstood them, attacked and exploited them. But they are great survivors that go back more than 70 million years. We must do everything we can to make sure that crocodiles live on, looking and behaving much the same as they do today.

Reading

1 three million/3 million/3,000,000 2 strangers
3 expressions 4 loyalty 5 opposition 6 stereotypes
7 coverage 8 panic 9 C 10 F 11 D 12 G 13 B

Writing

Sample answer

In the last few years, the Earth seems to have suffered more than its fair share of natural disasters. Events such as tsunamis, earthquakes and hurricanes have destroyed communities and ruined lives. These disasters have been attributed to the effects of climate change and global warming. People have been left feeling powerless against the strength of the elements. In such situations, it is normal to turn towards the government to do something, but in many countries no such help is forthcoming, despite their governments putting forward new proposals.

However, I think that it is possible for an individual to have an impact on what happens to the Earth. Even small things can help. For example, firstly, if everyone planted a tree, then this would help to counterbalance the destruction of the forests of the world. Secondly, if we all turned off our electrical appliances and turned down our heating, then think of all the energy we would save. Finally, if we all used public transport, or better still, cycled more, then think of the amount of fuel we would save. There is no need for grand gestures – just small ones can make a real difference.

The more we do to conserve energy, to reduce our use of fossil fuels and thus reduce the amount of greenhouse gas reaching the atmosphere, the greater the chance that global warming can be reduced, although perhaps not reversed entirely. To sum up, we must not feel defeated by the scale of the problem, but try to do our best to save the planet.

(263 words)

13 Choices

Unit topic	Choices
13.1 Test skills	Reading (AC): Locating information Multiple choice
Vocabulary	Collocations with adverbs
13.2 Test skills	Listening: Multiple choice Note completion Speaking Part 3
Grammar	Conditionals
Workbook contents	
1	Grammar: conditionals
2, 3, 4, 5, 6, 7, 8	Vocabulary

13.1 SB pages 86–87

1 Ask students whether they ever have problems choosing what to buy when they go shopping. Explain that they are going to read about a man who believes that more choice is probably less choice. Ask them to read through the statements in the questionnaire. There is no right answer, and students shouldn't take it seriously. The words *maximiser* and *satisficer* have been made up by Barry Schwartz, the writer of the article.

2 Encourage students to read through the text without worrying about the odd word they don't know. Make sure they time themselves.

3 Students should work through the questions. Questions 1–7 are testing Locating Information (Test folder 7) and questions 8–9 are testing Multiple Choice (Test folder 6). Students might find it useful to use a highlighter pen to underline where in the text they think the answer is.

Answers
1 A *But recently I was asked ... more and more dissatisfied.* (lines 6–9)
2 G *But no one wants to hear this ...* (lines 71–72)
3 C *psychologists and economists are puzzled by the fact that ...* (lines 34–35)
4 D *people are then upset by ...* (line 43)
5 B *Schwartz designed a questionnaire ...* (lines 18–19)
6 E *If there are few options ...* (line 53)
7 B *between what he terms 'maximisers' and 'satisficers'* (lines 19–20)
8 D
9 B

Extension activity

In the reading there are examples of negative prefixes: *dissatisfied, unstoppable, disappointing*.

Put the following adjectives in the correct column according to the negative prefix they take. One adjective can take two different negative prefixes, with a change of meaning. Which is it?

contented enthusiastic happy honest legal literate logical pleasant regular relevant replaceable reputable responsible used

dis-	un-	il-	ir-

Answers
Unused means 'not used'. *Disused* mean 'no longer used'.

dis-	un-	il-	ir-
discontented	unenthusiastic	illegal	irregular
dishonest	unhappy	illiterate	irrelevant
disreputable	unpleasant	illogical	irreplaceable
disused	unused		irresponsible

4 Students will come across adverb-verb collocations very often in academic writing. They should make sure they have a section in their vocabulary notebooks for this very important group of words.

Answers
1 highly 2 firmly 3 hugely/ (highly/totally)
4 anxiously 5 totally 6 widely 7 justly/ (hugely)
8 hardly

13.2 SB pages 88–89

1 Ask students to read through options 1–4 and then play the recording. Each speaker uses a different type of conditional. If students are unsure about the use of conditionals, it might be a good idea to elicit from them the four types and put them on the board so they can see the form.

Answers (see underlined text in script)
1 Speaker D 2 Speaker B 3 Speaker C 4 Speaker A

Recording script

Speaker A: When my grandfather was young, he had the chance to go to Paris to study the violin. I remember him telling me how excited he was – the only one in the family to win a scholarship. Then, overnight, great-grandfather lost all his money. My grandpa had to decide – he could still go to Paris, as it was fully funded, or he could stay at home and get a job to help the family. Well, you know the rest. But <u>if he had gone to Paris, who knows what would have happened – we might have had a famous musician in the family</u>.

Speaker B: I need to decide which college to apply to, but I'm finding it very difficult. My family want me to study something they think's useful, like medicine, and my tutor says that <u>if I train to be a doctor, I'll get a job fairly easily</u>, but the thing is, well, what I really want to do is Media Studies. I'm really into films – *making* them, not being *in* them – and, well, everything about the film industry, and I'd like to learn more. So, what do I do? Upset my family or toe the line?

Speaker C: My sister works for a large multinational in London. It's a really good job – most people would kill to have it – lots of money, but she does have to work 24/7. She wants to give it all up and go travelling – you know the thing – surfing in Hawaii, climbing Mount Kilimanjaro. I keep telling her not to be so stupid. After all, even she says <u>if she went on holiday for six months, they wouldn't keep her job open for when she returns</u>. You can't spend your life just hopping from plane to plane. She's mad.

Speaker D: How do I make choices? Well, I don't usually have any problem. <u>If I see something I like, I buy it.</u> Take last week. I was shopping with a friend and I saw the most gorgeous coat. It was a bit pricey, even for me, but I just had to have it, so out came the credit card again. I'll have to pay it off sometime, of course.

2   Play the recording again and ask students to write down the *If* sentence that each speaker uses.

> **Answers**
> A   *If he had gone to Paris, who knows what would have happened – we might have had a famous musician in the family.* (third conditional)
> B   *If I train to be a doctor, I'll get a job fairly easily.* (first conditional)
> C   *If she went on holiday for six months, they wouldn't keep her job open for when she returns.* (second conditional)
> D   *If I see something I like, I buy it.* (zero conditional)

3   Students should work through the questions.

> **Answers**
> 1 i   2 j   3 d   4 b   5 a   6 c   7 e   8 g   9 f   10 h

4

> **Possible answers**
> 1   Unless you wear something smart, you won't get a job.
> 2   I would have bought a new CD if I hadn't run out of money.
> 3   If I were you, I'd get a job rather than go to college.
> 4   If I had had the chance, I would have chosen a different course.
> 5   As long as you let me choose the film, I'll go to the cinema with you.
> 6   If I had to choose between studying at home and studying abroad, I'd choose the latter.
> 7   I won't go shopping unless you treat me to lunch.
> 8   I'll buy you a new jacket if you like.

5   Examples 7 and 8 are commonly found in letters. The correct versions feature the polite *would* in both sides of the sentence. Students should be familiar with this form and try to use it themselves.

> **Answers**
> 1   It **would** be best if the children were in bed when we go out tonight.
>   It is best if the children **are** in bed when we go out tonight.
> 2   You will not go wrong if you **choose** her for your secretary.
>   You **would** not go wrong if you chose her for your secretary.
> 3   If I ever **have** money, I **will spend** it wisely.
>   If I ever **had** money, I **would spend** it wisely.
> 4   What would happen if the cheque **went** missing?
>   What **would have happened** if the cheque **had gone** missing?
> 5   If you choose to live in the town centre, **you'll need** to pay more.
>   If you **chose** to live in the town centre, you'd need to pay more.
> 6   Unless we ~~will~~ hurry, we will be late.
> 7   I would appreciate it if you **would write** back to me.
> 8   I would be grateful if you **would/could** reply as soon as possible.

6   The pictures show two different types of shopping experience – one in a small shop with personal service and the other very impersonal in a large supermarket. Students should discuss which one they prefer.

7 There are four people speaking – Pete, Tom and Lucy, who are students, and their tutor. It should not make a difference to understanding, as it is very clear who is who. Part 3 of the Speaking Module often has up to four speakers, but two usually dominate.

8 Ask students to read through questions 1–3 and then 4–10.

> **Answers (see underlined text in script)**
> **1** A **2** C **3** B **4** CDs **5** confusion marketing **6** price; taste (in either order) **7** first impression **8** (your/their) parents **9** trend setter / trendsetter **10** designer clothes

Recording script

Questions 1–3
Tutor: Good morning. So, in our tutorial today we're looking at the nature of choice. Now, last week we were saying that, compared with 50 years ago, today we're totally surrounded by choice. We have it in the shops at a level which we've never previously had. But <u>if choice were to disappear, I mean if we were to live in an economy where we only had one type of biscuit on offer or one clothes shop in the vicinity, do you think we would really be worse off as a result?</u>
Pete: Oh, I think so, most definitely. It'd be so boring.
Tutor: Yes, I would argue that the very idea which <u>economics is based on is that people have different preferences,</u> and forcing people to buy a particular brand would make most people worse off. Unless we lived in a world where people happened to be identical and agree, which of course, happily, we don't.
Tom: But having too many choices can lead to problems – not having enough time, for example.
Tutor: Mm, <u>I read somewhere that in the US the average number of TV channels is about 55, and the average number that is viewed in a week in a typical American home is about 13, and if there are 99 channels, it is still about 13.</u> I think this is telling us something – it shows us the amount of time people are prepared to spend finding a programme.

****

Questions 4–10
Tutor: So, is the same true for washing powder or toothpaste, do you think?
Lucy: Certainly, as far as I'm concerned! I don't have time to spend deciding which sort of toothpaste I want to buy.
Tutor: Well, my view is that 50 kinds of different washing powder or 50 kinds of soap do not actually add to the quality of life, but in other areas – <u>such as CDs – then I might say yes, there are aspects of choice that do improve the quality of life.</u>
Pete: But what about things like choosing which mobile phone to get – that's a nightmare.

Tutor: Yes, there's definitely a problem when you're dealing with complex markets where there *appears* to be a large choice, but actually there isn't really – it's called <u>confusion marketing.</u> <u>With some mobile phone contracts, you need to be a trained mathematician</u> to work out which is the best deal!
Tom: Well, I think confusion marketing is one of the most irritating things I can think of. Each company offering a slightly different contract, so it's virtually impossible to compare prices. So how *do* people make a decision?
Tutor: Well, it seems to depend on what you're buying. There's a difference in decision-making between buying <u>a loaf of bread</u> and buying a house, for example. When you buy a loaf of bread, you generally use all the available information about it and then <u>choose the best option for you – probably based on price and taste.</u> However, psychologists say that, contrary to what you may think, <u>when you buy a house,</u> you make that decision in less than ten seconds – <u>that first impression counts most of all.</u> That's why people selling their houses are told to make some coffee so the house smells good, put fresh flowers out, make sure it's tidy, etc. First impressions matter a lot – it's the same when you buy a car or a holiday.
Pete: But what happens when there are two holidays and I want to choose between them? Is it better for me just to choose one immediately and save time, or put a lot of effort into finding out all I can about both holidays and making a rational choice?
Tutor: Well, generally, people use one of three basic strategies for dealing with choice. The first is simply to always <u>get what their parents have always bought in the past.</u>
Lucy: But I don't think many young people nowadays just follow what their parents did.
Tutor: Well, the second strategy is to <u>buy the latest thing – to be a trend setter.</u> More and more people seem to be doing this nowadays – you find people are throwing out perfectly OK TVs and other electrical equipment just because they're not totally up to date.
Pete: I know a lot of people who do that. Good for the economy, though – keeping people in work making even more stuff.
Tutor: Well, I guess that's one way of looking at it. The third strategy is to <u>buy something which is unique, something few people buy – designer clothes,</u> for instance. Of course, if you have real problems choosing, then you can actually pay people to choose for you. They spend their time finding the best deal and then present you with the information.
Tom: You'll still have the problem of how to choose the best person to find out the information for you, of course!

9

> **Suggested answers**
> 1 Yes, I quite agree with this idea. What I mean is that when I go into a shop, I find it completely mind-boggling when I have a huge choice, and in the end, I tend to walk out without buying anything.
> 2 I had to choose whether to have tea or coffee, whether to have an apple or a fattening pastry and also whether to go to the cinema tonight with a friend or stay at home and do some coursework.
> 3 Not really, nothing very important. I suppose I'm quite lucky in a way.
> 4 Well, first of all I weigh up all the evidence carefully. Then I go to bed. Let me put this another way: I think trying to sleep on a decision is probably the best way to come to a good conclusion.

Test folder 7

SB pages 90–91
Locating information

Make sure students fully understand the notes and advice.

1 Ask students to read the description of the passage, and paragraph A on page 90. Then ask them to read the rubric and the example on page 91. Make sure they understand that question 2 reflects *possible difficulties – such as resistance to their plans* in paragraph A. Ask them to complete the task in pairs.

Answers
1 E *It is an unstructured way of thinking, in which there is little criticism of ideas*
2 A (example)
3 D *It allows you to eliminate them, alter them, or prepare contingency plans to deal with problems that might arise ... make your plans 'tougher' and better able to survive difficulties ... spot fatal flaws and risks*
4 B *it has the benefit of blocking the confrontations that happen when people with different thinking styles discuss the same problem.*
5 F *people chairing meetings ... may direct activity into Green Hat thinking ... they will ask for Black Hat thinking*
6 B *As a result, your decisions and plans will be ambitious, creative and sensitive to the needs of others. They will be carried out effectively, and you will be prepared for the unexpected.*
7 C *analyse past trends, and try to work out from historical data what might happen in the future*
8 E *encourages you to think positively ... the optimistic viewpoint ... helps you to keep going when everything looks gloomy and difficult*

---

2 Ask students to read the rubric, skim the passage and carry out the task individually, then compare their answers in small groups before you check them all together.

Answers
1 C *they are not expected to do this all the time – when we meet them at parties or in the street, for instance.*
2 B *managers ... 'looking the part' by dressing differently from those below them in the company hierarchy*
3 D *Managers ... may feel under pressure to behave in an authoritarian manner, even if this conflicts with their personality and general approach to interaction with other people.*
4 A *one person may need to act as manager, husband, father, son, friend, and so on.*
5 E *once we know the relevant role of the other person, we assume that ... we, too, need to behave in certain ways.*
6 B *Clearly expectations are a product of a particular time and place*

---

14 The importance of colour

Unit topic	Colour
14.1	
Test skills	Listening:
	Matching
	Listening for specific information
	Writing extra (AC):
	Task 1: Describing changes
	Speaking Part 3
Vocabulary	Words and phrases related to change
	Colours
	Adjectives describing personality
Pronunciation	Linking words
14.2	
Test skills	Listening: Short-answer questions
Grammar	*-ing* forms and infinitives (2)
Vocabulary	Confused words
	Comment adverbs

Workbook contents

1, 2, 3	Reading
4	Grammar: *-ing* forms and infinitives
5	Vocabulary

14.1 SB pages 92–93

1 Draw students' attention to the pictures at the top of the page. These are of:
- the iPod Mini
- a Ferrari
- a bottle of ketchup.

Encourage students to discuss the use of colour in these pictures, e.g. which iPod Mini they prefer, etc. Can they name the colours of the rainbow? (**Answers:** red, orange, yellow, green, blue, indigo, violet) There will be more discussion on this subject in exercise 7, so don't spend too long on it at this stage.

2 Ask the class to look at questions 1–4 and try to predict the answers. Then to do the same for questions 5–8. For questions 5–8, students will have to write the name of a colour in each space. Explain that for questions 9 and 10, they will need to draw lines showing the popularity of blue and green vehicles over the period 1987–2001.

Play the recording and check answers. Ask students if they predicted the right answers.

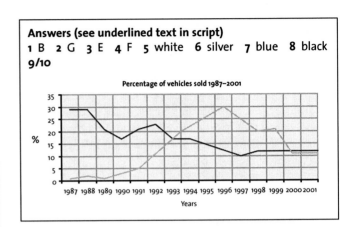

Percentage of vehicles sold 1987–2001

Recording script

Questions 1–4

Although the human eye can discern at least six million different colour shades, and theoretically there are an infinite number of colour possibilities, the colours which are popular at any given time will depend on a wide variety of factors – including technological advances, the economy and even politics. Colour fashions do not change abruptly, rather they are continually evolving, and one colour may be fashionable for up to ten or 12 years. Let's look now at some examples of colour trends.

When it comes to the world of work, most people are very traditional. Men go for suits, shirts and ties and, while there's a wide choice of colours for both shirts and ties – pink, purple and green proving popular recently – <u>it would seem that blue</u>, rather than black or grey, <u>is generally the first choice for their main outfit</u>. Apparently, it's a colour that appeals to people who are responsible, and is especially popular with bankers.

Now, offices always benefit from some colour. Even a small amount will improve mood and, <u>although most offices these days are generally a rather boring white</u>, by using a hint of colour – possibly with a green filing cabinet or red blinds at the windows – employers may find that their employees' stress levels are reduced and productivity is improved.

<u>Turning to national flags</u>, colour is of vital importance. The point made by one academic in the last century that 'national flags make use of only seven main colours: red, blue, green, and yellow, orange, black and white' remains true today. An analysis of the number of colours used on flags between 1917 and 1999 reveals that a combination of three colours is by far the most popular choice. The use of a single colour is negligible, but the use of four colours is increasing in popularity. <u>Most countries go primarily for red</u>, followed closely by white and then blue. Black, green and orange are among the least popular combinations.

<u>The iPod Mini</u> first appeared in January 2004. It came in a range of colours – blue, pink, green, silver and gold – which were supposed to appeal to different personality types. When it was first introduced, people were asked to vote on the Apple website for which colour they preferred, and <u>the silver one stole a stunning 46 per cent of the vote</u>, <u>with none of the other colours coming near</u>.

Gold was particularly low in the polls, with blue, pink and green all a rather poor second.

****

Questions 5–8

Next, cars. Much like fashion, colour preferences follow trends and fall in and out of favour as the years pass. In 2004, global colour-trend data showed that, interestingly, red and green were no longer popular, with less than 5% of vehicles manufactured using those colours, but <u>silver</u>, favoured often by first-time buyers, <u>was far and away the leader, being the colour of 38% of vehicles produced</u>. <u>White</u>, a favourite apparently with older, male drivers, <u>had 19.6% of the market</u>, followed by <u>black at 13.9</u>. Interestingly, in North America, white cars had the lowest collision rates, while black had the most. <u>The once trendy blue car</u> is declining in popularity worldwide, and in 2004 <u>made up only 9.3% of cars purchased</u>, perhaps because it had been found that in the USA particularly, blue cars were the most popular with car thieves.

****

Questions 9 and 10

Let's look now at the rise and fall in popularity of blue and green cars in Canada.

Let's take blue cars first. Blue cars began at a high of 29% from 1987 to 88. They then began to falter, with a fall to 21% in 1989 and a further fall to 17% in 1990. Sales picked up in 1991, when they rose to 21%, and reached a peak of 23% in 1992. There was then a gradual fall from 17% in 1993 and 94 to a low of 10% in 1997. Blue cars then remained more or less constant at 12% of the market until the end of 2001.

Turning now to green cars … from 1987 to 1990, sales of green cars were only very low – only 1%, with a high of 2% in 1988. There was an upturn in 1991, as sales hit 5%, growing to 20% in 1993. Sales continued to grow, reaching a peak of 30% in 1996. It was all downhill after 1996, though, with green-car sales back to 20% in 1998. Sales then rose slightly in 1999 to 21%, but plummeted to 11% by 2000 and then levelled off.

Photocopiable recording script activity
(**P** ⋯⟩ page 140)

Hand out copies of the recording script so that students can see how the language describing changes has been used. Students should monitor the amount of TV three students watch over the space of a month. (A class wall chart could be put up to be filled in.) At the end of the time period, students should all write a paragraph giving details of the changes that have occurred.

3 Students should be familiar by now with some of these words describing changes. Exercises 3 and 4 give practice in Task 1 of the Academic Writing Module.

Answers		
to go down	**to remain stable**	**to go up**
to decline	to be consistent	to grow
to weaken	to remain constant	to make progress
to plummet	to be steady	to pick up
to fall	to level off	to improve
	to remain unchanged	to rise

4

Sample answer
The chart shows the percentage of blue and green cars which were purchased between 1987 and 2001. First of all, blue cars. Sales began at a high of 29% in 1987–88. They then began to weaken, falling to 21% in 1989 and 17% in 1990. Sales made progress in 1991, when they rose to 21% and reached a peak of 23% in 1992. They then gradually declined from 17% in 1993–94 to a low of 10% in 1997. Blue cars then remained more or less constant at 12% of the market until the end of 2001.
Secondly, green cars. Sales of green cars from 1987 to 1990 were quite weak, with only 1% of the market, rising to a high of 2% in 1988. Sales began to improve in 1991, rising to 5% of vehicles sold, and then increased to 20% in 1993. They continued to grow, reaching a peak of 30% in 1996. Sales began to decline after 1996 and fell to only 20% in 1998. They then picked up slightly in 1991 to 21%, but then plummeted to 11% in 2000 and before levelling off.

5 Students often complain they can't hear where one word ends and another begins. This exercise builds awareness of what is happening when we are speaking in English.

Recording script

Examples
black_orange, red_apple, green_egg

Although blue can be quite a popular colour generally, it is the least attractive colour when it comes to food because of the way we have learnt to look at blue-, black- or purple-coloured foods. Psychologically, these foods resemble food spoilt by bacteria or food which is poisonous. However, one food giant is aiming to boost ketchup sales by introducing blue ketchup. The flavour remains unchanged and the price is a little higher than for the red ketchup, but it is popular with children.

6 This is a fun activity and should not be taken too seriously. Students will probably need to have an English-English dictionary for the words they don't know.

7 Students should spend ten to 15 minutes on this activity. They should try to use the phrases in the Useful language box. These are mainly phrases to do with generalising.

Possible answers
1 I haven't thought about it before, but I guess, yes, it may be possible to tell someone's personality by looking at their clothes. For example, if you wear black all the time, it probably means that, on the whole, you're a gloomy type of person, very pessimistic, but also that you are probably very strong-willed.
2 In my country, people generally wear white for weddings and black for funerals. Red is used for danger.
3 I think that, as a rule, colour plays an enormous part in our lives. What would the world be like without colour? Very sad and grey. We need colour to help cheer us up, to calm us, to make us happy. For instance, I've heard that some prisons have been painted pink and green in order to put the prisoners in a better mood.

4 Colour has a large role in advertising. We associate different products with their colour. Often people can't be bothered to remember the name of the product, but they do remember the colour of the packet.

14.2 SB pages 94–95

1 Students should be familiar with the concept of *-ing* forms and infinitives from unit 10. In this unit, the grammar is extended to look at verbs which change their meaning, depending on whether they are followed by an *-ing* form or an infinitive. Play the recording and elicit what is said about the colours. This first playing is for general understanding rather than anything more detailed.

Answers
Red and green: developed so humans could see red leaves or berries clearly in the forest. Some birds and fish can see in colour, but mainly in blue and yellow.

Up to 8% of men are colour blind. More humans suffer from colour-blindness than monkeys, so human beings may be losing their ability to distinguish red and green.

Recording script

Well, this morning I went to Dr Stanley's zoology seminar. It was quite interesting when I finally got there – on why man evolved the ability to see red and green colours. Apparently, it helped our ancestors to find food – you can see red leaves or berries more clearly among the green leaves in the jungle, or something like that anyway. Well, I always like to get to his seminars on time, but this morning I was running late – I didn't remember to switch my alarm clock on last night. I remember getting into bed, but that's about all, I was so tired. Well, as I say, I arrived late, and although I tried to be as quiet as possible, Dr Stanley stopped talking and just looked at me. I was so embarrassed. I told him I hadn't meant to be late. Well, I got a seat, and he started explaining about which other animals could see in colour – apparently, fish and some birds do, but mainly only blue and yellow. It's only primates that can see red and green as well as blue–yellow. Interestingly, he went on to say that more humans suffer from colour blindness than monkeys, so we may be losing our ability to distinguish red from green. Apparently, in some groups of people, up to 8% of men have red–green colour blindness. Anyway, he then stopped to show us a video, which meant switching off all the lights. I tried everything to keep awake – eating mints, pinching myself – but it was no good.

2 Play the recording again and ask students to work in pairs to answer the questions. They should try to answer using the same structure as in the recording. Draw students' attention to the structure following *remember*, *stop*, *went on* and *try*. Elicit the difference in meaning between *stop to do* and *stop doing*. Explain that other verbs also change meaning in this way. It is also worth explaining at this point that there are a very few verbs which have no difference in meaning when they are followed by a different structure.

Answers
1 zoology
2 no
3 She didn't remember to switch on her alarm clock.
4 He stopped talking.
5 He went on to talk about colour blindness.
6 He stopped to show a video.
7 She tried eating mints and pinching herself.

---

3 Ask students to work in pairs.

Answers
1 a She forgot to switch the alarm on before getting into bed.
  b She got into bed and now remembers it.
2 a He didn't talk any more.
  b He stopped what he was doing because he wanted to show a video.

---

4 This gives further practice. Ask the class to either give a paraphrase or synonym to explain the difference in meaning. Refer students to the Grammar folder (SB page 142) if they are having problems.

Answers
1 a *tried* + infinitive = attempted
  b *tried* + *-ing* form = experimented
2 a *went on* + *-ing* form = continued doing the same thing
  b *went on* + infinitive = did something else in addition
3 no real difference in meaning
4 a *I like* + *-ing* form = this is something I generally enjoy doing
  b *I like* + infinitive = this is an example of something I do regularly, often because I think it is a good thing to do

---

5 This exercise could be done in class or for homework.

Possible answers
1 When I couldn't wake up in time for school, I tried asking a friend to phone me.
2 When I realised I had forgotten my wallet, I tried to borrow some money for the ticket.
3 When I was young, I remember going to visit my grandparents on their farm.
4 I asked them to keep the noise level down, but they went on playing loud hip-hop all night.
5 At the weekends, I like to go shopping / going shopping.
6 Next time, you must remember to take your keys with you or you'll be locked out.

6

Possible answers
1 I first remember seeing the colour blue – it was a teddy bear that had a big, blue ribbon around its neck.
2 I often forget to take my diary with me to work.
3 I would try to make up with her as soon as possible.
4 I like to have a shower.

---

7 The words in this exercise are ones which are commonly confused by students. It is a good idea to make a poster and have these words on the wall of the classroom so that students can add to them.

Answers
1 *lent* (you *borrow* something from someone)
2 *Remind* (someone *reminds* you, you *remember* yourself)
3 *receipt* (a *recipe* has the instructions for cooking)
4 *raised* (*rise* has no object – the sun rises)
5 *countryside* (*nature* is the general term for animals, plants, etc.)
6 *check* (*control* is to order or limit someone's actions)
7 *effect* (*affect* is a verb and means 'to influence', 'to cause to change')
8 *economical* (*economic* relates to trade and industry)
9 *At the end* (*In the end* means 'finally', 'at the end of something')
10 *Standards of living* (this is an expression meaning the amount of wealth; *levels* refers to the height/amount/number of something)
11 *journey* (*travel* is more commonly used as an adjective not a noun, unless in *business travel/space travel*)
12 *discovery* (*invention* is of something new; *discovery* is of something that has always been there)

---

8 Ask students to read through the box on comment adverbs and look at the examples. Using a comment adverb correctly can lift their writing and speaking and make it seem more natural. This will help them to achieve higher marks in the exam.

Suggested answers
1 statistically 2 Personally 3 generously 4 logically
5 Interestingly 6 obviously 7 Disappointingly
8 Honestly 9 Surprisingly 10 wisely

---

9 Ask the class to form small groups and spend about ten minutes discussing a colour. Monitor to check they are using the comment adverbs appropriately.

Extension activity

Ask students, either individually or in small groups, to choose a colour and research it in detail. They should be prepared to give a talk on their colour to the rest of the class.

Writing folder 7

SB pages 96–97
Task 2: Making a general statement, giving examples and using comment adverbs

1 The first aim of this Writing folder is to increase awareness of generalising and to encourage students not to make sweeping statements which they do not have the information to support. More marks are to be gained if a more tentative approach is taken.

> **Answer**
> B is more general and formal.

2 Draw students' attention to the Useful language box.

> **Possible answers**
> 1 It is widely believed that blue is / Blue is thought to be a cold colour and it is often said that it shouldn't be used to paint living rooms.
> 2 It has been claimed that the colour of the packaging influences customers' choice of products.
> 3 Green tends to be the colour of environmental awareness.
> 4 It is widely assumed that if you drive a red car, you like speeding.
> 5 Broadly speaking / On the whole, more women than men wear bright colours.
> 6 I think that red tends to be the best colour for a national flag. / Red is generally agreed to be the best colour for a national flag.

3 This exercise looks at ways of incorporating relevant examples into writing. Make sure students try to use words/phrases from the Useful language box.

> **Possible answer**
> Colour blindness does not seem to affect a person's day-to-day life. People who are colour blind tend to adapt, and some people go through life without even knowing they are colour blind. The only problems that people with defective colour vision face are in some career choices. The following are examples of where there might be a problem: a career as a pilot, a police officer or a fire fighter may be impossible. For instance, it would be dangerous if a pilot couldn't tell the difference between red and green lights.

4
> **Possible answers**
> 1 For some types of animal, it is true to say that the male is more colourful than the female. Birds are the best illustration of this. There is a tendency for the male of each species to have very colourful plumage to attract the female. One clear example of this is the peacock, where the male bird is exceedingly beautiful and the female is very plain. Mammals such as bears, tigers and so on do not use colour as much as size and strength to attract the female.
> 2 Generally speaking, colour does help companies to sell their goods. If we look at packaging, for example, it would appear that certain colours help companies target particular consumers. Companies often favour bright, primary colours when they are targeting children and have a tendency to choose more sophisticated colours for young professionals. Another example of the way colour sells is in the use of yellow. It is widely believed that yellow, when placed on a supermarket shelf, will draw the eye more easily than any other colour.

5 Ask the class to read through the paragraph first before attempting to do the exercise.

> **Answers**
> 1 B   2 A   3 C   4 B   5 A

6
> **Sample answer**
> How often do we think, I mean really think, about colour? Personally, I believe there is a tendency for us to take colour for granted, to not acknowledge its importance. However, I very strongly believe that the world would indeed be a poorer place without it.
>
> For a start, we would no longer be able to see the colours of nature. What would the world be like without a beautiful blue sky, a blood-red sunset or a rainbow after a rainstorm? It would literally be colourless – a word that not only means 'without colour' but also 'not exciting' and 'uninteresting'. Clearly, not everyone has the time to sit around admiring Mother Nature and her colours, but life would be much poorer without the possibility of a free artistic display to cheer our lives up.
>
> Another thing worth mentioning is the way we look. If there was a world without colour, we would all look the same. Ideally, this would be a good thing, with the result that there would be no discrimination on the basis of the colour of our skin. However, personally, I think that there would be a strong tendency to find something else to discriminate over – possibly a person's height.
>
> Colour is something that adds life and beauty to our world. You only have to look around you to see that. For example, when you look into a child's bright blue eyes, or catch a glimpse of a young girl's shiny red hair. To sum up, I really have to say that a world without colour would definitely be a much, much poorer place.
> (267 words)

15 Social interaction

15.1 SB pages 98–99

Ask students to comment on the way the people in the pictures are relating to each other.

Possible answers
The first picture shows two women who are about to have a meal. They seem to be friends and are probably European, North American or Australian. They are going to eat in the kitchen, which is very informal, and would be unusual in some countries.

In the second picture, a group of people are having a barbecue. They appear to be in a public area, such as a park. At least one man is cooking. They seem very relaxed and friendly, and to be co-operating.

The third picture shows some people in Mongolia, eating from the same large cooking pot. Unlike the people in the other photographs, they are very close together. They look quite serious, as though they are concentrating on the food rather than on each other.

1 Ask students to discuss these questions in small groups and to expand their answers.

Possible answers
- I generally enjoy meeting new people if there's a chance to get to know them, but I prefer meeting one or two new people at a time, rather than a lot.
- I find it interesting to meet people from countries that I'd like to visit, because I can find out more about their country.

- When friends come to my home, I usually offer them a cup of tea or coffee, and try to keep my younger brothers and sisters away from them.
- When people invite guests to their home, it's usually for a meal in the evening. They might spend the whole evening sitting at the table and eating.

2 Ask students to read the rubric and to discuss possible problems and pleasures of staying with a family in another country. Make sure they understand *hospitality* (being friendly and welcoming to guests and visitors).

Ask students to skim the passage and check if any of their ideas about problems and pleasures are mentioned. After they have skimmed the passage, ask them if they have experienced anything that is mentioned.

Background information
Social anthropology is also called 'cultural anthropology', and is the study of different cultures and societies.

3 Ask students to read the rubric, the first line of the summary and lines 1–4 of the passage. Ask what other words from the box would more or less fit the meaning of space 0 (*homes, host, people, resident, villages*), and why *household* is the only possibility (the word needs to refer to something that can have members, and it must be singular).

Ask students to read the rest of the summary, the words in the box and the relevant part of the passage (from the beginning) and to complete the summary.

Answers
1	customs	*everyday life* (lines 2–3), *how people managed their lives* (line 4)
2	guest	*an honoured guest* (line 11)
3	duties	*shopping, cooking or domestic chores* (line 13)
4	wine	*Wine had already been made, generally by the men, who were also responsible for pouring it.* (lines 27–29)
5	meals	*large amounts of food were prepared in advance, usually by the women.* (lines 26–27)
6	groceries	*it was not always easy to buy food. Grocery stores ...* (lines 32–33)
7	markets	*people usually shopped in markets* (lines 34–35), *travelled to several locations* (line 38), *travelled across the city ... to the central market* (lines 16–17)
8	bus	*travelled across the city on buses to the central market* (lines 16–17), *frequent trips to the market on ... crowded buses* (lines 36–37)

Ask students to read questions 9–13 and find the answers in the passage.

4 Ask students to work in groups of three or four and to think of ways of talking about each part of the task (adding to the suggestions in the SB). Remind them that, in the test, what they say doesn't have to be true.

Ask students in each group to take turns to talk about the task for at least a minute.

Extension activity

Suggest that students find out about customs of hospitality in various countries, based on the topics that they have discussed. They could then write a short report comparing customs. Sources might include each other (in a multicultural class), TV programmes and the Internet.

In a multicultural class, students could instead each write a page about hospitality in their own country. These could be circulated, or put on the wall, so that they can read each others' reports.

15.2 SB pages 100–101

Ask students what the pictures show, and ask if they have had any similar experiences.

1 Ask students to discuss the questions in small groups.

2 Ask students to read the rubric, the options A–C and the example. Check that they understand why the answer is C (*come straight out with it* = 'say it in a direct, straightforward way').

Ask students to read questions 1–8. Remind them that they should only write A, B or C for the answer. Play the recording.

Recording script

Tutor: Good morning, everyone. Now, as I told you last week, our topic this morning is cultural differences and some of the aspects of behaviour you'll need to be aware of when you go abroad on business. Helen and Bill, you've prepared a short presentation, haven't you?

Helen: That's right. We've concentrated on three areas – Japan, the Arab countries and the USA – because they're important business partners for Australia, now or in the future. I should say first of all that we've had to simplify by making generalisations, but of course people vary a lot within each culture. And what we've learnt from our research is that one way of doing things is usually no better or worse than another. *We just tend to be more comfortable with the way we're used to.* OK. Now Bill's going to start with communication.

Bill: Right. Thanks, Helen. Um, information, particularly something negative, is communicated in different ways around the world. *In the US, people tend to speak and write fairly explicitly and frankly, and many people pride themselves on saying what they mean. If they want to say 'no', they come straight out with it.* But in some societies, a great deal of information is transmitted *non*-verbally. The Japanese, for instance, usually don't want to displease others with a negative answer, so they may not *say* 'no' – but it's still clearly understood if you can read the non-verbal signs.

There can be a big difference in appropriate eye contact, too, from country to country. *In the United States, if you look someone in the eye when they're speaking to you, you're thought to be honest and reliable.* Looking away or at the floor indicates that you aren't paying attention or you're guilty. But in Japan, an attempt to maintain eye contact isn't usually acceptable behaviour and may be taken as a sign of aggression. *Looking away is a sign of respect,* rather than of hiding something. On the other hand, in some Arab countries, such as in Saudi Arabia, eye contact is important and can help in communication. Helen …

Helen: Ways of shaking hands vary around the world, too. A weak grip, held for a relatively long time, is normal in Japan, and certainly doesn't mean the person is weak. In the United States, the way that someone shakes hands has long been taken as an indicator of their personality. *A firm grip is thought to show strength of character.*

Attitudes towards time vary. If you make an appointment with an Arab business person, you may find that your meeting begins long past the appointed time, though it'll probably last as long as necessary to conduct the business in hand. There, *time is a servant*, not a master, and the idea that a person should be ruled by the clock is amusing. But in the United States, time is money. *If someone's kept waiting for a meeting half an hour beyond the time that was agreed, it's seen as a signal that they aren't important.* So Americans try to avoid this happening.

People are expected to arrive in good time for a meeting in Japan. Being late demonstrates that you can't be trusted to keep your word or manage your time. But in the Arab tradition, punctuality isn't regarded in the same way. People can show up hours late, or not at all, and it won't be taken as an insult. Of course, a lot of Arabs, particularly business people, are aware that attitudes towards punctuality are different in other parts of the world.

In Japan, business meetings normally start with some casual conversation, because the Japanese are generally interested in getting to know the people involved. In America, though, meetings sometimes begin with phrases such as 'Let's get started'. Over to you, Bill.

Bill: OK, let's turn to personal space. When you're standing talking to someone, make sure you adopt the distance that's appropriate to the local culture. In the US and Britain, business people usually stand close enough to shake hands, about 75 to 90cm apart. In the Arab world, it's less, maybe under 30cm, and you sometimes see a British person backing away to maintain their preferred distance, while the Arab they're talking to keeps moving towards them, to maintain his or hers. The Japanese prefer a greater distance than either, perhaps 120cm, and may see the British as getting too close. One reason for maintaining that distance in Japan is to have room to bow when they greet someone – a custom that to some extent corresponds to the American habit of nodding.

Helen: And finally, you need to get used to the fact that in much of Asia, people gravitate towards other people in public spaces. For example, if you're sitting in a movie theatre surrounded by empty seats and a local resident enters, he's likely to sit next to you – it's considered appropriate in many parts of the world, but an American, for instance, would feel they were sitting much too close. And, er, that's as far as we've got.

Tutor: OK, thank you both. Now, are there any questions?

3   Ask students to read the rubric and task, and to complete the sentences as they listen. Play the recording: this is the same as the previous recording, but starts with *I should say first of all …* (in Helen's first speech) and ends at *So Americans try to avoid this happening* (half way through her second speech). Note that completing sentences is an IELTS task, but in the test the recording is played only once, and each task follows on from the previous one.

Answers (see italicised text in script)
1 comfortable   2 frankly   3 honest and reliable   4 respect
5 strength of character   6 servant   7 important

---

4   Point out to students that as well as talking about facts, we often talk about possibilities. Elicit examples (e.g. *I might invite some friends to lunch next week. I may ask them to help me cook.*) and ask students to read the Grammar box on page 100. Make sure they understand *speculate* (to guess possible answers to a question when you do not have enough information to be certain) – it is often used in Part 3 of the Speaking Module.

Ask students to rewrite answers 1–3 using *may* or *might (not)*.

Suggested answers
1   Customs may/might become more similar to those in other countries.
2   Shaking hands may/might not be so common in future.
3   People may/might copy the customs they see in foreign TV programmes.

Point out that modal perfects (modal verb + *have* + past participle) normally refer to the past. *May/might have done* can be used to talk about the past when you do not have enough information to be certain. Ask students to read the introduction to 4–6, and to rewrite the three sentences using *may* or *might (not) have*.

Suggested answers
4   People may/might not have eaten much foreign food.
5   People may/might have been more hospitable.
6   People may/might not have spent much time enjoying themselves.

---

5   Draw students' attention to the picture, which is part of the original poster for the film *If it's Tuesday, this must be Belgium*. Ask them to read the paragraph below the picture. Ask if the deduction in the film title is about the present or past (it's present), and whether it's saying something is true or impossible (true).

Ask students, in pairs, to read the task and find the right example for each explanation.

> **Answers**
> 1 b   2 a   3 d   4 c

Ask which modal verb is used to deduce that something is true (*must*) and which one to say something is impossible (*can't*).

Remind students that these are not the only meanings of *must* and *can't*. For further information, refer them to the Grammar folder (SB page 142).

6   Ask students, in small groups, to read the exercise and give some possible responses in each situation. Elicit a few examples.

> **Possible answers**
> 1   You must be tired. / You must have been out enjoying yourself.
> 2   He can't be a doctor – he told me he's a dentist.
> 3   You must be Sally Green.
> 4   Nur must have changed her email address.
> 5   No – he can't have received my message.

7   Elicit the meaning of *collocation* (words that are often used together, often for no obvious reason). Elicit the collocations in the three phrases (*large amounts, a great deal, a big difference*).

Ask students to put one of the adjectives (*big, large, great*) at the top of each column, and to answer the question.

> **Answers**
> **A** large   **B** great   **C** big
> (In columns A and B, some words collocate with *big*, but others don't.)
> *Great* is not normally used with physical objects.

8   Ask students to complete the passage with words from columns A and B in exercise 7.

> **Suggested answers**
> 1 honour   2 extent   3 number   4 amount   5 sum
> 6 advantage   7 distance   8 success

Test folder 8

SB pages 102–103
Classification

Make sure students fully understand the notes and advice.

1   Ask students to read the task. Ask them to think of ways of suggesting that someone is a colleague, friend or relative, without using those words.

> **Possible answers**
> * colleague: we work for the same company; we're in the same office; he/she's my boss
> * friend: we spend a lot of time together; we were at college together
> * relative: he married my sister; he/she is a family member

Ask students to complete the task. Remind them to write C, F or R for each answer. Play the recording.

> **Answers (see underlined text in script)**
> 1 R   2 C   3 F   4 C

Recording script

You will hear two friends discussing what to do at the weekend.

First, you have some time to listen to questions 1 to 4. (*pause*)

Now listen carefully and answer questions 1 to 4.

A What do you fancy doing on Saturday?
B We could go and see Douglas – I don't think you know him, but <u>we met a few years ago</u>, at my brother's birthday party. <u>We've stayed in touch</u> and generally get together every few weeks. He's crazy about football.
A Oh, well, I'm not sure – if you're going to talk about football!
B Or there's Rachel, I'm sure you'd like her, she's very friendly and easy to get on with. <u>She's actually my cousin</u>, though we don't see each other all that often. I sometimes bump into her on the way to work – she's with a company that's quite near mine.
A OK.
B In fact, if we go round to her place, we could go on to Suzanne's – <u>we work in the same department</u>. She's having a party Saturday evening, and she's invited everyone in the office, as well as lots of friends. I said I wasn't sure if I could go, but if you'd like to, I could give her a ring.
A I think I'd prefer something quieter.
B Well, how about going to stay with Jack for the weekend – he lives in a beautiful part of the countryside.
A Do I know him?
B I'm sure you do. Don't you remember? You met him at my firm's New Year's Eve party a couple of years ago. <u>His family lived next door to mine</u> when we were both children, so we've known each other for years. He works in the computer industry.
A Oh yes, he was there with a friend of his, wasn't he? What was her name – Melanie, wasn't it?
B That's right.
A So what was he doing at your office party?

B Well, <u>Melanie's our Finance Manager</u>. They've been friends for quite a long time.
A OK, well, why not give him a call?

2   Ask students to read the task. Check they are clear about the scenario (a student decides whether or not to include the five topics in an assignment she is working on). Play the recording.

> **Answers (see underlined text in script)**
> 1 B   2 A   3 C   4 C   5 A

Recording script

You will hear a student talking to her tutor about an assignment she is working on.

First, you have some time to look at questions 1 to 5. (*pause*)

Now listen carefully and answer questions 1 to 5.

Tutor: Morning, Catherine. Have a seat.
Catherine: Thanks.
Tutor: Have you decided yet what aspects of Social Interaction to cover in your assignment?
Catherine: Not really. I've read so much that I find interesting, I'm having trouble choosing.
Tutor: OK, what have you read about?
Catherine: Well, there's interaction in <u>families</u>. That's fascinating.
Tutor: Mm.
Catherine: I think I'd like to write a whole assignment about it, though, because there's so much to consider.
Tutor: Then <u>how about leaving it for now</u> and writing an assignment purely on that next semester?
Catherine: <u>That's a good idea. I'll do that.</u> Then there's how people interact in groups. I'd definitely like to write about that in this assignment.
Tutor: OK. It might be worth limiting it in some way, to <u>interaction in social groups</u>, for instance.
Catherine: <u>Right. Yes, I'll put that on the list.</u> But work teams are also very interesting. I'd be sorry not to include them.
Tutor: Maybe we should see what else you've thought about, and <u>come back to the question of work teams later</u>.
Catherine: Fine. Well, I read a good article about the sort of interaction we have with acquaintances – mostly about the people we recognise but don't necessarily know by name. It really opened my eyes to everyday behaviour, so I'd quite like to write about that. On the other hand, there are other things that I wouldn't want to leave out.
Tutor: I think you should consider how long the assignment is going to be, and how these different topics relate to each other.
Catherine: That's a point. Then <u>I'd better put off deciding about acquaintances for the moment</u>, until I've managed to plan this in more detail. But I think <u>friendship networks</u> are an important aspect of interaction, so <u>that's something I definitely want to include</u>.
Tutor: Right. Now have you considered …

3 Ask students to read the task, in particular noticing the three options A–C, then to skim the passage. Ask them to read the example and the underlined part of the passage. Then ask them to complete the task.

Answers

1 A *Most people also engaged in handicraft production in the home, the family being paid by a company to work* (paragraph 4); *home and workplace were physically separated* (paragraph 6)

2 C *their contributions to the family income were likely to make the difference between starvation and survival* (paragraph 2); *the already bad economic situation of families worsened* (paragraph 7)

3 A *Children worked from an early age, girls helping their mothers, and boys their fathers* (paragraph 3); *Few children now worked with their parents at home* (paragraph 7)

4 B *virtually all family members were engaged in agricultural work in one form or another, usually growing food for their own consumption* (paragraph 1); *Most people also engaged in handicraft production in the home* (paragraph 4); *Men, women and children were employed as individuals for a wage, often by different employers ... husbands, wives and children were also physically separated for a good part of their time* (paragraph 6)

5 A *School was an occasional or irrelevant factor in their lives* (paragraph 3) Note that although this may also have been true of the industrial period, this is not stated in the passage.

6 C *his wife and children, too, had an economic value as their contributions to the family income ...* (paragraph 2); *Men, women and children were employed as individuals for a wage* (paragraph 6); *children ... had generally become greater economic assets than before* (paragraph 7)

7 B *children's working hours were limited and their employment prohibited* (paragraph 7) There is no reference to restrictions in connection with the pre-industrial period.

8 A *The majority of English families of the pre-industrial age ... lived in a rural location* (paragraph 1); *... numerous factories in many towns and cities. These in turn encouraged migration from the countryside* (paragraph 5)

9 C *the husband, the undisputed master of the household* (paragraph 2); *men were still regarded as the head of the household* (paragraph 6)

---

16 Books, writing and signs

Unit topic	Books, writing and signs
16.1 Test skills	Reading (AC/GT): Classification True / False / Not given
16.2 Test skills	Listening: Form completion Speaking Part 2
Vocabulary	Books and writing
Grammar	Non-finite clauses
Pronunciation	Final consonants

Workbook contents

1	Reading
2, 3, 4	Vocabulary
5	Grammar: non-finite clauses

16.1 SB pages 104–105

1 Ask students, in small groups, to discuss the signs, using the Useful language box as far as possible.

Possible answers
Descriptions and meanings of the signs
1 This is a road sign. It's white with a red circle round the outside. It shows a car and a motorbike. The red circle means that something is prohibited – no motor vehicles are allowed to enter the street.
2 This is a thick black line forming a particular pattern, and it means *and*. The symbol is called an 'ampersand'.
3 This is another road sign. It's a triangle pointing upwards, surrounded by a thick red line. It shows a man with a spade and a pile of something that might be earth, sand or stones. It means that there are road works going on, so it's a warning to drivers to be careful.
4 This sign shows a dog on a white background, surrounded by a red circle, and with a red diagonal line across it. It means dogs are banned from this place, which might be a park or beach. (*It's a Canadian sign.*)
5 This is a square sign with a dark background. The meaning isn't very clear, because the white object in the sign could symbolise a castle or a pair of binoculars. (*In fact it's binoculars, and the sign means this is a good place for watching wildlife. It's an American sign.*)
6 This is a square sign, with a white pattern on it that I think represents a snowflake. I'm not sure, but it might mean that this is a good area for winter sports. (*It is. Again, it's an American sign.*)
7 This is an international sign, consisting of two horizontal lines of equal length, one above the other, and with a small space between them. It means *equals*, and is used in maths.
8 This is another road sign, and it's triangular, which means it's a warning. The black exclamation mark probably means that you're going to have a surprise, so you should be careful. It's a warning of danger.

Do you need to understand a particular language to understand them?
All these signs are intended to be easy to understand, whatever language you speak. So '&' means the same in all languages, whatever the word for *and* is. Most of the signs represent sentences, for example 4 'You mustn't bring a dog here' or 5 'This is a good place for watching wildlife', but the sentences could be in any language.

How easily can they be understood by someone seeing them for the first time?
It isn't obvious that red circles mean that something is banned or that triangles are warning signs. Some of the things that are shown are clear, like the motorbike and the dog, but the binoculars and snowflake are more difficult to interpret.

Can you think of ways in which they could be interpreted wrongly?
You might think that example 1 means you *can* drive here. Some people think 3 shows a man having trouble with an umbrella, so it could mean it's very windy. You might interpret the binoculars as showing the gate to a castle.

2 Ask students to read the rubric, then to skim the passage and decide if the signs (as a group) are more like Egyptian hieroglyphs, Chinese characters or letters of an alphabet.

Suggested answer
Hieroglyphs (1, 3, 4, 5 and 6) are representational, showing objects from the real world.
7 is symbolic, with the two equal lines meaning 'equals'.

Background information
Signs 2 and 8 fall into a different category, as they are thought to have developed from Latin words: '&' from *et* (meaning 'and') and the exclamation mark from *io*, which was an exclamation of joy.

3 Ask students to read the rubric, A–D and the example. Point out that although there are usually three options in a classification task in IELTS, it's possible to have four. Point out also that the answer is B according to the passage – even though the real answer may be C. Ask students to complete the task (1–6) in pairs.

Answers
1 C *Chinese ... Like many Egyptian hieroglyphs, the signs were originally pictures, and gradually became more abstract.* (lines 31–34)
2 B *Chinese characters are used ... in the unrelated languages of Japanese, Korean and, until the 20th century, Vietnamese.* (lines 36–39)
3 A *others indicate sounds* (lines 14–15)

4 B *The writing system consists of characters representing words, sections of words ...* (lines 34–35)

5 D

6 A *the third group are used to distinguish between two words that are otherwise identical: carve and retreat are represented by the same hieroglyph, but a knife symbol is added to show when the former meaning is intended, and a pair of legs to indicate the latter* (lines 15–20)

Questions 7–13: ask students to read and complete the task in pairs.

Answers

7	TRUE	*A totally new development in writing appeared in the Middle East about 3,700 years ago, when Egyptian hieroglyphs were well established. This was the North Semitic alphabet* (lines 48–51)
8	FALSE	*This was the North Semitic alphabet, which evolved in Palestine and Syria. The Phoenicians ... adapted it to form their own alphabet.* (lines 50–54)
9	TRUE	*This in turn spread into northern Africa to become the writing system of the Arabs, and north-west to Greece.* (lines 54–56)
10	NOT GIVEN	*The Greek letters were further modified to become the Cyrillic alphabets of Russia* (lines 57–58). This does not mean the languages are related, even though the alphabets are.
11	NOT GIVEN	*While most alphabets contain between 20 and 30 letters, the smallest, used in the Solomon Islands, contains only 11. Khmer, the official language of Cambodia, has the largest alphabet, with 74 letters.* (lines 68–73) This does not relate the number of letters to the number of words.
12	FALSE	*there is rarely great consistency between spelling and pronunciation* (lines 77–79)
13	TRUE	*the writing system has not kept pace with changes in pronunciation over the centuries.* (lines 81–83)

Extension activity

Ask students to find examples of signs that don't use words, and to work out why those particular signs are used. They could include a heart ♥ (meaning 'love'), a tick ✓ (meaning 'correct'), an arrow ➔ (showing direction), a knife and fork to mean food is available; computers have given rise to a lot of signs, such as an envelope to mean 'you have email(s)', a smiley face (showing a greeting) and so on.

Ask students to work out if any combinations of signs can be used to create more complicated messages. (This is rarely the case: combinations of signs, for instance in an airport terminal, normally give a list – 'this is the way to the restaurant and bank').

16.2 SB pages 106–107

1 Ask students whether they read reviews, e.g. of films, books, CDs, and whether they think they are useful and/ or interesting. Then narrow the discussion to book reviews.

Possible answers

Book reviews are published because people enjoy reading them and perhaps buy books recommended by reviewers.

Information might include: title and author, topic, genre (romantic novel, thriller, academic textbook, etc.), details of the author.

Opinions might include: reviewer's opinion of the quality of the writing, the accuracy and amount of information (in non-fiction), how easy it is to read.

2 Point out that some college courses include writing book reviews, and that the ability to assess books is likely to be essential in most courses.

Ask students to read the rubric and task. Play the recording as they complete the outline.

Background information

Professor Lord Robert Winston (born in 1940) is Professor of Fertility Studies at Imperial College School of Medicine, London University, and Head of the Department of Reproductive Medicine at the Hammersmith Hospital in London. He has presented a number of programmes for BBC Television, making science accessible to the general public – including ones on child development. *The Human Mind*, published in 2003, accompanies a television series of the same name. He was created a life peer in 1995, and so is a member of the House of Lords in the British parliament.

Answers (see underlined text in script)

1 *The Human Mind* **2** popular science **3** non-specialists
4 theories **5** function **6** personality **7** medical
8 stories **9** word list **10** goal

Recording script

Rachel: Oh, hello, can you spare me a few minutes, please?

Tutor: Yes, of course, Rachel. What can I do for you?

Rachel: It's about the book review you've asked us to write as part of the Academic Writing course. You said we should ask if we didn't know how to set about it.

Tutor: OK. Well, sit down, and let's talk about it. I presume you've chosen the book you want to write about.

Rachel: Yes.

Tutor: Good. Then have a look at this outline. If we talk it through and you make notes on it, it'll help you to structure your review. Right, first of all, what's the name of the book?

Rachel: *The Human Mind*.

Tutor: Ah yes, by Robert Winston. It was tied in with a very good television series, wasn't it? So you should start your review with the title and author. The next question is, what category would you put it in? For example, fiction, history, math …

Rachel: Well, I suppose it's science.

Tutor: Can you limit the field a little?

Rachel: Er, how about <u>popular science</u>?

Tutor: Yes, I think that's more helpful.

Rachel: Then I suppose the subject area is the brain.

Tutor: OK. And it's important to mention the intended readership, because you can't judge how effective a book is without considering who it's meant for.

Rachel: Well, it doesn't assume you know a lot about the subject, so <u>I'd say it's for non-specialists</u>. It was promoted in general bookshops.

Tutor: Right. Now the overview. What would you say Winston is trying to do?

Rachel: Er … it's very informative, but I think he's also telling us how to make the most of our brains.

Tutor: Then you should briefly discuss the main topics. I'd recommend mentioning the ones that you found the most significant and interesting.

Rachel: Mm-hm. Well, it starts by looking back at the last few thousand years, and <u>looks briefly at some of the theories that have been developed about the brain</u> and about its importance. It wasn't always considered as important as we now believe.

Tutor: True. And the next topic?

Rachel: I think it should be the structure and <u>activities of the brain that make it function</u>. I found that chapter very interesting, but it was probably the hardest to understand.

Tutor: Mm, I'd probably agree with you. Any more topics you want to mention?

Rachel: Oh, it covers so much, like the emotions, memory … but I think <u>the role of the brain in creating personality</u> should be mentioned, because I think that's an important aspect of the book. And then there's the advice on how we can use our brains to boost our intelligence. I've already started acting on some of the suggestions!

Tutor: Good luck! Now, let's look at the next section of your review, where you should analyse and evaluate the book. This is the main section, where you give your own opinions. This first point is really a question of whether we should take the writer seriously. A musician may be qualified to write about music, but not necessarily to write about the brain, for instance.

Rachel: Mm. Winston is a professor at the University of London, and <u>he's done a lot of research in various medical fields</u>. So he's very well qualified to write about this subject.

Tutor: What would you say are the strengths of the book?

Rachel: Mm … it's a complex subject, but he makes it as accessible as it can be for the general reader. That's partly because <u>he illustrates his points with a lot of stories</u>, both about well-known people, like Einstein, and from his own life.

Tutor: OK. Are there any other strengths you want to add?

Rachel: Er … <u>I was glad he included a word list</u> to explain the meanings of medical terms. And I didn't find any weaknesses.

Tutor: Mm. Right! Then that brings us to the conclusion. How would you sum up your overall response to the book?

Rachel: Well, I found it fascinating. I think Winston is quite <u>ambitious in the goal he's set himself, but he's succeeded in reaching it</u>.

Tutor: Well, there you are – you've got the skeleton of your review. Keep that in front of you while you're writing it up, and it should be fine.

Rachel: Thank you very much.

Tutor: You're welcome.

Photocopiable recording script activity
(**P** ⋯⟶ page 141)

Give students a copy of the recording script, and ask them to read it aloud in pairs. Then suggest that they choose another book that they both know, and adapt all or part of the script to suit that book.

3   Ask students to read the task card and the Useful language box. Check that they understand them. Point out that they can invent the book or the influence on themselves.

Give them one minute to prepare a short talk. Remind them to write down only key words or other brief notes. After a minute, ask them to take turns to talk to each other in pairs. Go round listening, without interrupting them. Make sure each person speaks for one to two minutes, so that they get used to speaking for that length of time.

4   Write on the board *People who use mobile phones in the library* and *People using mobile phones in the library* and elicit differences between *use* and *using* (*use* is a finite verb, it refers to the present and is plural – *people use* but *a person uses*; *using* is a non-finite verb (the present participle), so it doesn't refer to past, present or future, and doesn't show if the subject is singular or plural – *people using* or *a person using*).

Elicit the three non-finite verb forms (infinitive *to use*, present participle *using*, past participle *used*). Point out that these are used in many ways in English, particularly in academic writing. NB 'Present participle' and 'gerund' both refer to particular grammatical uses of the *-ing* form of a verb, and the terms can easily lead to confusion.

A non-finite clause normally consists of a non-finite verb form and other sentence elements, such as object, adverbial and (occasionally) subject.

Ask students to read the tinted box.

Elicit the correct versions of the two rules in the exercise, referring students to examples A and B in the tinted box.

> **Answers**
> 1 an active (example A)   2 a passive (example B)

5   Ask students to complete the exercise. Remind them to be careful with the spelling when the verb ends in *e*.

> **Answers**
> 1   concerning (active: could be paraphrased *some queries which concern the use*)
> 2   dated (passive: *your letter is dated 18 February*)
> 3   introduced (passive: *which were introduced*)
> 4   Attended (passive: *The conference, which was attended*)
> 5   Attending (active: *While she was attending*)

6 Ask students to read the pairs of sentences C–I. The sentences are paraphrases of each other, and the parts in italics are non-finite clauses. Ask why *having* + past participle is required in F and H (to make it clear that they refer to a time before the time of the main clause; in G, *after* serves the same function).

Draw attention to the position of *not* in E: negative non-finite clauses normally have *not* preceding the verb. Ask students to make the non-finite clause in F negative (*Not having grown up in Korea …*).

Refer students to the Grammar folder (SB page 142) for further information and examples.

Ask students to read the rubric and example of exercise 6. Check that they understand, then ask them to work through the exercise in pairs.

> **Answers**
> 1 facing learners of a foreign language
> 2 Having lived in Japan for many years,
> 3 required for your essay.
> 4 After being / Having been very variable for hundreds of years,
> 5 while travelling by plane or train.

7 Point out that, while some languages don't have consonants following vowels in the same syllable, in English this is very common. Speakers can easily be misunderstood if they don't pronounce these final consonants clearly.

Ask two or three students to read 1a and others to read 1b. Make sure they are clearly distinguishable. Continue similarly with one or two more pairs of sentences. Then ask students to work in pairs, reading each pair of sentences aloud to each other.

Play the recording and ask students to repeat the final word of each sentence immediately after hearing it.

Recording script

1 There's the sea.
  There's the seat.
2 It's a car.
  It's a card.
3 Is this the right day?
  Is this the right date?
4 It's the wrong tie.
  It's the wrong time.
5 How much did you say?
  How much did you save?

Ask students to take turns to read one sentence from each pair to their partner, who should identify it as 'a' or 'b'.

Writing folder 8

SB pages 108–109
Task 2: Being relevant and avoiding repetition

1 Students often fail to read the question carefully, especially under exam conditions. The result is that they often write quite a good essay, but it does not answer the question, and they lose marks. It is important to keep the title of the essay constantly at the forefront of the mind and not wander off the point.

> **Answers**
> The key words are:
> *With the increase in use of the Internet, books will soon become unnecessary.*
> *To what extent do you agree or disagree with this statement?*
> *Give reasons for your answer and include any relevant examples from your own knowledge and experience.*

Have students read the sample answer and mark the key and irrelevant points.

> **Suggested answer**
> It has been suggested that in the future the Internet will totally take over the role that has always been taken by books. Personally, I believe that this will, in fact, happen sooner than people think.
>
> It is often said that books are useful, but if we are talking about communicating news to the public, then in this case books are not so useful. ~~I don't often read books, even though I know they might help me. I find them boring, because most novels are really silly love stories.~~
>
> Personally, I think the Internet is very useful and I use it all the time both at college and at home. ~~I have had a computer for ten years and the one I have at the moment is an Apple Mac. It is particularly useful for finding information quickly and for keeping in touch with friends via email. I also use it to talk to people in chat rooms. People in chat rooms are really interesting and I have met many friends there. They give me a chance to practise my English which I find really interesting.~~ All the information I need I can find on the Internet. Some people say that it is hard to read from a screen but I don't have this problem.
>
> So in conclusion, I think the Internet is a good thing.

Commentary

There is very little on books in this essay – most information, and it is very lightweight and not very well developed, is about the Internet. The examples from own experience and knowledge are sketchy.

The first paragraph introduces the topic, but needs to be expanded, as the other paragraphs do not continue with this theme. The second paragraph seems to be comparing the Internet and newspapers rather than books, and the reference to novels is irrelevant. There needs to be a paragraph on the disadvantages and advantages of books, with some comparison of the Internet and books included. There is also repetition of vocabulary which shows the candidate has only a limited vocabulary range and will lose marks. However, the candidate has used pronouns, which do help in reducing the repetition of nouns.

This essay is really an answer to a question asking why you personally prefer the Internet to books, but even then the information is very limited. The examination task is also asking a general question which isn't answered – all the information we receive is about why the writer prefers the Internet. The conclusion is very poor, and the essay is too short.

2   Ask students to work in small groups or pairs and to discuss the question using the checklist in their books. They should aim to be relevant and not to wander off topic. Check they are using some of the language from the Useful language box.

3/4/5   Check that the class are familiar with the suggested alternative adjectives for exercise 3, with the concept of linking words for exercise 4 and pronouns for exercise 5.

Suggested answers

3   Adjectives (see numbers in answer below)
  1   *fascinating, absorbing, worthwhile, valuable, informative*
  2   Not adjectives used in 1: *helpful, effective*
  3   *tedious, predictable, uninspiring*
  4   *helpful, valuable*
  5   *helpful, valuable, efficient*
  6   *friendly, sociable, helpful*
  7   *absorbing, beneficial, helpful, worthwhile, effective*
4   Linkers
   but, and, so (see Writing folder 6 for alternatives)
5   Pronouns (see letters in answer below)
  a   *this* = the fact that the Internet will take over from books
  b   *they* = books
  c   *them* = books
  d   *it* = the Internet
  e   *the one* = the computer
  f   *It* = the computer / my Apple Mac
  g   *it* = the Apple Mac / computer
  h   *there* = in chat rooms
  i   *They* = chat rooms

---

underline (= adjectives, exercise 3); **bold** (= linkers, exercise 4); *italics* (= pronouns, exercise 5)

It has been suggested that in the future the Internet will totally take over the role that has always been taken by books. Personally, I believe that (a) *this* will, in fact, happen sooner than people think.

It is often said that books are (1) useful, **but** if we are talking about communicating news to the public, then in this case books are not so (2) useful. I don't often read books, even though I know (b) *they* might help me. I find (c) *them* (3) boring, because most novels are really silly love stories.

Personally, I think the Internet is very (4) useful **and** so I use (d) *it* all the time both at college and at home. I have had a computer for ten years **and** (e) *the one* I have at the moment is an Apple Mac. (f) *It* is particularly (5) useful for finding information quickly **and** for keeping in touch with friends via email. I also use (g) *it* to talk to people in chat rooms. People in chat rooms are really (6) interesting **and** I have met many friends (h) *there*. (i) *They* give me a chance to practise my English which I find really (7) interesting. All the information I need I can find on the Internet. Some people say that it is hard to read from a screen **but** I don't have this problem.

So in conclusion, I think the Internet is a good thing.

6

Sample answer

Although it is true to say that the Internet is expanding at an amazing rate, and much faster than anyone could have predicted, my feeling is that books will never disappear completely. I may be proved wrong, but I believe there will always be a place for books in the world.

Why do I think this? Well, I think we need to first of all look at the reasons we have books. They give us information, and the type of information they give us is perhaps the key to why they will always be with us. We are not talking here about news or weather. That can be obtained from the Internet or the TV and radio. We are also not talking about facts – we obtain those also from the Internet. So, what do we use books for? Well, personally, I read books for relaxation and for pleasure. You might say that I could read a book on the Internet instead, but I do not feel it would be quite the same thing.

The Internet has many uses, but I think it is very hard to imagine lying curled up on the sofa reading a computer screen for pleasure. Books are also easy to transport, generally light to carry, inexpensive and can be read anywhere. The same cannot be said about computers, although there may come a time when an easily portable computer with an easy-to-read screen becomes available.

Until that time, I firmly believe that books will not be replaced by the Internet.

(254 words)

Units 13–16 Revision

SB pages 110–111

The aim of this revision unit is to focus on the language covered in units 13–16. Exercises 2–5 can be done as a test in class or for homework.

Topic review

1 The aim of this section is to encourage students to speak, using the grammar and vocabulary they have learned in the previous four units. They should comment on the statements and expand their answers as much as possible. This is useful practice, because in the Speaking Module, they also need to give opinions and expand on what they say.

> **Suggested answers**
> 1 I suppose some people are better than others at considering alternatives and making the best decision. On the other hand, they might just be better at making the most of what happens after they've made the decision.
> 2 I think there are some areas where young children should choose, for example in what they eat. But I don't think they should choose in areas that they don't know much about, like what school to go to.
> 3 Some people think that something is going to taste bad if it's an unusual colour. But I think it makes food more interesting.
> 4 I try not to buy things that I don't need, but occasionally I see something that's so attractive that I must buy it, and the colour is part of what makes it look good.
> 5 Fashions change quite often, especially in clothing, and I agree that we tend to like what lots of people are wearing. If you see lots of people dressed in green, for example, it seems normal, and you start wanting to do the same.
> 6 People can use the same body language or gestures to mean different things. For example, you can smile because you're pleased to see someone, or because you want to seem friendly when you aren't. And that can happen within the same culture. So you can't always be sure what someone is thinking, whether they're from the same culture as you or another one.
> 7 I agree that it's important to be polite wherever you are, otherwise people might think you're rude or unfriendly when you aren't. And that could spoil your holiday, your business trip or whatever.
> 8 Yes, I believe it's important to learn about other countries and their customs, both so you're prepared for the fact that if you go abroad, things might be different, and also because it makes you realise that the way you do things in your own culture isn't the only way.
> 9 These days, people expect to be able to communicate very quickly, and I doubt if many letters will still be written in a few years' time. But it's important to be able to make your message clear in an email or text message. A lot of people write them very quickly without thinking.

> 10 Yes, I expect books and magazines will disappear fairly soon, because they'll be too expensive to print for the small number of people who want them. Instead, there'll be small, portable electronic devices, so that people can read whatever they want, wherever they are.

Grammar

2

> **Answers**
> 1 to grow   2 getting   3 being   4 worrying   5 to choose
> 6 to buy   7 to say   8 to be   9 to make
> 10 complaining

3

> **Answers**
> 1 catches   2 would/'d have been   3 pay   4 don't/won't mind   5 was/were (*could be* is also possible)   6 are/'re
> 7 don't have   8 would be   9 had been   10 keeps

4 The picture shows someone wearing clothing dyed with cochineal.

> **Answers**
> 1 used   2 Obtained   3 sucking   4 indicating   5 lighting
> 6 building   7 Realising   8 dyed

Vocabulary

5 In this exercise, students need to use the language that's appropriate to Task 1 in the Academic Writing Module. The description is a little longer than is required in the test.

> **Answers**
> 1 slide   2 picked up   3 levelled off   4 declining   5 was fairly steady   6 rose   7 fell   8 made steady progress
> 9 declined

Progress Test 4

Listening

Questions 1–6

How does the speaker describe the following pieces of advice?

A definitely a good idea
B definitely a bad idea
C probably a bad idea

1 Contact publishers directly.

2 Ask an author to recommend an agent.

3 Contact specialist agents.

4 Analyse books you don't like.

5 Try to write your first draft in a good style.

6 Keep your historical research to a minimum.

Questions 7–10

Complete the notes below.

*Write **NO MORE THAN ONE WORD** for each answer.*

> What helps to get a novel or short story published?
>
> • making the writer's **7** .... clear to readers
>
> • having enough **8** .... to remove irrelevant information
>
> • structuring the work to give readers a feeling of **9** ....
>
> • telling the story at a suitable **10** ....

Reading

Lapis lazuli

A Lapis lazuli is a type of rock whose name means 'stone of azure' – *lapis* meaning 'stone' in Latin. The second part of the name, *lazuli*, comes from the Persian word *lazhward*. This was originally a place name, but soon came to mean 'blue' because of its association with the stone. The English word *azure* also comes from this source.

B Lapis lazuli has had a long history. The ancient royal Sumerian tombs of Ur, located near the Euphrates River in lower Iraq, contained more than 6,000 beautifully executed lapis-lazuli statuettes of birds, deer and rodents, as well as dishes used to contain temple incense and possibly food and beads. Later, Egyptian burial sites dating from over 5,000 years ago were found to contain many lapis-lazuli jewellery items. Powdered lapis was favoured by Egyptian ladies as a cosmetic eye shadow. It was also once believed that lapis lazuli had medicinal properties. It was generally ground down, mixed with milk and applied as a dressing for boils and ulcers.

C Lapis lazuli is a rock and not a mineral because it is made up from various other minerals. (A true mineral has only one constituent.) The main component of the rock is lazurite, along with calcite, sodalite and pyrite. The most prized lapis lazuli is a dark, nearly blackish blue. However, pyrite, a commonly associated mineral, is often liberally sprinkled throughout the lazurite to create a striking combination of rich blue and brassy gold, and this is also much prized. Unfortunately, lazurite occurs most frequently in lighter shades, commonly mixed with streaks of calcite. Although attractive, this material is less desirable and consequently fetches a lower price. Often a stone with white calcite streaks is stained blue to improve the colour and increase the price, but this dye will fade with time.

D Although lapis lazuli can be found in Pakistan, in the Andes Mountains of Chile and around Lake Baikal in Russia, the finest examples have traditionally come from the Badakshan area of Afghanistan. This source of lapis may be the oldest continually worked set of mines in the world, the same mines operating today having supplied the pharaohs of ancient Egypt. The lapis is mined on the inhospitably steep sides of a long, narrow valley, sometimes only 200 metres wide and backed by jagged peaks that rise above 6,000 metres. Sparsely populated and covered with snow for much of the year, the barren region is inhabited by wild boar and wolves. The summer sun is scorching, but temperatures drop below freezing at night. Lazurite gem deposits occur in veins of black and white marble hundreds of metres thick. The gem veins, seldom exceeding 10 metres in length, lie in snow-white calcite.

E Ground to a powder and processed to remove impurities, lapis lazuli forms the pigment ultramarine. There is evidence of it being used as a pigment from as early as the sixth and seventh centuries AD from cave paintings found in Afghanistan. It has also been found in some tenth- and eleventh-century Chinese and Indian paintings. However, it is European painters who seem to have made most use of the material. Many of the blues, from medieval illuminated manuscripts to Renaissance panels, were derived from lapis lazuli. This clear, bright blue, which was one of the few blues available to painters before the 19th century, cost a princely sum. Only the highest quality of lapis with a high percentage of lazurite and few impurities was good enough to produce a rich ultramarine. The colour, however, could only be maintained within water solutions, gum Arabic and tempera (painting using egg as a medium for binding the pigment). However, as tempera painting was superseded by oil paint during the 15th century, painters found that the brilliance of ultramarine was greatly diminished when it was ground in oil and this, along with its cost, led to a steady decline in its usage. Since the synthetic version of ultramarine was discovered in the 19th century, production and use of the natural variety has almost ceased in painting.

F Lapis lazuli is still a very popular material today. It is made into a variety of hand-crafted objects such as carvings, spheres, beads, large gemstones and other fashionable items.

Questions 1–7

The passage has six paragraphs labelled **A–F**.

Which paragraph contains the following information? **NB** *You may use any letter more than once.*

1   a method of deceiving potential customers
2   why the removal of lapis lazuli from the ground is difficult
3   an example of the derivation of a word
4   a claim that lapis lazuli has not lost its appeal
5   reference to a claim that lapis lazuli could have health benefits
6   disadvantages of using lapis lazuli
7   an account of the constituent parts of lapis lazuli

Questions 8–13

Do the following statements agree with the information given in the passage? Write

TRUE	*if the statement agrees with the information*
FALSE	*if the statement contradicts the information*
NOT GIVEN	*if there is no information on this*

8   In ancient times, only royalty were allowed to wear lapis lazuli.
9   Lapis-lazuli mines are among the most ancient.
10 Lapis lazuli needs to be totally pure to be of value.
11 The quality of the lapis lazuli mined in other parts of the world is inferior to that of Afghanistan.
12 Ultramarine was a very expensive colour.
13 Most artists in the Renaissance painted with tempera.

Questions 14–16

Choose **THREE** letters **A–G**.

The list below gives some ways of using lapis lazuli.

*Which **THREE** ways are mentioned by the writer of the text?*

A   as make-up
B   as a charm against harmful influences
C   as an adornment
D   as a container
E   as a food colouring
F   as a modern painting ingredient
G   as a royal crown

Writing

Writing Task 2 (AC)

You should spend about 40 minutes on this task.

Write about the following topic:

> *Society today has more problems with the behaviour of teenagers than in the past.*
>
> *What do you think are the causes of this?*
>
> *What solutions can you suggest?*

Give reasons for your answer and include any relevant examples from your own knowledge or experience.

Write at least 250 words.

Progress Test 4 Key

Listening

1 C 2 B 3 A 4 A 5 B 6 A
7 enjoyment 8 confidence 9 suspense 10 pace

Recording script

You will hear a tutor talking to students in a creative writing class. First, you have some time to look at questions 1 to 6.

Now listen carefully and answer questions 1 to 6.

Now, you're probably all really keen to get your short stories or novels published. Well, take it from me, you're going to need plenty of luck, hard work and, above all, determination.

Let's assume for the moment that you've written your work. How do you set about getting it published? One way is to send it to a publisher. This sometimes works out OK, but publishing contracts are complicated, so you might later find that you've agreed to do something you weren't expecting. And often manuscripts sent directly to publishers don't get read at all, so it may not be worth doing.

Usually the best route to getting your book into the bookstores is to find yourself an agent. It's their job to get writers published, and they're in a better position to negotiate with publishers than you are. There are several specialist journals where you can find agents. Some people write to an author whose work they like, asking him or her to recommend an agent. But I'd strongly advise against it: so many people contact successful authors that it places unreasonable demands on them. One point to remember when you're contacting agents, though, is to send your work to someone who specialises in fiction. They're likely to know far more about what needs to be done than an agent who handles both fiction and non-fiction.

OK, now let's go back to the writing process itself, and I'll give you two or three pointers to think about. A really effective tool is to analyse published books – not just ones you admire, but also ones you don't. Break them down, paragraph by paragraph, working out the structure; where there's action, dialogue, background information and so on. Doing that helped me enormously with writing my own novels.

Another point to consider is the balance between story and style. Making the story work is the most difficult part of the process, so concentrate on that first. If you're thinking about style at the same time, you'll make it even harder to structure the story. Afterwards, it won't take all that long to rewrite your work and improve the style. Not every writer would agree, but that's what I think works best.

And thirdly, if your novel is set in the past, you'll need to do some historical research – having 19th-century characters using mobile phones isn't a good idea! But you risk spending the rest of your life doing research and never writing your novel. Remember, you aren't trying to educate your readers about life at that time – just aim to make sure nothing is too obviously wrong.

****

Before you hear the rest of the talk, you have some time to look at questions 7 to 10.

Now listen and answer questions 7 to 10.

Right, now I'll say a few words about what's likely to make a publisher interested in your novel or short story. Well, first and foremost, is the writer getting enjoyment from writing and putting that across to the readers? Most people think a writer needs to show freshness and originality, but let's face it, a lot of what's published isn't that different from other books.

Another important factor is keeping the amount of background detail to what's actually required. Writers need confidence, so they can say 'This or that isn't necessary. I'll cut it out.' An over-anxious approach can lead to writing that's too long and boring.

Then you must make sure the reader is presented with a question very early on, such as 'How will this character solve that problem?' The writing must keep the readers in suspense. That way, they keep reading, to discover what happens next and how that question is answered. If the solution to the problem is given in chapter five, why bother to carry on reading?

And you must keep your story moving quite fast. There's a danger of spending too long creating the world that the characters inhabit, when what you need is action. Of course, the pace shouldn't be the same all the way through – that would become monotonous – but you don't want your readers to lose interest.

Reading

1 C *Often a stone with white calcite streaks is stained blue to improve the colour and increase the price*

2 D *The lapis is mined on the inhospitably steep sides of a long, narrow valley ... freezing at night.*

3 A *The English word* azure *also comes from this source.*

4 F *Lapis lazuli is still a very popular material today.*

5 B *lapis lazuli had medicinal properties. It ... ulcers.*

6 E *the brilliance of ultramarine was greatly diminished when it was ... decline in its usage.*

7 C *The main component of the rock is lazurite, along with ... pyrite.*

8 NOT GIVEN Paragraph B talks about the Sumerian royal tombs containing beads, but also about the Egyptians wearing lapis-lazuli jewellery; it doesn't specify if the Egyptians were royal or not.

9 TRUE *may be the oldest continually worked set of mines in the world* (paragraph D)

10 FALSE *pyrite, a commonly associated mineral ... is also much prized.* (paragraph C)

11 TRUE *the finest examples have traditionally come from the Badakshan area of Afghanistan* (paragraph D)

12 TRUE *This clear, bright blue ... cost a princely sum.* (paragraph E)

13 NOT GIVEN Paragraph E talks about artists painting with tempera, but doesn't actually say how many of them did.

14, 15, 16 A, C, D (in any order)
   A *as a cosmetic eye shadow* (paragraph B)
   C *beads* (paragraph B), *jewellery items* (paragraph B), *beads* (paragraph F)
   D *dishes* (paragraph B)

Writing

Sample answer

Teenagers have always had a 'bad press', but perhaps today their reputation for wild behaviour has more basis in fact. However, I believe that society is not helping to make the situation better. In fact, it is making it worse.

In the past, children rarely had a childhood in the sense that they do today. Unless they were very rich, children were sent out into the fields and factories to work. They were then married at a young age – even as young as 14 – and as a result they had no free time to create problems for society.

Today, children in the developed world enjoy a lengthy childhood and then have no responsibilities until they reach their early 20s. Teenagers live at home, are looked after by their parents and have all their needs seen to. In my country, teenagers often have money to spend. They spend their 'pocket money', which can be quite substantial, on clothes, CDs and going out. However, some of them also have enough money for drugs and alcohol, and both of these substances have helped make a minor problem that much worse.

To find a solution to the problem of teenagers is not easy. We cannot insist they marry young or even send them to work in the fields. What we can do, though, is to make them realise they have a sense of responsibility to society and to limit the amount of money they have to spend. More emphasis on how to be a good citizen and on doing more sport would also help, along with a little more understanding on the part of society.

(271 words)

17 The body clock

<table>
<tr><td colspan="2">Unit topic   Sleep and the body</td></tr>
<tr><td>17.1
Test skills</td><td>Speaking Part 1
Reading (AC): True / False / Not
   given
Sentence completion</td></tr>
<tr><td>Vocabulary</td><td>Collocations with time</td></tr>
<tr><td>17.2
Test skills</td><td>Listening: Multiple choice
          Short-answer
          questions
Writing extra (AC):
  Task 2: Considering both sides of
  the argument</td></tr>
<tr><td>Grammar</td><td>Modal verbs: obligation, lack of
  obligation and prohibition</td></tr>
<tr><td colspan="2">Workbook contents</td></tr>
<tr><td>1, 2, 3, 4</td><td>Vocabulary</td></tr>
<tr><td>5, 6</td><td>Grammar: Modals: obligation,
  lack of obligation and prohibition</td></tr>
</table>

17.1 SB pages 112–113

1 Ask students to work through the exercise in pairs. They should try to incorporate some of the phrases from the Useful language box in their answers.

Possible answers
- If I could choose, I'd get up about 10.30.
- It depends – sometimes I'm really chatty and other times I can be terribly grumpy.
- I usually get up about 7.30 in the week, but at weekends it varies – it depends on what I need to do that day. I go to bed about ten in the week and often at weekends, too. I can never get enough sleep.
- I never go shopping late at night – what a waste of time!
- Yes, I think my country is so keen on shopping that people want to do it any time of the day or night. But you could argue that for some people it's really necessary, so why not?

2 The passage is about 650 words long and should take about two-and-a-half minutes to read through. Ask the class to read through the passage to find the answers to 1 and 2 and to get a general idea of what the text is about.

Answers
1 to regulate our waking and sleeping
2 Larks are alert in the morning; owls are alert in the evening.

Background information
Larks and owls are species of birds.

3 Students should read through the passage again to answer questions 1–8. The questions are in the order of the text.

Answers

1	NOT GIVEN	Paragraph 1 tells us what types of places are open at night, but there is no mention of demand.
2	NOT GIVEN	Paragraph 2 tells us that people maintain a natural rhythm if they are kept in isolation, but there is no mention of reacting to day or night – in fact, if people are in isolation, they don't know whether it is day or night.
3	FALSE	*is likely to cause ourselves both physical and pyschological damage (lines 18–19)*
4	TRUE	*Our prehistoric ancestors would have needed their biological clock to get them out hunting during the day and probably in bed around nightfall (lines 32–34)*
5	FALSE	*owls may pay a price for this in terms of health problems (lines 47–48)*
6	D	*needed their biological clock to get them out hunting during the day (lines 32–33)*
7	B	*Larks are 'morning people' – communicative from the time their eyes open (lines 44–45)*
8	E	*The fatigue ... is similar to that of jet lag (lines 54–56)*

Extension activity

The passage talks about *our prehistoric ancestors*. These are people who lived in 'pre-history'; that is, 'before' history. Put the following prefixes up on the board and ask the class to first of all decide what the prefix means and secondly, for homework, to find examples of words using these prefixes. Answers in brackets.

ante-	(before or in front of: *antenatal* = before birth)
anti-	(against: *anti-freeze* = to stop freezing)
bi-	(two: *bilingual* = able to speak two languages)
ex-	(from before: *ex-colleague* = former colleague)
hyper-	(too much: *hypersensitive* = too sensitive)
mega-	(extremely: *mega-rich* = very, very rich (informal))
micro-	(very small: *microclimate* = climate in a small area)
mono-	(one: *monolingual* = speaking one language)
poly-	(many: *polygamy* = having many wives)
post-	(after: *postgraduate* = after graduating)
semi-	(half: *semi-detached house* = attached to another house on one side)
sub-	(under: *sub-zero* = below zero)
trans-	(across: *transatlantic* = across the Atlantic)
ultra-	(extremely: *ultramodern* = very modern)

4 There are many collocations with *time* in English, and students often confuse them. Make sure that students understand that they can use each expression more than once.

Answers
1 run out of **2** waste/spend **3** give **4** Take
5 spent/wasted **6** passed **7** find **8** took **9** killed
10 run out of

---

5 The aim of this exercise is to get students to use the collocations they have learnt in the previous exercise. Try to get students to expand their answers and not just answer 'yes' or 'no'. Some collocations are very similar, and the difference between them may depend on the structure only, e.g. *pass the time*, but *kill time*; both have the idea of having to do something to make the time go faster/to fill the time.

Possible answers
1 I usually pass the time reading.
2 I think watching TV, especially football, is a complete waste of time. Also, playing snooker and knitting.
3 Yes, I usually set aside an hour or two every evening for my homework. That usually gives me enough time.
4 Yes, I read a newspaper every day – I usually spend about 20 minutes reading it at lunchtime.
5 Very often. I think most people run out of time because they spend too much time on the first exercise and don't give themselves enough time to do the last one.
6 I would spend my time travelling the world.

17.2 SB pages 114–115

1 The pictures are of people who often have to work at night: a security guard, a pilot, a fisherman and a nurse. Encourage students to talk about these jobs and find out whether they would enjoy working the nightshift.

Possible answers
I wouldn't mind doing the nightshift if it was for a long period – for example, for a month. What I wouldn't like is to work two nights, then work three days, as I would find that very disorientating.

Advantages of working the nightshift
Being paid more
Fewer problems travelling to work
Quieter at work
Fewer interruptions

Disadvantages of working the nightshift
No social life
Hard to get a proper sleep pattern
A feeling of being sidelined – not being at the centre of things
Hard to go shopping, have your hair cut, etc.

---

2 Give students time to read through the questions and point out the different tasks; questions 1 and 2 are multiple choice; 3–5 require a short answer and 6–8 also

require a short answer. Play the recording once only. You will hear the recording for questions 1–5 and then for questions 6–8.

Answers (see underlined text in script)
1 A **2** B **3** wear/wearing dark glasses **4** take a bath
5 unplug the telephone **6** 20 minutes
7 operate machinery **8** 4 a.m.

Recording script

Questions 1–5

Do you work at times other than the usual 'nine-to-five' business day? If so, you are not alone – there are millions of nightshift workers across the world who don't have to travel to work in the rush hour. Nightshift workers perform critical functions in hospitals, on police forces and as emergency personnel, and in the transportation and manufacturing industries. In addition, they're meeting the demand for 'round-the-clock' service in an age of global interaction. In the USA, for example, more than 22 million people work nightshifts, and that number is growing by 3% each year.

However, nightshift workers still need to get a reasonable amount of sleep. When shifts fall during the night (11 p.m. to 7 a.m.), the worker is fighting the natural wake–sleep pattern. It will be hard for them to stay alert at night and <u>harder for them to get to sleep and stay asleep during the day than it is for daytime workers.</u> Night workers get less sleep than daytime workers do, and the sleep is less restful. Sleep is more than just 'beauty rest' for the body; it helps restore and rejuvenate the brain and organ systems so that they function properly. Chronic lack of sleep harms a person's health, on-the-job safety, task performance, memory and mood.

For humans, the desire to sleep is strongest between midnight and six a.m. <u>Many people are alert in the morning, with a natural dip in the mid-afternoon.</u> It's not surprising that ten to 20% of nightshift workers report falling asleep on the job, usually during the second half of the shift. That's why people who work all night may find it difficult to sleep for part of the day, even though they're tired.

If you're a night worker, there are several steps you can take to help you fall asleep and stay asleep. First of all, <u>wear dark glasses.</u> If you put these on just before leaving work, it can help enormously. They'll get the eyes gradually used to the dark and make it easier to fall asleep when you get into bed. In addition, <u>take a bath</u> just before getting into bed. This will soothe and relax you, preparing your body for sleep. Last but not least, <u>unplug the telephone</u> – there's nothing worse than having your much-needed sleep interrupted by a casual caller.

****

Questions 6–8

Nightshift workers face special problems in trying to maintain family relationships and social and community ties because they have to work anti-social hours. It becomes difficult to balance work, sleep and personal time. The need to sleep during the day could mean nightshift workers have to miss out on family activities. But this doesn't have to be the case – with a bit of effort, it should be possible to reschedule some of them.

But nightshift workers must try to have a regular sleep schedule, even on weekends. However, if they can't get enough sleep or feel drowsy, <u>naps can also be helpful. Twenty minutes is about right.</u> Naps shorter than that – perhaps five minutes – are not really long enough. Some people feel groggy or sleepier after a nap. These feelings usually go away within ten minutes, while the benefits of the nap may last for many hours.

Nightshift workers should try to have someone to work with – someone they can chat to while they're working. This work-buddy can help to keep them alert. Whatever they do, they mustn't operate machinery when feeling sleepy. To help guard against this, they should exercise during breaks and eat three normal meals. Finally, most nightshift workers find that the worst time is the period around 4 a.m. This is a natural low for all humans, and workers especially should be aware of it.

If you want to know more about how to handle working on the nightshift, then take a …

3 Ask the class to match the sentences (1–6) with the explanations (a–f). For this exercise, some knowledge of modals for obligation is assumed, i.e. that students are familiar with the form and basic use of *must* and *have to*.

> **Answers**
> 1 c   2 e   3 f   4 a   5 b   6 d

4 The aim of this exercise is to establish the difference between *have to* and *must*. Both *must* and *have to* are used in British English to talk about obligation. In the US, *have to* is more common. Refer students to the Grammar folder if they are having difficulty.

> **Answers**
> 1 That's what the rules say; someone else has the authority – strong obligation coming from outside, from laws, regulations and other people's orders. We also say *have got to*.
> 2 Obligation coming from the speaker.
> 3 It is unnecessary.
> 4 It is not allowed.

5 This exercise can be done in class or given for homework.

> **Answers**
> 1 You mustn't smoke in the factory.
> 2 You don't have to leave home early to beat the rush hour now.
> 3 We have to begin the nightshift at 9.30.
> 4 All workers must wear a hard hat on site.
> 5 'You mustn't make personal calls,' said the manager to the staff.
> 6 I don't have to get up tomorrow.
> 7 When I work nights, I have to do my shopping on the Internet.
> 8 I don't have to go to the bank in the daytime as I can ring them at any time now.

Extension activity

Ask students to write a list of the rules of your college for new students. They should incorporate both the grammar and vocabulary from this unit in their list.

6

> **Sample answer**
> (This is slightly longer than required. You are not penalised for a slightly longer answer, only for too short an answer.)
>
> There is no doubt that today people are becoming accustomed to being able to access services like banks and shops at all hours of the day and night. Personally, I am not sure that we can say categorically that this has a negative effect on society. I believe that there are definite advantages to living in a 24-hour society.
>
> In the past in my country, most people worked from nine to five, from Monday to Friday, and had the weekend free for leisure. Sunday was a total day of rest, and all the shops and businesses were closed. However, today we have a situation where every day is the same. This change has come about because of the need for greater production in industry and also from consumer demand.
>
> One of the main arguments in favour of 24-hour opening is that people today work hard and want to play hard. They have no time to shop when they are at work and need to be able to buy clothes, have their hair cut and so on when they are free. The labour market is also more flexible today than in the past, and there are more people willing to work unsocial hours. In addition, the Internet has enabled people to shop and bank when businesses are normally closed. I often shop online after midnight when I have difficulty sleeping and I do not think I am unusual in this.
>
> To conclude, I believe that times have changed and that we have to accept that life goes on 24 hours a day, not just 12. This does not necessarily mean that we become less productive – in fact, I believe it means we can become more productive and we have more control over both our working and social lives.
>
> (295 words)

Test folder 9

SB pages 116–117
Speaking

Make sure students fully understand the advice. Ask them to read what is said about Part 1.

1 Ask students to read the rubric and comments A–F. Play the recording as they choose an option for each answer.

> **Answers**
> 1 C 2 A 3 F 4 E 5 B

Recording script

1 A Do you work or are you studying?
 B I work in a restaurant. Um, I used to work in an office, but when I came to this country, it was easier to get a job in a restaurant. I enjoy it quite a lot, although you have to work long hours and the pay isn't very good. Now I'm thinking about going into restaurant management as a career.
2 A How you do spend your free time?
 B Swimming.
3 A How long have you been studying English?
 B Most people in my country start learning English quite early at school, when they are six or seven.
4 A Why do foreign tourists visit your country?
 B I don't really know, but maybe some are interested in culture, and others come to go shopping.
5 A What is your favourite type of food?
 B (*long pause*) I like pizzas, but I prefer traditional food from my own country.

2 Ask students to discuss suitable answers with a partner, then to ask and answer the questions together.

> **Possible answers**
> 1 I come from Beijing, which is the capital. It's in the north-east of the country.
> 2 There are plenty of opportunities for certain types of work, for instance in the construction industry.
> 3 Luckily I've never needed to work at night, but just before exams I sometimes study until midnight, or even later.
> 4 Often night work is well paid, and that attracts people who need the money. Others work at night to fit in with family commitments.
> 5 I think I'd get very sleepy about two or three o'clock in the morning. I wouldn't like to try working at night.

3 Ask students to read what is said about Part 2 and then to read the rubric and task card for exercise 3. Ask them to make notes about why it is, or isn't, a good talk, as you play the recording.

> **Possible answer**
> It is a good answer, because it focuses on the topic, uses a range of grammatical structures and vocabulary, there is a brief introduction and conclusion, and the speaker varies the intonation, speed and volume to sound interesting. There are a few mistakes, but they don't make it difficult to understand what is said. The candidate is Chinese and has lived in Britain for a number of years.

Recording script

A I'd like you to describe an occasion when you did something that you don't normally do.
B Yeah, let me tell you an experience I will never forget. Two years ago, when I went back to see my parents in China and, um – you know, in the Chinese culture, we shake hands, we say hello, but we never, er, kiss each other or even hug each other – even between parents and children. But because I have been living in this country for so long and get used to the way people, you know, show their affection and friendliness to each other. And I haven't seen my mum for a long time, so, um, when I saw my mother, she was greeting me from the door, I went over and gave her a big hug, and she was kind of very … nervous and … and a bit embarrassed, you know, she just … she behaved somewhat differently than normal and she didn't know what to say. But I know at that moment she would feel very warm, you know, from a daughter, a hug from the daughter. And, um, so that is something that I wouldn't normally do or I have never … I had never done before then.
A Have you done it again since then?
B Yes, I did, when my mother came to visit me this summer.
A Do you think other people should have a similar experience?
B I think they should. I think the Chinese and the British should learn from each other for the good things they do.

4 Ask students to read the card and to spend no more than two minutes planning a talk. Remind them only to write key words or brief notes. Ask them to form pairs, and to take turns to give the talk to each other.

Elicit short answers to the two 'rounding-off' questions.

> **Possible answers**
> • I prefer surprises, because if you know what's going to happen, you may be disappointed.
> • It's best if people only have three or four special occasions a year. Otherwise they stop being special.

5 Ask students to read what is said about Part 3 and then to read questions 1–3 in exercise 5. Make sure they understand, then play the recording so that they can assess the candidate's answer.

> **Possible answer**
> These are excellent responses to the questions, giving examples and using a range of structures and vocabulary. When the candidate didn't understand question 3, she asked the examiner to repeat it, and was then able to answer. It is all right to do this in the Speaking Module.

Recording script

A Could you describe how society can benefit from people working at night?

B Yes, I think talking about working at night, I can think of policemen as a necessity for security for the society, and also as, er, cab drivers for people to transport, er, travel from one place to another, and all these are necessary because without them, life would be more difficult.

A Can you compare going to the cinema or other entertainments at night with going to the same entertainments by day?

B I think it's the atmosphere that is different, saying if you are going to a concert or cinema at night, and then the lights, the atmosphere, you know, and sometimes you have the music. It just make you feel, well, brilliant, you know. After a long day's work, it's relaxing, it's entertaining, it's fun.

A What would you recommend people to do if they have to work at night?

B Can you repeat that question, please? Sorry, I didn't quite catch …

A What would you recommend people to do if they have to work at night?

B First, I would recommend that they get enough sleep, so that they can maintain a high level of energy at night, to achieve the best performance when they do what they do.

A Thank you.

Ask students to read questions 4–8 and to discuss possible answers in small groups.

> **Possible answers**
> **4** Nowadays, people are far more likely to accept that night work is essential, because we want all sorts of things to be available at night – from hospitals to supermarkets.
> **5** In some families, the parents go out to work at different times, so that there's always one of them available to look after the children. But it's difficult for them to do things together as a family.
> **6** In a 24/7 society, buses and trains need to operate all night. Without them, it would be very difficult for people to get to work, to provide the services we demand.
> **7** It's difficult to tell, but on the whole I think we're more likely to move back towards working during daylight hours, except for emergency services.
> **8** People could be offered higher salaries for working at night, or could work fewer hours for the same salary.

18 The tourist boom

Unit topic	Travel and tourism

18.1	
Test skills	Speaking Part 1
	Listening: Summary completion
	Table completion
	Writing extra (AC):
	Task 1: Comparing and contrasting
Pronunciation	Pronouns as objects of phrasal verbs
Vocabulary	Collocations related to travel
18.2	
Test skills	Writing extra (GT):
	Task 1: Letter of complaint
	Speaking Part 2
Grammar	Phrasal verbs
Workbook contents	
1, 2	Reading
3, 4	Vocabulary
5	Grammar: phrasal verbs

18.1 SB pages 118–119

1 The pictures are of backpackers, a cruise ship off a tropical beach, Bondi beach in Australia, tourists in Prague and Guatemala, and Mount Everest in the Himalayas. Encourage the class to discuss the pictures and monitor to provide additional vocabulary, if needed. Then go on to the paired discussion.

Possible answers
- I think there are many advantages to getting away from the daily routine. You see new people and places, and this helps to put life into some sort of perspective.
- Workers in my country usually get about four weeks' holiday a year.
- A good tourist is someone who leaves nothing behind them – no litter especially.

2 The recording is similar to a Part 4 Listening in the test. Give the class time to read through all the questions and then play the recording once only.

Answers (see underlined text in script)
1 technology 2 wealth 3 developed 4 skiing
5 art galleries 6 (the) railway 7 (the) Internet
8 literature/writers 9 garlic 10 drama (festival)

Recording script

Questions 1–5

Travel and tourism is the largest industry in the world, but calculating its economic impact is quite difficult. The one thing everybody can agree on, though, is that it's huge.

There are two things which have influenced the growth of tourism. These are firstly social factors and secondly, technology and the way it's developed. Let's consider the social factors first of all. Demand for tourism is determined mainly by the amount of wealth a country has, which is why countries such as Japan, Australia, the USA and western European countries have contributed most in terms of tourist numbers in the past. However, growing wealth in developing countries will mean that demand for holidays abroad will take off there in the near future, boosting tourism enormously.

That said, the majority of tourists are still from what are called the 'developed nations'. However, studies show that their numbers will not rise much further in the next few decades because their populations are fairly stable. As a result, there'll be a growth in the number of retired people who'll have more time on their hands. This'll influence the kind of tourism wanted: fewer skiing holidays will be required, but there'll be an increase in the number of people wanting to visit art galleries.

****

Questions 6–10

Let's turn now to the second factor in the growth of tourism. The technology that sustains mass tourism today is the jet plane. Air travel has opened up the world. In 1970, scheduled planes carried 307 million passengers. Today, there are four times as many. In fact, cheaper and more efficient transport has been behind the development of mass tourism from its beginnings in Britain in the 19th century. The first package tours were arranged in 1841 by Thomas Cook, an entrepreneur whose company subsequently became one of the world's largest tour operators. In his day, it was the railway that allowed his business to flourish.

Today, technology is proving very important in other ways, as well as in transportation. In the past, people went to a travel agent to find and book their holiday. Now, many of these people are bypassing the high-street travel agent and booking their holidays themselves on the Internet. Airlines have been keen to encourage this direct approach, as it keeps down their costs, and increasingly high-street travel agents are finding their business is disappearing.

These days there may be more tourists to go round, but there is also more competition among destinations as cities, countries and continents all compete for tourist revenue. But becoming a tourist destination is not quite as straightforward as it might seem. For example, Ireland used to sell itself as a place to go to and enjoy the beautiful countryside. However, it soon discovered that it was attracting young student backpackers without any money. So how did Ireland set about increasing revenue from tourism? Well, the Irish Tourist Board came up with the idea of promoting the country's literature, using the names of writers such as Oscar Wilde and James Joyce to appeal to older, richer tourists who would spend their money in the hotels and restaurants of the country.

However, there are other ways of appealing to tourists. The US is dotted with places that claim to be the capital of something or other (sometimes things which may seem rather strange: Crystal City, for example, is the world capital of the vegetable broccoli, and then there's Gilroy – <u>famous for its garlic</u>). These towns are trading on a single gimmick to attract the tourists. Festivals are another way to bring them in – literary, food, art – they're all staged for one reason only: to attract tourist revenue. Many a town has sought to copy the success of Stratford, Ontario, which was transformed from a small, run-down blue-collar town to a bustling cultural centre by the efforts of Tom Patterson, who managed to persuade a British director to stage their first <u>drama festival</u> in 1953.

But then boosting a city through tourism is nothing new. In 18th-century England, Bath Spa became fashionable after the owners of the hot baths employed Beau Nash, the trendsetter of his day, to promote the city. I want to end the lecture there for today. Now, next week …

Photocopiable recording script activity
(**P** ⋯⟶ page 142)

Hand out the worksheets and make sure all students have access to an English-English dictionary. Ask students to find the following words/phrases in the recording script. They should try to work out the meaning of the words/phrases from the context first of all, and only then use a dictionary to check the meaning. (Answers are given in brackets.)

1 <u>boosting</u> tourism (increasing/improving tourism)
2 time <u>on their hands</u> (time to spend/waste)
3 <u>sustains</u> mass tourism (supports)
4 allowed his business to <u>flourish</u> (develop successfully)
5 are <u>bypassing</u> the high-street travel agent (avoiding/ignoring)
6 not quite as <u>straightforward</u> (simple)
7 a single <u>gimmick</u> (something to attract people's attention)
8 a small, <u>run-down blue-collar</u> town (shabby/poor town for workers)

3 Play the extract and point out the lack of stress on the pronoun. Then play each phrase and ask the class to repeat after each one. Students should then practise each phrase together in pairs.

Recording script

Example: Festivals are another way to bring them in.
1 give it up
2 cut them down
3 bring her round
4 work it out
5 pick him up
6 let me through
7 fill them in
8 ask us out

4

> **Possible answers**
> 1 I hate smoking. I'm going to give it up.
> 2 Those trees are rotten – cut them down.
> 3 The girl's fainted – bring her round.
> 4 The bill's very high – I'll use a calculator to work it out.
> 5 The baby's on the floor – you'd better pick him up.
> 6 It's an emergency – let me through.
> 7 Look at all these forms – I'll have to fill them in.
> 8 I hope those boys ask us out.

5 This exercise can be done in class or for homework.

> **Answers**
> 1 long-haul 2 sightseeing 3 tour 4 student 5 travel
> 6 far

6 Point out that the figures give the average amount of money spent by a British household on their holidays in one year (2002).

> **Suggested answer**
> Although all age groups spent much more on holidays abroad than on holidays at home, some age groups spent up to five times as much on overseas trips as they did on holidays in the UK. The biggest spenders on holidays abroad were the 50 to 64 age group. They spent nearly £800 per household, compared with almost £700 for the next age group (30- to 49-year-olds) and around £600 for the 65- to 74-year-olds. The lowest spending group on overseas holidays was the elderly, at less than £200 a year.
>
> When it came to holidays within the UK, the age group who spent the most was the 65- to 74-year-olds, followed by the 30 to 64 age group. In contrast, the under-30s spent the least on UK holidays – only around £100 a year.
>
> In conclusion, it would appear from the graph that spending on overseas holidays rose with age to reach a peak between the ages of 50 and 64, whereas for holidays in the UK, a peak was reached later, between the ages of 65 to 74.
> (179 words)

18.2 SB pages 120–121

1 Although students are usually familiar with phrasal verbs as vocabulary items, they often do not realise that phrasal verbs have their own grammar rules. Draw students' attention to the box with the explanation and check for understanding, then ask them to work through the exercise. It might be helpful to explain at this point the terminology of 'subject' and 'object', 'transitive' and 'intransitive'.

> **Answers**
> 1 came up with   2 take off (*intransitive, no object here*)
> 3 keeps down

2 Ask students to discuss the sentences in pairs and then go through their answers.

> **Answers**
> 1 made up her face (= used cosmetics; object)
> 2 passed out (= lost consciousness; no object)
> 3 make out her handwriting (= understand; object)
> 4 checked in (= registered; no object)

3 Read through the explanations together with students and then do the first sentence on the board so that they understand what they have to do.

> **Answers**
> 1 It was hard to make the cruise ship out through the fog.
>   It was hard to make it out through the fog.
> 2 A rival took the student travel company over when it went bankrupt.
>   A rival took it over when it went bankrupt.
> 3 Can I put Maria forward as a suitable replacement for Lisa?
>   Can I put her forward?
> 4 My father set the holiday company up in 1967.
>   My father set it up in 1967.
> 5 We'll have to take extra staff on when it's high season.
>   We'll have to take them on when it's high season.
> 6 Josh was asked to give free tickets out to the guests.
>   Josh was asked to give them out to the guests.

4 Explain to the class what a three-part phrasal verb is and ask them for some examples, such as *go down with, fall back on, get along with, catch up with, come up against, back out of,* etc. Ask students to work in pairs and to match the sentences (1–6) with the meanings (a–g). They should refer to the Grammar folder (SB page 143).

> **Answers**
> 0 f are looking forward to
> 1 e came up against
> 2 d went down with
> 3 a make up for
> 4 c woke up to
> 5 g put up with
> 6 b face up to

5 This task can be done in class or for homework.

> **Answers**
> 1 which 2 due/still 3 since 4 before 5 who
> 6 already 7 for 8 if

Extension activity
Students should work in small groups to identify something at the college that could be improved – for example, the canteen, the library or the computers. They should then work together to make notes for points to be made in a letter to the Principal. Each student then uses the notes to write a letter for homework.

6 Students can prepare this talk in class or at home. If possible, they should try to record themselves speaking so that they can analyse their mistakes. Notice that most of the talk is taken up by the final point, but that all the points are mentioned. A memorable trip could be a holiday, a business trip, a trip to an exhibition – it doesn't really matter, as long as the reason why it was memorable is given in detail.

> **Sample answer**
> When I was 15, I went on a skiing trip with the school. There were about 20 of us altogether, and we went to Engelberg in Switzerland. It was December and very cold. First of all, we went by coach to Dover and then we caught a ferry to Calais. It was very stormy when we crossed the English Channel, and I remember feeling very seasick. We then went by train to Basle and then by another train to Engelberg. It took ages – probably nearly 38 hours. It was a relief to get to Engelberg, where we stayed in a comfortable youth hostel. I shared a room with five other girls, and my best friend was on the bunk below mine.
>
> We spent the whole week learning to ski. I was not very good at this. I had never been on skis before and found it quite exhausting. Anyway, by the end of the week, we were all able to ski fairly well – or at least, get up the mountain and come down again without falling over too many times. Every morning, we had a ski lesson and we were free every afternoon. We generally spent this time shopping.
>
> So, what made this trip memorable? Well, lots of things really. My age at the time was an important factor. I felt very unsure of myself and unfortunately my ski outfit didn't help. I had had to borrow the outfit belonging to my aunt. She is nearly 1.9m tall, and I am only 1.6m. I also particularly remember the New Year's Eve party at the youth hostel. We all had a good time singing and dancing, and the next day was spent feeling too exhausted to ski.
>
> However, there were great things to remember about the holiday – the night we went on a midnight sleigh ride and saw people skiing down the mountainside carrying torches. Then the night we went to a restaurant and had fondue and the largest meringues I had ever seen for dessert. We all made great friends with the other people in the hostel, and in fact, one of my friends married a Swiss boy that she met on that holiday (they waited until she was 20 before getting married!).
>
> (373 words = approx. one and a half minutes)

Writing folder 9

SB pages 122–123
Task 2: Connecting ideas 2 – cause and result

The introduction gives examples of how the various cause and result connectors are used. Direct students to unit 3 of the Student's Book for further exercises on cause and result.

1 There are no correct answers to this exercise. Encourage students to use their imaginations. It might be a good idea to try to elicit reasons to put on the board for question 1.

Possible answers
1 The hotel has used so much water to keep the golf course green that this has led to a water shortage on the island.
2 A new airport has been built, and as a consequence people have found jobs there and now have more money to spend.
3 As a result of global warming, skiing centres are having to close early in the season because of lack of snow.
4 The badly trained staff and dirty kitchen have resulted in the hotel guests being ill.
5 We tipped the museum guide really well because he was so knowledgeable and helpful.
6 The art gallery is only opening in the morning as a consequence of staff shortages.

2

Suggested answers (more than one answer is possible)
1 There has been a rise in hotel construction over the past decade, which / and this has led to increased traffic congestion and water pollution.
A rise in hotel construction over the past decade has led to increased traffic congestion and water pollution.
2 An increase in housing development has resulted in a reduction in agricultural land.
3 Because of the rapid urbanisation in some Mediterranean islands, local culture has suffered.
Local culture has suffered because of the rapid urbanisation in some Mediterranean islands.
4 Growth in air transport connected to tourism has resulted in an increase in acid rain, global warming and local pollution.
5 The development of marinas has caused changes in sea currents and coastal erosion.
6 As a result of a large increase in tourists attracted to the area, the local people can find jobs more easily.
7 The hotel can't get enough staff. As a consequence, it can only open for a short season.
8 The visitors have complained about poor service. As a result, the management have decided to give the staff extra training.

3 Students should read through the text carefully before attempting the exercise. Only one answer is correct for each. The exercise tests a range of linking words.

Answers
1 B 2 A 3 C 4 A 5 A 6 B 7 C 8 A 9 A 10 B

4 This exercise can be done for homework or in class as practice for the test. This sample has been done in the form of a case history.

Sample answer
There is no denying that tourism today is big business. However, people are beginning to question whether tourism is, in fact, a good thing for a country or not. Does it cause more problems than it solves or is it the solution to all problems? I'm going to answer this question by looking at a place that I know well – Cornwall.

Cornwall is situated in the south-west of the United Kingdom. Its main industries for many years were tin mining and china-clay extraction, but both of these industries declined in the early 20th century. As a result, there has been unemployment and hardship. There is still some sea fishing, but less and less as time goes on.

Cornwall is an area of outstanding natural beauty and so attracts tourists in very large numbers. The council does everything it can to bring in the tourists in order to boost the economy. As a result, in the summer, the narrow roads are jammed with tourists, and the small towns are full of cafés and souvenir shops. Many people have also bought holiday homes in the county.

However, in the winter, the area takes on a different look. The towns are empty, and it is difficult for locals to buy ordinary goods, as most of the shops have been turned into souvenir shops. Many villages are ghost villages as the holiday cottages are empty. Consequently, community services such as schools and post offices close, and local people move out.

In conclusion, I think it is important for an area or country to think long and hard about tourism. Yes, it can be a force for good, but it needs to be managed. Without good management, tourism can cause serious problems.

(287 words)

Unit topic	Methods of transportation
19.1	
Test skills	Speaking Parts 2 and 3
	Listening: Sentence completion
	Note completion
	Labelling a diagram
Vocabulary	Transport and driving
Pronunciation	Rhythm
19.2	
Test skills	Speaking Part 3
	Reading (AC/GT):
	Flow-chart completion
	Sentence completion
Grammar	Unreal present and future
Workbook contents	
1, 2	Reading
3	Grammar: unreal present and future
4	Vocabulary

19.1 SB pages 124–125

Ask students what they think of the methods of transport in the pictures. The first shows a stretch limo (limousine) in New York, USA; the second a subway (underground) train in Washington DC, USA; and the third cyclists in Ho Chi Minh City, Vietnam.

> **Possible answers**
> Stretch limos are most often used by celebrities, and there may only be a few people inside. Like all cars, they damage the environment, but they're comfortable and don't get crowded.
> Trains do relatively little damage to the environment, but they can get crowded and they're restricted to fixed lines.
> Cycling is healthy and doesn't harm the environment, but it isn't very pleasant in the rain or in cold weather.

1   Ask two or three students to answer the two questions. (NB Discussing the questions in exercises 1, 2 and 3 will help students to develop their answers for both Parts 2 and 3 of the Speaking Module.)

> **Possible answers**
> I'd rather travel by train than bus or plane, because you can see the countryside and you can walk around if you want to.
> I cycle in fine weather, for short distances, but if I'm travelling a longer distance or the weather is bad, I go by car.

2   Ask students to form small groups, then to read the rubric and example, and think of ways of comparing two forms of transport.

> **Possible answers**
> Cars are far more convenient than buses, because you can go from your home to your destination without changing.
> Trains have a very good safety record – far better than cars.
> It's much cheaper to travel by bus than by car, if you consider all the costs, including buying the car and insurance.
> Planes are very harmful for the environment, because of the gases they emit – ships do much less damage.

3   Make sure students understand *congested*, then ask them to read the rubric and discuss the suggestions in small groups.

> **Possible answers**
> • **Banning non-essential traffic** would greatly reduce the number of vehicles, but would make it very difficult for people to get to where they need to go.
> • **Making driving very expensive** would encourage people to find cheaper alternatives, like cycling or public transport. On the other hand, it would be much more difficult for people living in rural areas and people without much money.
> • **Improving public transport** would reduce the number of private cars being used, but would need a lot of investment by the government, and people would probably object to paying higher taxes.
> • **Encouraging people to live near their work** would make life less stressful for people who commute to the same place every day. However, people won't want to move home every time they change jobs, if their new job is in a different area.

4   This exercise will help students to understand the listening passage. Ask them to read the rubric, explanations 1–3 and the words in the box, then to write each word under the appropriate explanation. Point out that the words in each set are similar in meaning, rather than being exact synonyms. Encourage them to use English-English dictionaries for words they don't know.

> **Answers**
> 1   crash, collision
> 2   elevation, levitation, suspension
> 3   disruption, disturbance, interruption

5   Elicit answers to the questions, and ask students to look at the picture and identify the features of a monorail.

6 Ask students to read the rubric and questions for 1–4, and to work out what kind of information is required.

Possible answers
1 a description of the tracks, e.g. *expensive, concrete*
2 things that can be transported, e.g. *goods, people, animals*
3 a year, probably in the 20th century
4 a number, to give a speed – probably about 200–300

Play the first part of the recording as students complete the sentences.

Answers (see underlined text in script)
1 elevated 2 passengers/people 3 1901 4 430

Ask students to read the notes for questions 5–9 and work out what kind of information is required. Point out that the heading 'Disadvantage' suggests that the previous notes are all advantages.

Possible answers
5 something bad, e.g. *a crash*
6 something that affects the environment negatively, e.g. *damage, emission of greenhouse gases*
7 an example of busy places, e.g. *town centres*
8 a good quality, e.g. *cheap, good value*
9 a possible disadvantage, e.g. *a track, a driver*

Play the second part of the recording as students complete the notes.

Answers (see underlined text in script)
5 (a) collision
6 pollution
7 shopping centres/centers (*shopping malls* is also acceptable, as it has the same meaning, but students should be encouraged to write the exact words they hear)
8 reliable
9 fixed route

Ask students to read the next part of the rubric, then look at the diagram of a monorail and notice what each number refers to. Ask them to try in pairs to label the diagram with words from the box, using an English-English dictionary to help them.

Without checking their answers, ask them to read the final part of the rubric, then play the third part of the recording as they check their answers, and write the actual words they hear (if they are different).

Answers (see underlined text in script)
When words used in the recording are different from those in the box, they are given in brackets.
10 pillar (*columns*)
11 beam
12 walkway (*for people to walk along it*)
13 vehicle (*car*)
14 operating unit (*operating units called bogies*)

Recording script

Questions 1–4

Tutor: OK, let's begin. First, Hannah is going to give a short introduction to monorails, then Stuart will talk about some of their advantages. Finally, Sharon will describe a particular type of monorail. Right, Hannah, over to you.

Hannah: Thanks. Well, monorails are a bit like railways, but there's just one rail, which is wider than each of the rails of a railway. Actually, 'mono' means 'one', which is how it got the name. Some monorails are at ground level or in subway tunnels, though in most cases the track is elevated. The vehicles are always wider than the track. In some types of monorail, the vehicles run *on* the track, like a normal train, and in other types they're suspended from it.
Some monorails are used to transport freight, but the majority carry passengers. A lot of them take visitors around amusement parks – there are plenty of these all round the world – and some form part of an urban transport system. Most of these are in Japan. Monorails were first constructed in the 19th century, though the one that's been in operation for longest dates from 1901. It's in the town of Wuppertal, in Germany. The vehicles are electrically operated, but a different kind of technology is used by one fairly new monorail. This went into service in 2004, between the city of Shanghai, in China, and its airport. Here, too, the energy source is electricity, but it's used to create a magnetic field which propels the train forwards. And while they're travelling, the trains are levitated, which means they're suspended about one centimetre above the track. This technology is called 'maglev', short for 'magnetic levitation'. Though the trains are capable of going at over 500 kilometres an hour, they regularly travel at up to 430. Right, that's a short introduction to monorails, and now it's Stuart's turn.
****

Questions 5–9

Stuart: Thanks, Hannah. I'm going to say something about the advantages of monorails.
The most important point is, of course, safety, and here monorails score very highly. Unlike trains, the design of monorails means that derailment is virtually impossible. And as they're normally quite separate from pedestrians and road traffic, there isn't any danger of a collision.
Nowadays, we're far more concerned about the environment than we used to be, and monorails have advantages over many other forms of transport. They're electrically operated, so they don't cause the pollution that cars and buses do, though admittedly some pollution is produced by the electricity generating stations.
The vehicles move much more quietly than trains, because they normally use rubber tyres. This allows stations to be situated in busy areas like shopping centres without creating disturbance.

From an economic point of view, monorails have a lot going for them. For one thing, construction of all the elements takes place off-site, so installation can be very fast and cause very little disruption. Once they're up and running, they're very cost-effective to operate. And as they're not held up by traffic jams or accidents, they're far more reliable than trams and especially buses. On the other hand, monorails have the same disadvantage as other railways, that they operate over a fixed route: the vehicles can't transfer to the road. So routes can't be changed without constructing a new monorail, and people have to get to and from the stations, so they may not be as convenient as buses or, in particular, private cars.

So those are some of the disadvantages, and now I'll hand over to Sharon.

****

Questions 10–14

Sharon: OK. Most monorail systems consist of a single track, with the vehicles moving either on top of the track or suspended from it, as Hannah said. One advantage is that the track is narrow, so it's particularly suitable for towns and other built-up areas. But it may mean that two tracks have to be constructed, one for travel in each direction.

An alternative is a single track which can be used for travel in both directions, and this diagram shows a monorail of this type. In this particular example, the track is elevated, so it's supported on a series of columns, made of concrete reinforced with steel. They stand about five metres above ground level and are generally positioned about 40 metres apart. The track itself consists of a series of horizontal concrete beams, each 25 metres long, and joined end to end. They're two metres wide and almost as high. They're hollow, to reduce their overall weight, so part of the internal space can be used for data cabling. There's enough room on the top of the track for people to walk along it in an emergency, and handrails can rise to provide support for people using it.

As this is a two-way system, each side of the track supports a car. The cars are a bit like balconies on the side of a building: they're cantilevered from the side of the track, and because their weight is balanced, they can't fall. But unlike balconies, of course, they *can* move.

The car is connected with the track by several operating units called 'bogies'. These are what make the car travel, and each one contains a range of equipment, including an electrically powered motor, a braking unit and three sets of wheels, which engage the car with the track.

So with this system, there's one track, and the big advantage is that it can have cars travelling along it in both directions at the same time.

Tutor: Right, thank you, all of you. Now let's open it up to questions.

> **Photocopiable recording script activity**
> (**P** ⋯⟶ page 143)

As a way of revising vocabulary, give students the section of the script with some words gapped, then ask them, in small groups, to work out the missing words.

> **Answers**
> Several of the answers are used elsewhere in the passage, so in most cases the spelling should be correct. Some other possible answers are given in brackets.
>
> **1** ground **2** suspended (*hanging* has a similar meaning, though is less formal) **3** freight (goods) **4** urban
> **5** technology **6** magnetic **7** capable **8** impossible
> **9** pedestrians **10** cause (produce, create, generate)
> **11** situated (placed, sited, located, constructed)
> **12** construction **13** disruption (disturbance) **14** jams
> **15** changed (altered, modified)

7 Say the two sentences aloud, making the time interval between the stressed syllables *put* and *wa* the same as the interval between *bought* and *ti*. Point out that in English, stressed syllables tend to come at fairly regular intervals, however many unstressed syllables come in between (in the first example, there is one unstressed syllable, *a*, and then three, *it in my*). This is not the case in all languages.

Ask students to read the explanations following the examples, then to read sentences 1–5 aloud to each other in pairs. Go round listening and encouraging students to say each sentence without gaps, and keeping the time intervals between stressed syllables roughly the same.

Play the recording. Ask students to repeat each sentence immediately after hearing it.

Recording script

1 I've bought a ticket.
2 I've put it in my wallet.
3 I'm waiting for the train.
4 I've been waiting for the train for half an hour.
5 I seem to spend my life waiting for the train.

19.2 SB pages 126–127

1 Elicit answers to the questions.

> **Possible answers**
> We travel far more often than in the past, and far greater distances. For instance, many people go on holiday or business to other continents.
>
> People's lives may have been less stressed when they could only travel slowly, because they had to work close to their homes.

2 Ask students what they think the picture shows. Don't give them the answer – tell them they will find out by reading the passage. Ask them to read the rubric and skim the passage. Then ask them again what the picture shows (it's a clock on the main railway station in Bristol, in the west of England, showing national time, 5.50, and Bristol time, 11 minutes behind it). Elicit one-sentence summaries of the passage.

3 Ask students to read the rubric and flow chart for questions 1–6, then to complete the flow chart.

Answers

1	unreliable	*All these devices were unreliable.* (line 15)
2	watches and clocks	*Until late into the 18th century, very few people could afford watches and clocks* (lines 16–17)
3	coaches	*the guards on these coaches carried timepieces* (lines 32–33)
4	London time	*In November 1840, the Great Western Railway ordered that London time should be used in all its timetables and at all its stations ... It was usually referred to as 'railway time'.* (lines 66–72)
5	standard time	*it was not until 1880 that Parliament introduced a standard time* (lines 92–94)
6	conference	*the International Meridian Conference in 1884* (lines 104–105)

Ask students to read the task for questions 7–12 and complete the sentences in pairs. Remind them that the sentences must be grammatical, must make sense and must reflect the meaning of the passage.

Answers

7 F *Across Britain there is a difference in time of approximately half an hour from the eastern to the western extremities.* (lines 23–25)

8 C *When travel and communications were slow, these local time differences were of little importance* (lines 26–28)

9 H *These timepieces were adjusted to gain about 15 minutes in every 24 hours when travelling from west to east, to compensate for the local time differences. And they were adjusted to lose 15 minutes in 24 hours when returning.* (lines 35–40)

10 D *A baby born in London early on Saturday morning might officially be a day younger than a baby born a few minutes later in Dublin – where it was still Friday evening.* (lines 48–53)

11 B *the railways, the telegraph companies and the Post Office – and it was the first of these that started the process of standardising time in Britain.* (lines 58–61)

12 G *The last major resistance to standardisation came from the legal profession, which operated by local time for many years.* (lines 84–87)

Extension activity

Give students this list of headings and ask them to choose the best one for each paragraph, filling in the line number where the appropriate paragraph begins. There is one extra heading.

A One group of people refuses to change (*paragraph from line ....*)

B A growing need for accurate time-keeping (*paragraph from line ....*)

C The difficulty of measuring time (*paragraph from line ....*)

D Local time is a problem for several types of business (*paragraph from line ....*)

E A device to measure time at different speeds (*paragraph from line ....*)

F The region that suffered the greatest problems (*paragraph from line ....*)

G A company starts using the same time for its activities (*paragraph from line ....*)

H When accurate time-keeping wasn't important (*paragraph from line ....*)

I A law introducing the same time throughout the country (*paragraph from line ......*)

J Why it isn't the same time everywhere (*paragraph from line ....*)

K Countries begin to work together (*paragraph from line ....*)

Answers
A 79   B 41   C 10   D 55   E 26   F (extra heading)
G 62   H 1   I 88   J 19   K 103

4 Write *If we had wheels instead of feet, we wouldn't need bicycles* on the board. Elicit from students the fact that this means we *don't* have wheels, and so *do* need bicycles. Explain that the 'unreal present' refers to things that aren't true, and the 'unreal future' means things that probably won't come true.

Ask students to read the questions and to answer them as they listen to the recording. When checking the answers, don't quote from the script, as students need to listen to it again for exercise 5.

Answers (see underlined text in script)
1 No   2 No   3 Yes   4 Yes

Recording script

Mr Smith and his car

Mr and Mrs Smith have got two cars. Mr Smith loves his car. Virtually every time he leaves his home, he goes by car, even for fairly short distances. His car is quite old, but <u>if he had plenty of money, he'd buy the car of his dreams,</u> a black sports car.

Every day, during the rush hour, Mr Smith drives to work and back, and Mrs Smith drives to *her* work and back, in a different direction. They drive at the same time as thousands of other people. This of course creates traffic jams, which have got much worse in the last few years. Mr Smith thinks <u>it's high time the problem was solved</u> before there's complete gridlock on the roads. He hopes that the government will build some new roads, to reduce congestion. However, he doesn't think motorists should pay for road-building: <u>he would rather the money came out of general taxation.</u>

In fact, Mr Smith can't see any alternative to greater investment in roads. He finds driving so much more convenient than public transport. <u>He sometimes travels by train, but he wishes they weren't so crowded and didn't stop at so many stations.</u> Mr Smith really enjoys driving. <u>He often says to himself, 'If only I didn't need to earn a living,</u> and could spend much more time in my car.'

5   Ask students to complete the sentences with words from the recording. Play it again.

```
Answers
1 had   2 was   3 came   4 weren't; didn't stop
5 didn't need
```

6   Ask students to work out the rule, based on the examples in exercise 5.

```
Answer
Past
```

7   Ask students to read the tinted section about *wish* and *would*. Check that they understand the significance of *wish* + *would* in A, compared with *hope* + *will* in B.

For further information and examples, refer students to the Grammar folder (SB page 143).

Ask students to read the rubric and example for exercise 7. Elicit another wish for the same situation, e.g. *I wish people didn't use their cars so much.*

Ask students, in pairs, to think of one or two wishes for the two situations.

```
Possible answers
1   I wish Ann would phone me when she says she will.
2   I wish John would return the book I lent him a year ago.
```

8   Ask students to think of other situations where a wish could be expressed.

```
Possible answers
You live a long way from your college or work: I wish I lived
nearer my college/work.

You have to take a test, and you don't want to: I wish I
didn't have to take the test.

In every lesson, your teacher sets you some homework, but
you think it's too much: I wish my teacher didn't set so
much homework.
```

Test folder 10

SB pages 128–129
Labelling diagrams and maps

Make sure students fully understand the notes and the advice on listening. Point out that there is no significant difference between diagrams, maps and plans: they are all graphic.

1 Ask students to read the rubric, study the plan and orientate themselves (they should start at 'from baggage claim'). Ask them what the plan shows (the arrivals section of an airport terminal). Ask them to read the questions, then to fill in the answers as they listen. Play the recording.

> **Answers (see underlined text in script)**
> 1 E   2 I   3 J   4 F   5 L   6 C

Recording script

You will hear a telephone conversation between two friends about a meeting in an airport terminal.

First, you have some time to look at questions 1 to 6. (*pause*)

Now listen carefully and answer questions 1 to 6.

Jean: Jean Clark speaking.

Tom: Hello, Jean, it's Tom.

Jean: Hello, Tom. Nice to hear from you. I'm looking forward to your visit.

Tom: Me too. In fact, that's what I'm calling about. I've booked my flight, so I can give you my arrival time now.

Jean: Good.

Tom: I'm due to land at 15.20 on June the 7th. But I expect you'll be at work, so don't worry about meeting me.

Jean: Well, I can get to the airport a couple of hours later, so if you don't mind waiting, it won't be for very long.

Tom: OK, that's fine.

Jean: You won't want to carry your suitcase around, so you might like to put it in a locker. When you come out of the baggage-claim area, you'll see a big clock just ahead of you. Turn right into Lobby East, and you'll come to a sign to the car park on your left. There are some lockers just after that passageway.

Tom: Good. I don't suppose there's much to do at the airport, but a cup of coffee would be nice.

Jean: Well, if you go from the clock into Lobby West, you'll see various shops and things on both sides. The first two on the left are both cafés. The second one is more popular, but I prefer The Coffee House – the staff are much friendlier, and they serve better coffee. It's the first one you come to.

Tom: OK. I've made a note of that.

Jean: Oh, but you'll need some local currency. Will you be bringing any with you?

Tom: I thought I'd draw some out when I arrive. I presume I can get some money at the airport.

Jean: Mm, let me think … Um yes, there are several cash machines close together. Imagine you're going from the clock into Lobby East, and they're immediately to the right, before the hotel.

Tom: Oh, right.

Jean: You might like to go to the exhibition space. It's only small, but there are usually some interesting paintings by local artists. It's at the end of Lobby West. You can see the entrance facing you as you walk along.

Tom: That sounds as though it's worth a visit. I'd also like to buy some CDs. Do you know if there's a store in the terminal?

Jean: Yes, there are a couple. There's one more or less opposite the exit from the baggage claim, on the corner of Lobby West.

Tom: Oh, do they stock classical CDs?

Jean: Oh, no, I don't think they do. But there's another store that does. From the clock go along Lobby East, then turn right just after the hotel. You'll see the store – it's opposite the side of the hotel. It's very small, but there's a reasonable selection.

Tom: That's great. I'm sure I can fill in the time before you arrive. Where shall we meet?

Jean: There's a quiet lounge – no mobile phones allowed! Would that be OK with you?

Tom: Perfect.

Jean: It's beside the main exit, in Lobby East. I'll see you in there about 5.30 on the 7th.

Tom: Great. Look forward to seeing you, Jean. Bye.

Jean: Bye, Tom.

2 Make sure students fully understand the advice on reading, then ask them to skim the passage and to study the diagram and complete the task.

> **Answers**
> 1 lighting — *The lighting is at the top of the tunnel, virtually at its highest point (paragraph 2)*
> 2 concrete lining — *The wall is made up of four main elements … on the inside of the tunnel, a concrete lining. (paragraph 2)*
> 3 base slab — *The road surface lies on the base slab (paragraph 3)*
> 4 mains drainage — *Mains drainage, just below the road surface on one side (paragraph 3)*
> 5 fire main — *The fire main is at the side of the tunnel, at the level of the road surface. (paragraph 3)*

20 Moving abroad

<table>
<tr><td colspan="2">Unit topic</td><td>Immigration and Emigration</td></tr>
<tr><td colspan="3">20.1</td></tr>
<tr><td>Test skills</td><td colspan="2">Speaking Part 3</td></tr>
<tr><td></td><td colspan="2">Reading (AC): Global multiple choice</td></tr>
<tr><td></td><td colspan="2">Locating information</td></tr>
<tr><td></td><td colspan="2">Flow-chart completion</td></tr>
<tr><td colspan="3">20.2</td></tr>
<tr><td>Test skills</td><td colspan="2">Listening: Note completion</td></tr>
<tr><td></td><td colspan="2">Short-answer</td></tr>
<tr><td></td><td colspan="2">questions</td></tr>
<tr><td>Vocabulary</td><td colspan="2">Phrasal verbs</td></tr>
<tr><td>Grammar</td><td colspan="2">Position of adverbs</td></tr>
<tr><td colspan="3">Workbook contents</td></tr>
<tr><td>1, 2</td><td colspan="2">Reading</td></tr>
<tr><td>3</td><td colspan="2">Vocabulary</td></tr>
</table>

20.1 SB pages 130–131

Ask students what the picture shows. (Immigrants arriving by ship in New York in the late 19th century.)

1 Ask students to suggest answers to the questions, either in small groups or as a class.

Possible answers
- to join friends or family; to get a better job; to increase their income; to learn a foreign language; to gain religious or political freedom; to study; to improve their social status
- They work, and the taxes they pay contribute to national income; they provide skills that may be in short supply; they help to make the country more cosmopolitan, e.g. by adding to the variety of food and festivals.
- People might move because of conflicts in their own country; as countries like India and China become richer, they may attract immigrants from poorer countries.

2 Ask students to match the words with the definitions, in pairs.

Answers
1 b   2 c (one aspect of migration)
3 e (another aspect of migration)   4 a   5 d

3 This reading passage, with 13 questions on it, is like one section of the Academic Reading Module, so students could be given 20 minutes to deal with it, as practice for the test. Remind them to skim through the passage first and to read the rubrics carefully.

Answers
1 B *While some theories about migration emphasise individual choice, and others focus on the influence of governments and business, it is more realistic to understand migration in terms of a complex interaction among all these elements.* (lines 21–25)
2 F *People begin to see their life as being based in the new country. This is particularly true of migrants' children: once they go to school in the new country, learn the language and make friends, it becomes more and more difficult for the parents to return to their homelands.* (lines 57–62)
3 C *While some theories about migration emphasise individual choice, and others focus on the influence of governments and business, it is more realistic to understand migration in terms of a complex interaction among all these elements.* (lines 21–25)
4 I *migrants may find it hard to save as much as they require, and stay on in the hope of succeeding eventually.* (lines 81–83)
5 E *Social networks based on family or a common place of origin help to provide housing, work, assistance in coping with bureaucratic procedures and support in personal difficulties.* (lines 44–48)
6 D *For instance, migration from some North and West African countries to France is linked to earlier French colonisation* (lines 34–36)
7 B *It is hardly ever a simple individual action, in which a person decides to move in search of a better life, leaves the home country and quickly becomes assimilated in the new country.* (lines 11–15)
8 H *They want to save enough in a higher-wage economy to improve conditions at home, to buy land, build a house, set up a business, or pay for education.* (lines 72–75)

(The model referred to in questions 9–13 is described in paragraph J.)
9 earnings *First, young workers move in order to work abroad temporarily, and send money home.* (lines 89–90)
10 friendships *Secondly, the stay is lengthened, and social networks are developed* (lines 91–92)
11 reunion *Thirdly, the original migrants' families join them* (line 93)
12 belonging *there is an increasing orientation towards the new country* (lines 94–95)
13 residence *And finally settlement becomes permanent.* (line 97)

Extension activity

Ask students to find words in the passage with the following meanings. The answers are in the order that they are first used in the passage.

1 first, at the beginning
2 importance

3 having an impact on, making a difference to, influencing
4 (to) stress
5 connections (*two words required*)
6 not having enough of something
7 made less strong
8 develop
9 for a limited time
10 lack of success
11 for a long time, forever
12 extended

> **Answers**
> 1 initial (lines 4, 41)   2 significance (line 8)
> 3 affecting (lines 17, 20)   4 emphasise (line 21)
> 5 links (lines 32, 63, 66), ties (line 34)   6 shortage (line 40)
> 7 weakened (line 64)   8 evolve (line 70)
> 9 temporarily (lines 72, 90)   10 failure (line 81)
> 11 permanent (lines 86, 97)   12 lengthened (line 91)

20.2 SB pages 132–133

1   It would be useful to have a map of Canada and a picture of the Canadian flag. Elicit answers to the questions.

> **Answers**
> 1 Ottawa   2 Toronto   3 English and French
> 4 Pacific (west), Arctic (north), Atlantic (east)   5 maple

2   Draw students' attention to the pictures of the two people they are going to hear about, Azim Lila and Tatyana Litvinova.

Ask students to read the rubric, box of words and notes for questions 1–5. Play the first part of the recording as they complete the task.

> **Answers (see underlined text in script)**
> 1 coast   2 education   3 challenges   4 jobs   5 talents

Ask students to read the rubric and questions for 6–12. Then play the second part of the recording as they write the answers.

> **Answers (see underlined text in script)**
> 6 chemistry   7 research   8 (twin) sister
> 9 (their) homework   10 speeches   11 countryside
> 12 kindness

Recording script

Questions 1–5

Azim Lila spent his childhood in East Africa, in a remote part of Tanzania. He lived at the end of a dirt road by the sea, far from the capital and other big towns, just as his great-grandparents had done. His life was hard, but now he feels that overcoming the difficulties he faced was the most valuable experience in his life and made him stronger.

When he was growing up, his parents gave him love, support and encouragement. Above all, they taught him something very important: you need to learn if you want to achieve your dreams.

When Azim was nine, his family left Tanzania and settled in Canada, which they found demanding. They needed to adjust to life in a new cultural context and develop their understanding of other people and cultures. They had to find employment and speak a different language. Most importantly, Azim believes, they had to develop a positive attitude.

At the same time, Canada presented unparalleled opportunities, but Azim's family weren't affluent. All the same, he was able to attend York University, thanks to scholarships and part-time work, which meant that he could complete his studies without disruption. He won several awards, and he was also selected to represent Canada in the Far East, as a member of a trade mission to China.

In Azim's opinion, Canada has changed his life. He sees Canada as a country that takes pride in encouraging everyone to discover their skills and capabilities. He describes this as a distinguishing feature of the country, a country that believes in diversity, self-expression and pluralism.

****

Questions 6–12

Tatyana Litvinova is Russian, and now lives in Canada, where she's currently an Assistant Professor at the University of Alberta.

She studied at one of the top universities in Moscow, and is a graduate in chemistry. She and her husband and their two sons moved to Canada in 1998, mainly because she thought there would be better opportunities to get funding for research. She was appointed to a position in a science laboratory.

Of course, she missed her family, especially her twin sister. They'd never been separated before, and Tatyana found it very difficult not to be able to speak to her every day. At that time, it was quite expensive to make international calls.

At first, her greatest problem was her lack of English. Not being able to understand or express herself fully made it difficult for her to register her children in school, and she couldn't give them the support they needed with their homework. All that soon changed, however.

She learned to speak English in quite an unusual way, by joining a Toastmasters' Club and paying close attention to the speeches that people made. She found it a very enjoyable experience.

Tatyana has always felt welcome in Canada, and that's what makes it a very special place for her. While she enjoys living in big cities, she loves the wonderful countryside, and the similarities between Canada and Russia: both are very big countries, and the people living in them come from all over the world.

Tatyana says that she still loves Russia, but she loves Canada too, in a different way. She's never felt she was a second-class citizen. She feels great affection and respect for Canadians, above all for the kindness they've invariably shown her. Whenever she had a problem, there was always someone willing to help her. Because of that, she believes that anyone who truly wants to settle in Canada will find a way.

> **Photocopiable recording script activity**
> (**P** ⋯⟶ page 144)

Give students the recording script, and suggest they write a series of sentences or a short essay comparing Azim's and Tatyana's lives.

Some similarities
They have both attended university at some time in their lives.
They both seem to be very close to their families.
They both moved to Canada with their families.
They both faced various challenges when they moved to Canada.
They both feel very positive about Canada.

Some differences
Whereas Azim comes from Africa, Tatyana is from Europe.
Azim lived in a remote part of his home country, while Tatyana lived in the capital, Moscow.
Azim went to university in Canada, but Tatyana attended university in Russia.
Azim went to Canada as a child, whereas Tatyana was an adult.

3   Ask students to discuss the questions in small groups.

Possible answers
Becoming part of the community makes it easier for immigrants to get a wider circle of friends and to be involved in all aspects of life in the country. On the other hand, they may not feel fully part of the community, their ties with family members (particularly those living in the home country) may be weakened, and if they have to use a foreign language, they may find it frustrating.

Feeling part of the country immigrants have come from maintains their emotional links with family, friends, culture and language. On the other hand, it may make them feel homesick if they spend many years in the new country.

4   Point out that there are no extra phrasal verbs in the box, so when students do the exercise, they should try to work out the meanings of any they aren't familiar with. Ask them to read the rubric, words in the box and passage, and to fill in the spaces.

Answers (definitions in brackets)
1   lived up to (was as good as previously expected)
2   turned out (was in the end)
3   deal with (do something about)
4   look forward to (wait for something with pleasure)
5   put up with (tolerate)
6   hold on to (keep, retain)
7   work at (make efforts to do something)

5   Write on the board *Recently I went to Canada, I recently went to Canada* and *I went to Canada recently*. Point out that adverbs can be used in three positions – at the beginning of the sentence (or clause), with the verb and at the end, as in the three examples above. *Recently* can occur in all three positions. However, some adverbs normally occur with the verb.

Ask students to read the introduction and rubric, and to complete situations 1–3 by choosing from rules a–c. Ask students to match the rules with the relevant parts of the examples.

Answers
1   c (1st example: *were both*)
2   b (2nd example: *soon found*)
3   a (3rd example: *had never been*)

6   Ask students where *currently* should go in the first sentence (after the auxiliary verb, *is* – see rule 3 in exercise 5), then ask them to read the rubric and complete the exercise.

Answers (Relevant rules 1–3 are given in brackets)
1   Tatyana Litvinova **is currently working** at the University of Alberta. (*rule 3*)
2   Before emigrating to Canada, Tatyana **had never been separated** from her sister. (*rule 3*)
3   Years after moving to Canada, she **still loves** Russia. (*rule 2*)
4   However, she **is still** happy with her life in Canada. (*rule 1*)
5   Some people **have hardly ever left** their home before deciding to emigrate. (*rule 3*)
6   Because of my new job, I **almost changed** my mind about emigrating. (*rule 2*)
7   Since moving inland, I **no longer go** to the beach every day. (*rule 2*)

7   Ask students to read the rubric and correct the errors in the positions of adverbs.

Answers (Relevant rules 1–3 are given in brackets)
1   We **can also see** from the chart that the number of immigrants rose sharply. (*rule 3*)
2   An immigrant who **already has** work experience will find it easier to get a job. (*rule 2*)
3   People who are living in a foreign country **can still find** happiness in their lives. (*rule 3*)
4   *correct*
5   I **particularly like** meeting people. (*rule 2*)
6   Immigrants **will sometimes miss** people and things from their old home. (*rule 3*)
7   It **will still be** very cold next month. (*rule 3*)
8   The number of immigrants to Canada **has also been affected** by economic conditions in other parts of the world. (*rule 3*)

8   Divide the class into teams of the same size. You might like to offer a small prize to the winning team. Give the class five minutes to answer as many questions as they can. Each team should write down their answers on one sheet of paper. After five minutes, ask teams to exchange their answer sheets and to mark each other's answers. Elicit the answers.

Answers

1 A: New Zealand   B: USA   C: Australia
   (Give $\frac{1}{2}$ mark if two are correct, no mark if only one is correct.)
2 a musical instrument (a long, wooden wind instrument played by Australian Aborigines to produce a deep sound)
3 Canberra (Sydney is sometimes wrongly thought to be the capital, because it is the largest city.)
4 koala (or 'koala bear'. It lives in trees and looks like a small bear with grey fur.)
5 North Island and South Island

6 the kiwi (It is a flightless bird; the people of New Zealand are nicknamed 'kiwis'.)
7 sheep (There are roughly 12 times as many sheep as people. Kangaroos are native to Australia, not New Zealand.)
8 Spanish (There are about 35 million people of Hispanic origin in the USA, and around 26 million of them speak Spanish as their first language.)
9 a type of music (a type of folk music from the southern USA, typically played on banjos and guitars)
10 eight years (Presidents are elected for a four-year term and can be elected for a maximum of two terms.)

Writing folder 10

SB pages 134–135
Preparing for the IELTS General Training and Academic Writing Modules

Ask students to read through the Advice box carefully and check they have understood each point.

1 Students should work through these examples in pairs and discuss the errors.

Answers

1 I am agree that people should be allowed to travel to find work.
2 If people have **a lot of / a great deal of** experience, I think they can become citizens quite **easily**.
3 Young people **who** are new to a country have to learn many things about it.
4 There are many **places**, for example in factories, in where they can work.
5 In some countries people they can be stay there as long as they want (to).
6 The families are not as close as they **used to be / once were, due to / because of** widespread emigration.
7 It is known that every problems / **every problem** come(s) from poor communication.
8 You need **a large amount of / a great deal of / a large sum of** money for taxes, for clothes, for food, for everything in **a** new country.

2

Answers

1 growing   2 children   3 First of all   4 such as
5 and so on   6 educational systems   7 Children
8 receive   9 Secondly   10 enrich   11 Admittedly
12 a considerable amount   13 fees   14 accommodation
15 a great deal   16 In addition   17 suffer from loneliness
18 However,   19 for educational purposes   20 study
21 fluently   22 problem   23 an appropriate
24 Money permitting   25 most suitable   26 At this time
27 independently   28 more effectively

Task 1

Sample answer

The charts show us the changes in both the numbers of immigrants to the United States in the late 19th and early 20th centuries, together with changes in the country of origin of those immigrants.

Apart from a slight fall of approximately half a million in the 1860s, there was a steady rise in the number of people emigrating to the USA from the 1850s to the 1880s. Numbers fell sharply in the 1880s, by almost one and a half million, but then climbed dramatically to a peak of nearly nine million in the period from 1900 to 1910. This was followed by a steady decline in immigrants until the 1930s.

In 1882, the majority of immigrants were European, with large numbers arriving from Germany, Britain and Ireland. However, by 1907, a large proportion of immigrants were from Russia, Italy and Austria-Hungary – about a quarter of the total number of immigrants were from each of those countries. Also, there was a smaller proportion of non-European immigrants in 1907 than in 1882.
(171 words)

Task 2

Sample answer

Although it is true to say that people are crossing borders in search of work, I am not sure that it is true to say that it is at a greater rate than ever before, or that there will come a time when there are no borders.

The decision to emigrate is not an easy one, and people who emigrated in the past did not take that decision lightly. They were driven to emigrate because of persecution or famine or lack of work. People are still having to take that decision and proportionally, probably in fewer numbers than in the past when large numbers of people emigrated to the United States.

Today, we have a situation in most of Europe where people are moving from country to country with few, if any, restrictions, as a consequence of the European Union. The Union is being expanded rapidly, and more and more countries are being invited to join. This has resulted in an exchange of ideas and experience, which can only be a good thing.

However, I am not sure that this will happen worldwide. Many countries guard their borders jealously, and some live in fear of what they see as an invasion of people from another country or culture. I, personally, think that this way of thinking will take many years to overcome and that we

will not see the removal of all borders at any time soon. In fact, I think that it is possible that more and more restrictions will be put in place to prevent people moving freely. This may be very pessimistic, but I think it is very difficult to know what will happen in the future.
(280 words)

Units 17–20 Revision

SB pages 136–137

The aim of this revision unit is to focus on the language covered in units 17–20. Exercises 2–7 can be done as a test in class or for homework.

Topic review

1 Students should comment on the statements and expand their answers as much as possible. This is useful practice, because in the Speaking Module they also need to give opinions and expand on what they say.

> **Possible answers**
> 1 I agree, because I'm usually so busy that a day without worrying about the time is very relaxing. But I've never tried it.
> 2 I think entertainments should be available 24 hours a day, because different times suit different people – depending on their work and whether they're 'larks' or 'owls'.
> 3 Wasting time can help you to relax, so it's useful – as long as you haven't got anything urgent to do.
> 4 It would be best if there wasn't pressure on people to work at night, but it would mean making people realise that they really don't need to go shopping at night.
> 5 A job in tourism might give you the opportunity to travel abroad and to meet lots of people, but it can be very hard work.
> 6 Children can learn a lot from travelling abroad, but I think they need to be helped to see what's interesting, and how it's different from their own country.
> 7 Commuting to work can be very stressful, and I'd much rather be able to walk to work. For one thing, I wouldn't have to get up so early in the morning.
> 8 I don't think people would be willing to give up flying, so it's probably more realistic to develop planes that are more environmentally friendly.
> 9 I think it would be great if people could live anywhere, as long as they could find homes and jobs.
> 10 I entirely agree with this. Multicultural cities have different types of restaurants, music, festivals and all sorts of things.

Vocabulary

2

> **Answers**
> 1 taken over   2 deal with   3 put forward   4 set up
> 5 take on   6 keep; down

3

> **Answers**
> 1 forward to   2 up against   3 up to   4 up with
> 5 up with   6 away with   7 up to   8 up for

Grammar

4

> **Answers**
> 1 deal with it   2 *correct*   3 came across it
> 4 give them out   5 work at it   6 *correct*   7 make it out
> 8 went down with it

5

> **Answers**
> 1 monorails are hardly ever involved in accidents
> 2 I nearly always travel by public transport
> 3 are rarely able to sleep well during the day
> 4 The passengers were all asleep
> 5 It has often been said
> 6 We can only hope
> 7 the special offer on tickets is no longer available
> 8 I almost missed the plane.

6

> **Answers**
> 1 don't have to   2 must   3 must (*have to* is also possible, but less likely, as this is described as a rule)
> 4 must (as for 3)   5 mustn't   6 must / has to
> 7 doesn't have to   8 have to

7

> **Answers**
> (Other verbs might also be possible, but they should all be in the past simple tense.)
> 1 had   2 made   3 came/travelled   4 didn't live   5 wore
> 6 went   7 didn't make   8 bought/had

Progress Test 5

Listening

Questions 1–6

*Complete the notes using **NO MORE THAN THREE WORDS**.*

George Mortimer Pullman and the Pullman carriage.

1831	Pullman born in USA. Father's profession: **1** ....
1859	arrived in Chicago
	changed standard carriage design to make a **2** .... carriage
	carriages lit by **3** ....
1862	went to Colorado gold fields and ran a **4** ....
1865	built the Pioneer rail carriage
	built new factory outside Chicago
1880–1884	built a **5** .... for his workers
1894	business began to decline, and workers **6** ....
1897	Pullman died

Questions 7–10

*Complete the table using **NO MORE THAN THREE WORDS AND/OR A NUMBER**.*

George Nagelmackers and the Orient Express

Date	Event	Details
1868	visited USA	travelled in Pullman carriage
1883	started Orient Express	one car for **7** .... and one for luggage
		passengers completed journey to Istanbul by **8** ....
1905	journey time reduced	opening of a 20km-**9** ....
1950s and 1960s	company declined, due to competition from **10**	

OBJECTIVE IELTS INTERMEDIATE – THIS PAGE MAY BE PHOTOCOPIED © Cambridge University Press, 2006

PROGRESS TEST 5 **127**

Reading

Every year, over five million visitors go to Banff National Park in Canada, an area that includes part of the Rocky Mountains. The town of Banff, which is situated inside the park, has a resident population of 7,000, and is host to the vast majority
5 of those visitors. Tourism directly or indirectly employs virtually everyone in the town and has enormous economic benefits for the region and for Canada as a whole. It's a multimillion-dollar industry that ranges from large, upmarket hotels, ski resorts and tour operators to restaurants, galleries,
10 guides and much more.

Only a small proportion of those millions of visitors leave the streets, shops or ski slopes to actually experience the wilderness first-hand. For the vast majority of visitors, Banff is merely a great place to shop, ski or party, with pretty scenery
15 and the occasional deer that wanders along the streets.

There are many ecological problems affecting the park, and while the press on this topic has generally been too sensational, the basic story is true. The town and the highway and railway that slice through the park are all barriers to
20 wildlife movement. Habitats have been destroyed, leading to a decline in natural food supplies: because of this, and because of highway mortality, large carnivores – bears and wolves – have almost disappeared from the river valley where Banff is located; meanwhile, deer and elk populations have increased
25 unchecked. The whole ecosystem is out of balance and in danger of collapsing – yet tourism operators continue to market Banff as an unspoilt ecological paradise.

In 1997, a number of businesses and concerned citizens in Banff came together to find a way of preserving and
30 protecting the park without destroying tourism. Their view is that, in the face of current human population increases and worldwide ecological damage, healthy ecosystems will increasingly become major tourism destinations, and that it is therefore essential to preserve the natural landscapes and
35 ecosystems of the national park. To this end, they developed the Banff Heritage Tourism Strategy (HTS).

The strategy sets out guidelines for a form of tourism that doesn't harm the environment. One of its central policies is to educate tourists before they go to Banff, so that they have
40 realistic expectations and can behave appropriately once they are there.

The other main thrust of the strategy is to convince tourism service providers within the park that if they are to continue to be successful, they need to re-think what they offer and act in socially and environmentally responsible ways. One 45 recommendation is that hotels and restaurants should teach their front-line staff about the natural and human history of the park, so that they in turn can influence the behaviour of tourists. However, individual businesses will need to work towards the objectives in their own ways: coach-tour 50 companies, for instance, may take a very different approach from car-hire companies.

To date, several tourism operators have accepted the proposals and are making progress in a number of respects, including training their staff and helping visitors to 55 understand the implications of being in a national park.

Parks Canada – the government agency responsible for maintaining national parks – is now taking a tougher, more pro-active attitude towards managing the park, in line with HTS thinking. For the past 50 years, it has had an active fire- 60 suppression policy, which limited the natural growth of plants, but it is now bringing the essential role of forest fire back into the park's ecology through the use of controlled fires. Other initiatives include closing several facilities around Banff town that were barriers to wildlife movement; setting limits on how 65 many people can visit certain beauty spots such as Moraine Lake; and using various tactics to scare deer and elk out of the town (where the animals had moved to escape predators).

The ecology of Banff National Park is now improving, as a result of the efforts of the HTS group and Parks Canada. 70 However, the strategy does not currently have broad acceptance. There are many obstacles and many opposing points of view. There needs to be much more dialogue among the various interested parties before the park is safe for future generations, and this dialogue is ongoing. 75

Questions 1–7

Do the following statements reflect the claims of the writer in the reading passage? Write

YES	*if the statement reflects the claims of the writer*
NO	*if the statement contradicts the claims of the writer*
NOT GIVEN	*if it is impossible to say what the writer thinks about this*

1 Most visitors explore the wilderness areas of the park.

2 Press coverage of the problems in Banff National Park has affected the number of tourists.

3 Tourism operators give a misleading impression of the park in their marketing.

4 The HTS group believes that eco-tourism is likely to grow in the future.

5 Parks Canada has changed the way it manages the park.

6 The HTS group is pleased with the amount of progress it has achieved so far.

7 The strategy of the HTS group has the support of all interested parties.

Questions 8–12

*Choose **FIVE** letters **A–K**.*

Which **FIVE** of these policies does the HTS group support?

A developing alternatives to jobs in tourism

B preventing any increase in the number of hotels

C introducing more bears and wolves into the area

D reducing the number of tourists

E giving information to tourists in advance of visits to Banff

F changing the services offered by tourism companies

G giving hotel workers a role in protecting the park

H reducing the use of cars

I burning some sections of the park

J encouraging tourists to visit certain beauty spots in the park

K removing some animals from the town of Banff

Question 13

*Choose the correct letter, **A**, **B**, **C** or **D**.*

Which of the following is the most suitable title for the reading passage?

A Damage done to the tourism industry in Banff National Park

B The growing popularity of eco-tourism in Banff National Park

C Why tourism is so important for the economy of Banff National Park

D The struggle to ensure a long-term future for tourism in Banff National Park

Writing

Writing Task 1 (AC)

You should spend about 20 minutes on this task.

The graph below shows the numbers of people moving into and out of the UK between 1993 and 2002.

Summarise the information by selecting and reporting the main features, and make comparisons where relevant.

Write at least 150 words.

International migration into and out of the UK

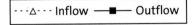

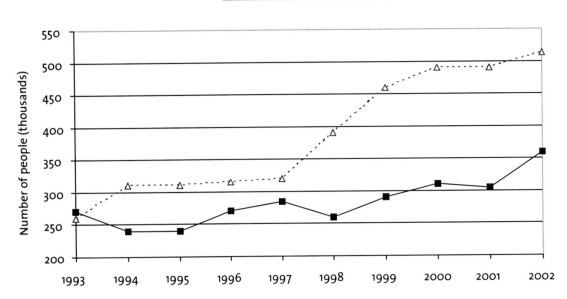

Progress Test 5 Key

Listening

1 (a) builder   2 sleeping/sleeper   3 candles   4 store
5 town   6 went/were on strike   7 mail   8 ferry   9 tunnel
10 air travel / planes / airplanes / aeroplanes

Recording script

You will hear someone talking about rail travel. First, you have some time to look at questions 1 to 6.

Now listen carefully and answer questions 1 to 6.

Man: Today we're going to be talking about luxury rail travel. It all started with George Pullman, didn't it?

Woman: Yes, the man who began luxury train travel was called George Mortimer Pullman. He was born in the USA on the 3rd March 1831, the son of a <u>builder</u>. However, when he arrived in Chicago in 1859, he spent his first few years there raising offices and houses and constructing new foundations. This was necessary because much of the Chicago area was only a metre or so above the level of Lake Michigan, and the streets were often flooded. Pullman took the money he earned from this and moved on to develop a new venture – railroad carriages. Pullman began by remodelling two standard passenger carriages into <u>sleeping</u> carriages. His first service was between Chicago and Bloomington, Illinois. Heating came from wood-burning stoves, and the light from <u>candles</u>. Steam heating replaced the wood stoves only in the 1880s, and electric lights came in in the 1890s.

Business grew slowly but steadily until the Civil War. In 1862, he left Chicago for the Colorado gold fields, where he opened a <u>store</u> and in his spare time continued to develop his ideas about railway carriages. Returning to Chicago, Pullman constructed the 'Pioneer' carriage in 1865, which became a classic in rail history.

Orders began to pour in, and Pullman built a new plant on the shores of Lake Calumet, several kilometres from Chicago. Between 1880 and 1884, in an effort to make it easier for his employees, he constructed a <u>town</u> near the factory. All the houses were leased, employees weren't allowed to buy, and Pullman sold water and gas to his own workers at a ten per cent premium.

The railroad-carriage business made him a fortune. Pullman only leased his carriages, never sold them. With over two thousand of them on the rails, his company was worth $62 million by 1893.

When business fell off in 1894, Pullman cut jobs, wages and working hours, but not house rents. His employees <u>went on strike</u>. This was eventually broken by government troops. Pullman's reputation was ruined. A government report condemned him for refusing to negotiate and for creating economic hardships for his workers. Pullman died in 1897.

****

Before you hear the rest of the talk, you have some time to look at questions 7 to 10.

Now listen and answer questions 7 to 10.

Woman: So, how are Pullman and the Orient Express connected? Well, it all started in 1868 when Georges Nagelmackers, the son of a Belgian banker, visited the USA, and while there, he travelled in the railway carriages built by an American called George Mortimer Pullman. He was very impressed, and on his return to Europe, Nagelmackers decided to start Europe's first luxury train service. This, in fact, took another 13 years because of problems in Europe, but finally, in 1883, he launched the Orient Express.

The train consisted of two baggage cars, one for <u>mail</u> and the other to hold passengers' luggage. Then came two sleeping cars and the dining car, which was lit by gas chandeliers.

The original route was from Paris to Romania via Munich and Vienna. In Romania, passengers were taken across the Danube to Bulgaria to pick up another train to Varna, from where they finished the trip to Constantinople, modern-day Istanbul, by <u>ferry</u>.

It wasn't until 1889 that there was a direct rail line to Istanbul. Then, in 1905, the journey time between Paris and Venice was cut when a <u>tunnel</u> – at just over 20km, the world's longest – was completed. This allowed the introduction of a more southerly route via Milan, Venice and Trieste to Istanbul.

The journey between Paris and Istanbul took several days. Passengers relaxed in their compartments, where they had wash basins and comfortable beds. The fares were very high, but then so was the level of comfort. The train was a great success.

The Orient Express went into decline in the 1950s and 60s as <u>air travel</u> became cheaper and faster. However, it continued to operate until 1977. In 1982, the route was reborn when the company was bought by James Sherwood.

Reading

1 NO *Only a small proportion of those millions of visitors leave the streets, shops or ski slopes to actually experience the wilderness first-hand.* (lines 11–13)

2 NOT GIVEN Nothing is said about the effect of press coverage on the number of tourists.

3 YES *The whole ecosystem is out of balance and in danger of collapsing – yet tourism operators continue to market Banff as an unspoilt ecological paradise.* (lines 25–27)

4 YES *healthy ecosystems will increasingly become major tourism destinations* (lines 32–33)

5 YES *For the past 50 years, it has had an active fire-suppression policy, which limited the natural growth of plants, but it is now bringing the essential role of forest fire back into the park's ecology through the use of controlled fires.* (lines 60–63)

6 NOT GIVEN Nothing is said about how the group feels about the amount of progress.

7 NO *the strategy does not currently have broad acceptance. There are many obstacles and many opposing points of view.* (lines 71–73)

8–12 E, F, G, I, K (in any order)
   E *educate tourists before they go to Banff* (line 39)
   F *if they are to continue to be successful, they need to re-think what they offer* (lines 43–44)
   G *hotels and restaurants should teach their front-line staff about the natural and human history of the park, so that they in turn can influence the behaviour of tourists.* (lines 46–49)
   I *but it is now bringing the essential role of forest fire back into the park's ecology through the use of controlled fires.* (lines 62–63)
   K *using various tactics to scare deer and elk out of the town* (lines 67–68)

13 D

Writing

Sample answer

This graph, covering the period 1993 to 2002, shows the inflow of immigrants into Britain and the outflow of emigrants. Apart from the first year, inflow consistently exceeded outflow, and both figures showed an upward trend.

In 1993, inflow stood at a little over 250,000, slightly below outflow. In the following year, immigration overtook emigration, remaining at a little over 300,000 until 1997. Emigration fell in 1994, was unchanged in 1995, then gradually rose until 1997, narrowing the gap between the two figures. The gap widened considerably in 1998, when outflow declined, while inflow began to rise steeply and continued to be greater than in the first part of the period.

In 1999, the previous year's fall in outflow was reversed. In that year and the next, inflow increased more sharply than outflow. In 2001, inflow remained virtually unchanged, while outflow declined slightly. In the following year, both figures rose to their highest levels of the period, with inflow exceeding 500,000 and outflow reaching just over 350,000.

(167 words)

Photocopiable recording scripts

Unit 1, 1.2, Exercise 10 photocopiable recording script

Man: Good morning. Computer Solutions.

Woman: Oh, hello. My printer's broken, and I need to get a new one. Someone gave me your number, and I was wondering whether you could help me.

Man: No problem. We stock printers suitable for both home and office.

Woman: Well, I'm a student. I just need one for my coursework. How much do they cost?

Man: An inkjet printer will probably be good enough for what you want – it'll do text and pictures. They start at £80 and go up to £250.

Woman: Mm. Quite a good price range, then. I can spend about £150. Can I get a good one for that?

Man: Yes. I'd go for the Trion i860. It had good reviews, and we've had no complaints about it.

Woman: The i860. I'll come in and have a look. What time are you open to?

Man: Normally we close at 5.30, but today, being Saturday, it's 8.30.

Woman: And where exactly are you?

Man: In Hollowridge – 15 Park Lane.

Woman: Fifteen Park Lane, got that. Is that in the town centre?

Man: Yes, opposite the cinema.

Woman: OK, and is it easy to park? If I buy the printer, I'd want to take it home with me today.

Man: No problem. There's a car park quite near, just at the back of the supermarket.

Woman: OK. Oh, one more thing – do you take credit cards?

Man: Cash only, I'm afraid. Will that be all right?

Woman: Yes, but I mustn't forget to go to the bank before I come! Oh, by the way, what's your name?

Man: Jack Stanway. That's S-T-A-N-W-A-Y. There are two Jacks here, so when you ask for me, give my surname, too.

Woman: OK, I will.

Man: I work in the office, but you need to go to the third floor, where the printers are. Just ask for me there, and I'll come out and see what I can do to help. See you later.

Woman: The third floor. Great – thanks for your help. Bye.

Unit 3, 3.2, Exercise 2 photocopiable recording script

You will hear an Englishman telephoning an Australian friend who also lives in England.

Robin: Hello?

Jerry: Hi, Robin, it's Jerry.

Robin: Jerry! Nice to hear from you. How're you doing?

Jerry: Fine, thanks. Guess what? I'm going on holiday to Australia next month!

Robin: Wow, that's great!

Jerry: I thought you might be able to give me some ideas about what to do while I'm in Sydney. That's where you come from, isn't it?

Robin: That's right. And I wish I was there now, instead of here in the cold.

Jerry: What's the temperature likely to be there?

Robin: Oh, next month it'll be around 25 degrees. If you went during the British summer, and the Australian winter, it would only be about 16 degrees.

Jerry: I'm looking forward to some warm weather.

Robin: So how long are you staying in Sydney?

Jerry: Only a couple of days. I'm going to spend a month touring Australia.

Robin: Sounds good. Well, you'll need at least a morning exploring the harbour area – it's fascinating. I really like the Pylon Lookout: the entrance is on the bridge. It's got an interesting display on how the bridge was built, and the panorama of the harbour from the observation area is spectacular.

Jerry: Right, I'll do that.

Robin: And of course you can see the Opera House – that and the bridge are Sydney's most famous sights.

Jerry: Do you know if there are any tours of the Opera House?

Robin: Yes, there are. As far as I remember, there's one every 30 minutes, and you spend around an hour exploring different parts of the building, depending which tour it is.

Jerry: Uh-huh. Do I need to book tickets in advance?

Robin: No, just buy them at the Opera House, from the Guided Tours office. You'll see the signs to point you in the right direction.

Jerry: Right, I'll do that. It'll be interesting to find out how the Opera House is run.

Robin: Then I reckon you should walk round the Rocks. It's the oldest part of the city, and always crowded with tourists of all nationalities, as well as local people. The cafés and restaurants keep very busy. Whenever I go back to Sydney, I enjoy sitting outdoors with a cup of coffee, watching the people passing by.

Jerry: Yes, that sounds like a good idea.

Robin: Oh, and I almost forgot – it's the Dragon Festival next month. You should arrange to be in Sydney that weekend. You'll have a great time.

Jerry: What is it?

Robin: You don't know the Dragon Festival? It's to celebrate the Chinese New Year. There are races between lots of traditional wooden boats, decorated with dragons' heads and tails. Each boat has something like 20 people rowing it, and over 2,000 people take part altogether.

Jerry: Uh-huh.

Robin: Crowds of people go to watch. The opening ceremony is pretty exciting, too, with drums and dancing. Why don't you check the dates on the Internet?

Jerry: I will. It sounds great. Well, thanks for the suggestions, Robin. I'm looking forward to my holiday.

Robin: Have a good trip and call me when you get back to the UK. Bye.

Jerry: Bye.

Unit 6, 6.1, Exercise 3 photocopiable recording script

Questions 1 and 2

My lecture today is on motivation at work. If managers are to improve the running of their organisation, it's important for them to understand what motivates the workforce – to know how to satisfy both the high flyers and those who have lower ambitions or ability.

First of all, let's look at the model of how motivation works. You will see that every member of the workforce has needs or expectations, and these needs and expectations will affect each person's behaviour. For example, they will work harder if they know that they will be rewarded – that is, if they can achieve their goals of higher pay or promotion. The achievement of these goals will, in turn, lead to job satisfaction. This then feeds back into the worker's needs or expectations.

****

Questions 3–5

Over the years, the development of different theories of management and different approaches to organisation has affected the way we view motivation. In the 19th century, the writer Frederick Taylor put forward the theory that workers were only interested in making money. In contrast, in the early 20th century, researchers found that people went to work to satisfy a *range* of different needs, and not simply for financial reward. One need, in particular, was emphasised – the social need. An early study done on a coal-mining company, for instance, showed that people generally were happier and worked more productively if they were able to work in teams.

****

Questions 6 and 7

One important 20th-century theory of motivation was that put forward by Maslow in 1943. Maslow identified five important needs which he placed in a triangle: at the bottom of the triangle, he put what he called 'basic needs': good pay and pleasant working conditions. Then, above the basic needs, he put 'security needs' – safe working conditions and job security. His third need he called 'social' – the need to have friends at work and get on with the boss. Fourth were 'status needs' – a job title and social recognition. Finally, at the top of the triangle, Maslow identified the need for advancement – to have a challenging job with opportunities for promotion. His theory isn't perfect, but it's a convenient framework for viewing the different needs and expectations of work that people have, and, what's more, I believe it's still valid today.

****

Questions 8–10

During an early 21st-century survey of full-time employees, when asked what gave them job satisfaction, 72% said having an inspirational leader. Fifty-five per cent of those questioned found satisfaction in the challenging nature of their work, 50% by being paid well, and 40% said flexible working hours. Consequently, we can see that this indicates that today, an employee's opinion of the quality of the leadership in their workplace is an important factor influencing belief in the company as a good place to work.

Motivation varies over a person's working life and also according to where they live. Studies show that people have different goals in different countries. For example, a good lifestyle would appear to be more important in Spain than it is in Sweden. Financial security is more important in the US than in the UK. Social contact at work is important to workers in both Germany and in Australia, but not of top importance in Britain and Italy. As to high status, this is more important in the USA than to Europeans. These results indicate clear differences between countries, but I think they shouldn't be taken too seriously.

There have been many theories which have attempted to explain the nature of motivation. These theories are all partially true, and by and large all help to explain the behaviour of certain people at certain times. However, none really provide all the answers. The best a company can do is to provide people with the right environment to be self-motivated. If they are self-motivated, they will perform well.

Unit 8, 8.2, Exercise 2 photocopiable recording script

Example

Leisure activities are as varied as crossing the Arctic, or collecting foreign coins, or a visit to a museum. Research into people's experience of leisure has revealed that people get a number of different kinds of enjoyment from leisure, some of which I'll briefly talk about now. But bear in mind that most activities will provide several types of experience.

We often talk about leisure as giving the opportunity for relaxation. Yoga is generally relaxing, both physically and mentally, as is stamp collecting. Relaxation tends to be associated with undemanding activities, but many leisure activities are far from relaxing.

Questions 1–9

At the opposite end of the spectrum is 'flow', the name given to a very intense experience, where you're completely absorbed in what you're doing and lose track of time. This often comes from activities where people set themselves challenges to test and improve their skills, as in rock climbing. Many activities that provide flow carry a considerable physical risk, which is likely to add to the experience – paragliding is just one example. But the same intensely emotional experience may occur in a very different activity, like chess. It isn't the activity alone which provides the experience, but also what the participant brings to it.

Another feature of many leisure activities is the introduction to a whole new social network, providing companionship with other like-minded people. New friends can be made through joining a music club, for instance. And social relationships can be strengthened through a shared interest in football. The media open up this experience to everyone who wants to participate, even if they don't play.

Then there's the pleasure that some people get from being in communion with nature, either alone or with companions. Surfing, for example, is likely to focus your entire attention on the sea, while one of the more relaxing ways of relating to the natural world is bird-watching.

Leisure activities can also provide an opportunity to express creativity. Again, these can be solitary or companionable. Painting is often done alone, although many people join a club that can give them encouragement and tips for improvement, while

drama is normally a combined effort, with a performance as its goal.

****

Questions 10–14

An essential aspect of leisure is that we can pick hobbies to suit our personality, our needs and our wallet, and we can drop them at any time. This control is crucial, as people benefit from feeling that they're making their own decisions. That's one reason why children need to choose their own hobbies, instead of having them imposed by their parents.

With large numbers of people wishing to spend time on leisure activities, there's a growing demand for the organiser – whether it's a cinema or a dance class – to ensure that participants have a full experience. It isn't enough just to show a film: customers want to be able to find out in advance what's on, travel to the cinema easily, feel welcome when they arrive and have the chance to buy popcorn to eat during the film.

People may enjoy an activity – a dance class, for instance – but drop it because these other parts of the experience have been overlooked. They're likely to enjoy themselves much more if they're made to feel welcome and there's an opportunity to socialise when the dancing ends.

Like cinemas, the retail sector is making efforts to package a variety of experiences. Many people go shopping for pleasure and spend far longer comparing and discussing products than they do actually buying. This has even gained a name in recent years – 'retail therapy' – reflecting the view that it makes people feel better.

Shopping used to be purely practical: we bought what we needed. But that's no longer enough. Many shopping centres now ensure shoppers are provided with entertainment as well. This is good for business, as it attracts more customers, who stay longer and spend more.

And is leisure good for us, or simply a waste of time? According to psychologists, participating in leisure activities makes us healthier, both physically and mentally, and increases the pleasure we gain from life. So we've got good reason to carry on with our hobbies!

Unit 10, 10.1, Exercise 2 photocopiable recording script

Woman: Can I help you?

Girl: Yes, please. I'm looking for the accommodation officer. Do you know where she is?

Woman: I don't, I'm afraid. *I* can probably help you. My name is Joanna Swift. Do sit down.

Girl: Thank you. I'd like to move into a college room in October. Can you tell me a bit about what's available?

Woman: Certainly. We have two blocks for women students. The first is Ridgeway House. There are two types of room – an ordinary bedroom with desk, etc., which is $230 a week, that's with food, of course, but not en-suite facilities, and then there's the bigger study bedroom which is $270 a week.

Girl: Mm. I think I'm more interested in the cheaper room. But are they very small?

Woman: Well, they're not very big, but there's a large common room with a TV on each floor, so there's somewhere to go and talk to friends or see the news. The university campus is a five-minute bus ride, or 20 if you walk.

Girl: Oh, that's not so far.

Woman: No, but there is something that you may find a problem – I'm afraid Ridgeway House is closed in the summer but not the winter vacation.

Girl: Oh, that *is* a problem, actually. I need somewhere for the whole year.

Woman: Mm. International House may suit you better. It's much cheaper – only $130 to share a room or $150 for a single room. Food isn't included in the price, but there's a kitchen on every floor and washing machines on the ground floor.

Girl: That sounds better, but I wouldn't want to share. I'm such a tidy person, you know, I would find sharing difficult. I'd like to have a single room, if one is available.

Woman: There are a few singles still available for next year, but you'll have to make up your mind fairly soon, as it's such a popular hall. Why don't you go and take a look? The address is 27 Whitaker, that's spelt W-H-I-T-A-K-E-R, Place.

Girl: Yes, I'll do that.

Woman: There are also quite a few facilities you might be interested in. There's an outdoor swimming pool for the warmer months and an all-weather volleyball court.

Girl: I think I'm probably more interested in having access to a computer.

Woman: No problem – there's a computer room situated in the basement. It's run by volunteers and is always open in the evenings and at weekends. Now, I should tell you that there's really only one rule in International House, and that is that no smoking is permitted anywhere on the premises. They also have an unofficial policy of no noise after ten o'clock at night.

Girl: That won't be a problem. I will go and have a look and then come back. Would I need to pay a deposit today?

Woman: It would be better, and you also need to fill in the application form. The fee is $25, which you pay now, with a further $100 deposit when you get the key. I'm sure you'd enjoy living there – it's a lovely building and was only finished last year.

Girl: It sounds brilliant. Thank you very much for your help.

Unit 11, 11.2, Exercise 2 photocopiable recording script

Animals have played a major role in human society for many thousands of years – as food, to help in hunting and to provide companionship – and their importance is reflected in our mythology. Many cultures have myths in which animals play a significant role in the creation of the earth and everything on it: for example, a snake is a major figure in the mythology of the Aboriginal people of Australia.

There's a long tradition of animals appearing in literature and, nowadays, in films, too. Sometimes they appear as themselves, as in 'wild animal stories', a popular literary form in the USA in the first half of the 20th century. These stories aimed to give a realistic view of animals and their lives, although the standpoint was occasionally somewhat romanticised. And many authors have written stories arguing the need to give animals greater protection, often by reducing the amount of pollution human beings create.

In this literary approach, the *actual* physical qualities of a species are presented, but animals are often used *symbolically* in literature, particularly in fables. These are short stories, usually written to make a point about a moral issue, often through satire of how human beings behave. Impossible events take place: most characters are animals that have a command of language, and behave in other respects, too, like human beings, while keeping their own physical shape.

Fables are thought to have originated in the Middle East two to three thousand years ago, and they're also found in the ancient literatures of Iran, India and other cultures. Aesop, who lived in Greece in the sixth century BC, wrote a large number of fables that still retain their popularity, and many other writers have followed in his footsteps. In English literature, a much longer fable is George Orwell's political satire *Animal Farm*, published in 1945.

Animal Farm is unusual in being a fable for adults. Far more often, the target audience is children, and fables provide them with examples of good and bad behaviour. *The Just So Stories*, written by the British author Rudyard Kipling in the late 1890s, are typical of the genre. As in the same author's *Jungle Book*, the stories contain many animal characters. *The Just So Stories* focus on how the Earth began, and of the people and animals who live on it, and recommend certain ways of behaving.

Let me give you an example. One story, 'How the Camel got his Hump', is set at the time when animals were first domesticated. A dog, a horse and an ox work for a man, but the camel, who lives alone in the middle of the desert, is lazy and refuses to work. As a result, the other three animals have a heavier workload. They complain to the magical creature in charge of all deserts, who tells the camel to work. The camel simply replies 'humph'. So the magical creature punishes him by giving him a hump on his back. This holds enough food for the camel to work for three days without eating, to make up for the time he's missed. The moral of the story is that everyone ought to work, in order to contribute to the common good.

© Cambridge University Press, 2006

Unit 12, 12.1, Exercise 6 photocopiable recording script

Man: Hello, Grayson's Adventure Days. How can I help you?

Woman: Oh, good morning. I want to book an activity day as a birthday present for my father, so could you give me an idea of the sorts of things you organise, please?

Man: What a great present! Do you want the activity to take place in a particular location?

Woman: No, anywhere in the country would be OK.

Man: Right. Well, how about bungee jumping? That's our most popular activity.

Woman: Ah-ha.

Man: After a safety briefing, you're securely fastened to the correct bungee rope for your weight. Then the crane takes you up to a height of 50 metres in a cage, and you jump from it.

Woman: You make it sound so easy!

Man: In fact, some people change their minds at the last moment. But for the really brave, you can also book our special, which is one normal bungee jump and then a backwards one. It's quite an experience!

Woman: I can imagine! Is it available every day?

Man: We do bungee jumping all year round, on over 120 dates, and in various locations, but you should try to book about four weeks in advance, if possible, as it's very popular.

Woman: OK. And are there any age restrictions? It'll be my father's 50th birthday, so I hope he isn't too old.

Man: No, he certainly isn't too old, but we'll require a certificate from a doctor, to confirm that he's in good health.

Woman: Oh, he's very fit, so that won't be a problem. How much is it?

Man: It costs £57 per person for the standard jump, and 97 for the special.

Woman: Right. Now, I've heard of something called 'zorbing'. Do you do that, too?

Man: Yes, we do. That's another very popular activity.

Woman: What exactly is it?

Man: Well, you're securely attached in the centre of a zorb, either alone or with another person. A zorb is over three metres high, and it consists of one ball inside another, both made of clear plastic, so you can see out through them.

Woman: And what happens next?

Man: You roll down a hill, at speeds of up to 50 kilometres an hour. You can also choose the hydrozorb experience, where 25 litres of water is thrown inside with you, and you aren't attached, so you slide around in the water while you're rolling.

Woman: Wow! I'm sure my father would enjoy that. What about the dates?

Man: The zorb rides take place between April and October, but just at weekends.

Woman: Are there any restrictions, I mean, for height or weight?

Man: Your father needs to be at least 160cm tall and weigh no more 110 kilos.

Woman: Oh, that's fine. How much does it cost?

Man: Zorbing is £50 per person.

Woman: And is hydrozorbing the same price?

Man: No, that's £65.

Woman: Right, I'd better give my father details of both the bungee jumping and zorbing, and let him choose, and then I'll get back to you.

Man: Fine. We tend to get fully booked, especially at this time of year, so you ought to book well in advance.

Woman: OK, I'll get back to you in the next few days. Thanks very much for your help.

Man: No problem. Bye.

Woman: Bye.

Unit 14, 14.1, Exercise 2 photocopiable recording script

Questions 1–4

Although the human eye can discern at least six million different colour shades, and theoretically there are an infinite number of colour possibilities, the colours which are popular at any given time will depend on a wide variety of factors – including technological advances, the economy and even politics. Colour fashions do not change abruptly, rather they are continually evolving, and one colour may be fashionable for up to ten or 12 years. Let's look now at some examples of colour trends.

When it comes to the world of work, most people are very traditional. Men go for suits, shirts and ties and, while there's a wide choice of colours for both shirts and ties – pink, purple and green proving popular recently – it would seem that blue, rather than black or grey, is generally the first choice for their main outfit. Apparently, it's a colour that appeals to people who are responsible, and is especially popular with bankers.

Now, offices always benefit from some colour. Even a small amount will improve mood and, although most offices these days are generally a rather boring white, by using a hint of colour – possibly with a green filing cabinet or red blinds at the windows – employers may find that their employees' stress levels are reduced and productivity is improved.

Turning to national flags, colour is of vital importance. The point made by one academic in the last century that 'national flags make use of only seven main colours: red, blue, green and yellow, orange, black and white' remains true today. An analysis of the number of colours used on flags between 1917 and 1999 reveals that a combination of three colours is by far the most popular choice. The use of a single colour is negligible, but the use of four colours is increasing in popularity. Most countries go primarily for red, followed closely by white and then blue. Black, green and orange are among the least popular combinations.

The iPod Mini first appeared in January 2004. It came in a range of colours – blue, pink, green, silver and gold – which were supposed to appeal to different personality types. When it was first introduced, people were asked to vote on the Apple website for which colour they preferred, and the silver one stole a stunning 46 per cent of the vote, with none of the other colours coming near. Gold was particularly low in the polls, with blue, pink and green all a rather poor second.

****

Questions 5–8

Next, cars. Much like fashion, colour preferences follow trends and fall in and out of favour as the years pass. In 2004, global colour-trend data showed that, interestingly, red and green were no longer popular, with less than 5% of vehicles manufactured using those colours, but silver, favoured often by first-time buyers, was far and away the leader, being the colour of 38% of vehicles produced. White, a favourite apparently with older, male drivers, had 19.6% of the market, followed by black at 13.9. Interestingly, in North America, white cars had the lowest collision rates, while black had the most. The once trendy blue car is declining in popularity worldwide, and in 2004 made up only 9.3% of cars purchased, perhaps because it had been found that in the USA particularly, blue cars were the most popular with car thieves.

****

Questions 9 and 10

Let's look now at the rise and fall in popularity of blue and green cars in Canada.

Let's take blue cars first. Blue cars began at a high of 29% from 1987 to 88. They then began to falter, with a fall to 21% in 1989 and a further fall to 17% in 1990. Sales picked up in 1991, when they rose to 21%, and reached a peak of 23% in 1992. There was then a gradual fall from 17% in 1993 and 94 to a low of 10% in 1997. Blue cars then remained more or less constant at 12% of the market until the end of 2001.

Turning now to green cars … from 1987 to 1990, sales of green cars were only very low – only 1%, with a high of 2% in 1988. There was an upturn in 1991, as sales hit 5%, growing to 20% in 1993. Sales continued to grow, reaching a peak of 30% in 1996. It was all downhill after 1996, though, with green-car sales back to 20% in 1998. Sales then rose slightly in 1999 to 21%, but plummeted to 11% by 2000 and then levelled off.

Unit 16, 16.2, Exercise 2 photocopiable recording script

Rachel: Oh, hello, can you spare me a few minutes, please?

Tutor: Yes, of course, Rachel. What can I do for you?

Rachel: It's about the book review you've asked us to write as part of the Academic Writing course. You said we should ask if we didn't know how to set about it.

Tutor: OK. Well, sit down, and let's talk about it. I presume you've chosen the book you want to write about.

Rachel: Yes.

Tutor: Good. Then have a look at this outline. If we talk it through and you make notes on it, it'll help you to structure your review. Right, first of all, what's the name of the book?

Rachel: *The Human Mind.*

Tutor: Ah yes, by Robert Winston. It was tied in with a very good television series, wasn't it? So you should start your review with the title and author. The next question is, what category would you put it in? For example, fiction, history, maths …

Rachel: Well, I suppose it's science.

Tutor: Can you limit the field a little?

Rachel: Er, how about popular science?

Tutor: Yes, I think that's more helpful.

Rachel: Then I suppose the subject area is the brain.

Tutor: OK. And it's important to mention the intended readership, because you can't judge how effective a book is without considering who it's meant for.

Rachel: Well, it doesn't assume you know a lot about the subject, so I'd say it's for non-specialists. It was promoted in general bookshops.

Tutor: Right. Now the overview. What would you say Winston is trying to do?

Rachel: Er … it's very informative, but I think he's also telling us how to make the most of our brains.

Tutor: Then you should briefly discuss the main topics. I'd recommend mentioning the ones that you found the most significant and interesting.

Rachel: Mm-hm. Well, it starts by looking back at the last few thousand years, and looks briefly at some of the theories that have been developed about the brain and about its importance. It wasn't always considered as important as we now believe.

Tutor: True. And the next topic?

Rachel: I think it should be the structure and activities of the brain that make it function. I found that chapter very interesting, but it was probably the hardest to understand.

Tutor: Mm, I'd probably agree with you. Any more topics you want to mention?

Rachel: Oh, it covers so much, like the emotions, memory … but I think the role of the brain in creating personality should be mentioned, because I think that's an important aspect of the book. And then there's the advice on how we can use our brains to boost our intelligence. I've already started acting on some of the suggestions!

Tutor: Good luck! Now, let's look at the next section of your review, where you should analyse and evaluate the book. This is the main section, where you give your own opinions. This first point is really a question of whether we should take the writer seriously. A musician may be qualified to write about music, but not necessarily to write about the brain, for instance.

Rachel: Mm. Winston is a professor at the University of London, and he's done a lot of research in various medical fields. So he's very well qualified to write about this subject.

Tutor: What would you say are the strengths of the book?

Rachel: Mm … it's a complex subject, but he makes it as accessible as it can be for the general reader. That's partly because he illustrates his points with a lot of stories, both about well-known people, like Einstein, and from his own life.

Tutor: OK. Are there any other strengths you want to add?

Rachel: Er … I was glad he included a word list to explain the meanings of medical terms. And I didn't find any weaknesses.

Tutor: Mm. Right! Then that brings us to the conclusion. How would you sum up your overall response to the book?

Rachel: Well, I found it fascinating. I think Winston is quite ambitious in the goal he's set himself, but he's succeeded in reaching it.

Tutor: Well, there you are – you've got the skeleton of your review. Keep that in front of you while you're writing it up, and it should be fine.

Rachel: Thank you very much.

Tutor: You're welcome.

Unit 18, 18.1, Exercise 2 photocopiable recording script

Questions 1–5

Travel and tourism is the largest industry in the world, but calculating its economic impact is quite difficult. The one thing everybody can agree on, though, is that it's huge.

There are two things which have influenced the growth of tourism. These are firstly social factors and secondly, technology and the way it's developed. Let's consider the social factors first of all. Demand for tourism is determined mainly by the amount of wealth a country has, which is why countries such as Japan, Australia, the USA and western European countries have contributed most in terms of tourist numbers in the past. However, growing wealth in developing countries will mean that demand for holidays abroad will take off there in the near future, boosting tourism enormously.

That said, the majority of tourists are still from what are called the 'developed nations'. However, studies show that their numbers will not rise much further in the next few decades because their populations are fairly stable. As a result, there'll be a growth in the number of retired people who'll have more time on their hands. This'll influence the kind of tourism wanted: fewer skiing holidays will be required, but there'll be an increase in the number of people wanting to visit art galleries.

****

Questions 6–10

Let's turn now to the second factor in the growth of tourism. The technology that sustains mass tourism today is the jet plane. Air travel has opened up the world. In 1970, scheduled planes carried 307 million passengers. Today, there are four times as many. In fact, cheaper and more efficient transport has been behind the development of mass tourism from its beginnings in Britain in the 19th century. The first package tours were arranged in 1841 by Thomas Cook, an entrepreneur whose company subsequently became one of the world's largest tour operators. In his day, it was the railway that allowed his business to flourish.

Today, technology is proving very important in other ways, as well as in transportation. In the past, people went to a travel agent to find and book their holiday.

Now, many of these people are bypassing the high-street travel agent and booking their holidays themselves on the Internet. Airlines have been keen to encourage this direct approach, as it keeps down their costs, and increasingly high-street travel agents are finding their business is disappearing.

These days there may be more tourists to go round, but there is also more competition among destinations as cities, countries and continents all compete for tourist revenue. But becoming a tourist destination is not quite as straightforward as it might seem. For example, Ireland used to sell itself as a place to go to and enjoy the beautiful countryside. However, it soon discovered that it was attracting young student backpackers without any money. So how did Ireland set about increasing revenue from tourism? Well, the Irish Tourist Board came up with the idea of promoting the country's literature, using the names of writers such as Oscar Wilde and James Joyce to appeal to older, richer tourists who would spend their money in the hotels and restaurants of the country.

However, there are other ways of appealing to tourists. The US is dotted with places that claim to be the capital of something or other (sometimes things which may seem rather strange: Crystal City, for example, is the world capital of the vegetable broccoli, and then there's Gilroy – famous for its garlic). These towns are trading on a single gimmick to attract the tourists. Festivals are another way to bring them in – literary, food, art – they're all staged for one reason only: to attract tourist revenue. Many a town has sought to copy the success of Stratford, Ontario, which was transformed from a small, run-down blue-collar town to a bustling cultural centre by the efforts of Tom Patterson, who managed to persuade a British director to stage their first drama festival in 1953.

But then boosting a city through tourism is nothing new. In 18th-century England, Bath Spa became fashionable after the owners of the hot baths employed Beau Nash, the trendsetter of his day, to promote the city. I want to end the lecture there for today. Now, next week …

Unit 19, 19.1, Exercise 6 photocopiable recording script

Well, monorails are a bit like railways, but there's just one rail, which is wider than each of the rails of a railway. Actually, 'mono' means 'one', which is how it got the name.

Some monorails are at **1** _____ level or in subway tunnels, though in most cases the track is elevated. The vehicles are always wider than the track. In some types of monorail, the vehicles run on the track, like a normal train, and in other types they're **2** _____ from it.

Some monorails are used to transport **3** _____ , but the majority carry passengers. A lot of them take visitors around amusement parks – there are plenty of these all round the world – and some form part of an **4** _____ transport system. Most of these are in Japan.

Monorails were first constructed in the 19th century, though the one that's been in operation for longest dates from 1901. It's in the town of Wuppertal, in Germany. The vehicles are electrically operated, but a different kind of **5** _____ is used by one fairly new monorail. This went into service in 2004, between the city of Shanghai, in China, and its airport. Here, too, the energy source is electricity, but it's used to create a **6** _____ field which propels the train forwards. And while they're travelling, the trains are levitated, which means they're suspended about one centimetre above the track. This technology is called 'maglev', short for 'magnetic levitation'. Though the trains are **7** _____ of going at over 500 kilometres an hour, they regularly travel at up to 430. Right, that's a short introduction to monorails, and now it's Stuart's turn.

****

Thanks, Hannah. I'm going to say something about the advantages of monorails. The most important point is, of course, safety, and here monorails score very highly. Unlike trains, the design of monorails means that derailment is virtually **8** _____ . And as they're normally quite separate from **9** _____ and road traffic, there isn't any danger of a collision.

Nowadays, we're far more concerned about the environment than we used to be, and monorails have advantages over many other forms of transport.

They're electrically operated, so they don't **10** _____ the pollution that cars and buses do, though admittedly some pollution is produced by the electricity generating stations.

The vehicles move much more quietly than trains, because they normally use rubber tyres. This allows stations to be **11** _____ in busy areas like shopping centres without creating disturbance.

From an economic point of view, monorails have a lot going for them. For one thing, **12** _____ of all the elements takes place off-site, so installation can be very fast, and cause very little **13** _____ . Once they're up and running, they're very cost-effective to operate. And as they're not held up by traffic **14** _____ or accidents, they're far more reliable than trams and especially buses.

On the other hand, monorails have the same disadvantage as other railways, that they operate over a fixed route: the vehicles can't transfer to the road. So routes can't be **15** _____ without constructing a new monorail, and people have to get to and from the stations, so they may not be as convenient as buses or, in particular, private cars.

Unit 20, 20.2, Exercise 2 photocopiable recording script

Questions 1–5

Azim Lila spent his childhood in East Africa, in a remote part of Tanzania. He lived at the end of a dirt road by the sea, far from the capital and other big towns, just as his great-grandparents had done. His life was hard, but now he feels that overcoming the difficulties he faced was the most valuable experience in his life and made him stronger.

When he was growing up, his parents gave him love, support and encouragement. Above all, they taught him something very important: you need to learn if you want to achieve your dreams.

When Azim was nine, his family left Tanzania and settled in Canada, which they found demanding. They needed to adjust to life in a new cultural context and develop their understanding of other people and cultures. They had to find employment and speak a different language. Most importantly, Azim believes, they had to develop a positive attitude.

At the same time, Canada presented unparalleled opportunities, but Azim's family weren't affluent. All the same, he was able to attend York University, thanks to scholarships and part-time work, which meant that he could complete his studies without disruption. He won several awards, and he was also selected to represent Canada in the Far East, as a member of a trade mission to China.

In Azim's opinion, Canada has changed his life. He sees Canada as a country that takes pride in encouraging everyone to discover their skills and capabilities. He describes this as a distinguishing feature of the country, a country that believes in diversity, self-expression and pluralism.

****

Questions 6–12

Tatyana Litvinova is Russian, and now lives in Canada, where she's currently an Assistant Professor at the University of Alberta.

She studied at one of the top universities in Moscow, and is a graduate in chemistry. She and her husband and their two sons moved to Canada in 1998, mainly because she thought there would be better opportunities to get funding for research. She was appointed to a position in a science laboratory.

Of course, she missed her family, especially her twin sister. They'd never been separated before, and Tatyana found it very difficult not to be able to speak to her every day. At that time, it was quite expensive to make international calls.

At first, her greatest problem was her lack of English. Not being able to understand or express herself fully made it difficult for her to register her children in school, and she couldn't give them the support they needed with their homework. All that soon changed, however.

She learned to speak English in quite an unusual way, by joining a Toastmasters' Club and paying close attention to the speeches that people made. She found it a very enjoyable experience.

Tatyana has always felt welcome in Canada, and that's what makes it a very special place for her. While she enjoys living in big cities, she loves the wonderful countryside, and the similarities between Canada and Russia: both are very big countries, and the people living in them come from all over the world.

Tatyana says that she still loves Russia, but she loves Canada too, in a different way. She's never felt she was a second-class citizen. She feels great affection and respect for Canadians, above all for the kindness they've invariably shown her. Whenever she had a problem, there was always someone willing to help her. Because of that, she believes that anyone who truly wants to settle in Canada will find a way.

Acknowledgements

The authors would like to thank Catriona Watson-Brown for her helpful suggestions and careful editing.

Thanks also go to Annabel Marriott at Cambridge University Press for her constant diligence and support, and to Stephanie White at Kamae for her creative design solutions.

The authors and publishers would like to thank the teachers and consultants who commented on the material:
Australia: Stephen Heap; Brunei: Caroline Brandt; Spain: Chris Turner; Taiwan: Daniel Sansoni; United Arab Emirates: Paul Rawcliffe; UK: Jan Farndale, Roger Scott, Rob Shaw, Clare West

The author and publishers are grateful to the following for permission to reproduce copyright material. It has not always been possible to identify the sources of all the material used or to contact the copyright holders and in such cases the publishers would welcome information **from the copyright owners**.
Apologies are expressed for any omissions.

p. 26: Statistics Finland for the adapted graphs 'Mobile phone possession' and 'Use of mobile phones for the sending and receiving of text messages', taken from www.stat.fi.

The publishers are grateful to the following contributors:
Catriona Watson-Brown: editorial work

Lightning Source UK Ltd.
Milton Keynes UK
UKOW01f2311290114

225538UK00005B/107/P

9 780521 608725